The Encyclopaedia of 21st Century Signal Boxes

A definitive illustrated record of
all Network Rail mechanical and heritage
signal boxes

by
Michael Rhodes

The Encyclopaedia of 21st Century Signal Boxes by Michael Rhodes

Published by Platform 5 Publishing Ltd, 52 Broadfield Road, Sheffield, S8 0XJ. England.
Printed in England by The Amadeus Press, Cleckheaton, West Yorkshire
ISBN: 978 1 909431 66 9

Front cover:- *The 1899-built Wooferton Junction signal box basks in the autumn sunshine as Class 60 No. 60079 passes with the morning Dee Marsh to Margam steel train in October 2013. The box here was initially fitted with a 62-lever frame, subsequently expanded to 75 levers but reduced to today's 39 levers following closure of the junction and goods sidings.* M. Rhodes

Back cover top:- *Class 66 No. 66712 passes Speke Junction signal box with a Dagenham to Garston car train on 11 August 2016. The box opened in 1907 and contained an 86-lever frame to control the main line and the entrance to Speke Yard, which once contained over 30 sidings. The loco will run round its train in the few loops that now remain.* M. Rhodes

Back cover bottom:- *Your author hard at work, cooking breakfast in Reedham Junction box for another very helpful signalman. The gentleman is vegan, so I made him a fritata from vegetables I'd picked that morning in the garden and he deigned to eat the eggs as they were freshly laid for me by our hens!* M. Rhodes

Above:- *One of the inspirations for this book was West Anglia Operations Manager, Steve Ashling, who asked in 2010 if I might like to record the last months of operation of the signal boxes between Norwich and Ely, to produce a memento for the 50 or so signallers along the line. Many years earlier, in 1996, Steve is seen working the night shift in his then post as resident signalman at Reedham Junction.* M. Rhodes

Contents

Introduction and Acknowledgements

An encyclopaedia such as this needs some explanation. I have to start by saying "I never meant to write this book"! I hope the reader will allow me to explain. This book has been the result of the kindness and generosity of railway men and women over nearly five decades. My fascination with the humble signal box started back in 1972 when I realised that we had a signal box in walking distance from my home in Cardiff at Heath Junction. From the moment I tentatively knocked on the door and asked if I could look inside the box I was hooked. Not just that but it was a great place to shelter from the elements if one was hoping to photograph some of the passing coal trains and also in a pre-TOPS world, the only place to find out where the coal trains had got to. I soon found that the signal boxes at Radyr Junction and Radyr Quarry Junction were much better for observing freight trains and spent many happy hours in these during the 1970s.

In 2018 it is hard to imagine a world with no "Realtime Trains", no internet and no idea where trains might have got to. I remember one day, standing in a field overlooking Harringworth Viaduct, certain that there was a morning train from Toton to Acton and worrying that if I gave up it would immediately appear. The train eventually came at 1600 after an 8 hour wait, because it was running as an out-of-gauge load with the head code 8X26. Because of incidents such as this, my visits to signal boxes became more frequent as this was the only way to obtain information. More often than not signalmen in the 1970s and early 1980s were exceptionally welcoming and often offered tea and biscuits and hours of fascinating conversation to impromptu visitors. It may have helped that nearly all my visits were to freight-only lines with infrequent traffic, but I see from my notebooks that I wandered into the panel box at Cardiff, and also at Port Talbot, something that would be unheard of in the 21st century.

I digress and will try to explain how this book came to be written. It was back in 2010 when I found I had some time on my hands and the Operations Manager for West Anglia, Steve Ashling, asked if I might like to record the last months of the signal boxes between Norwich and Ely in order to produce a memento for the 50 or so signallers along the line. I had first met Steve in 1996 when he was in his first post as a resident signalman at Reedham Junction. Steve rose through the ranks rapidly, moving to Liverpool Street in one jump from Reedham and then becoming a senior manager with Network Rail. Indeed it was Steve who saved my bacon in 2000 when he moved our stranded London-bound train onto the slow lines at Stratford and allowed me to get to a lecture in the Royal College of Surgeons. The idea to record the Norwich to Ely line was a superb one and proved an enjoyable project and a successful book was produced.

Several of the signalmen who had worked between Norwich and Ely, moved to the mechanical signal boxes along the Wherry lines in 2012. As a result, the Local Area Operations Manager (LOM), Tim Randell, asked if we could produce a similar record of the Wherry line boxes and this is nearing completion for the 2019 resignalling of these routes. If this was all that had happened in the last decade, then there would only be a book about East Anglia, but projects such as this one are partly undertaken by design, but mainly in my view by serendipity.

In 2012, I was contacted via Flickr by Alex Fisher, a signalman from Great Rocks Junction, asking if I might be able to provide images for his book about Wath marshalling yard. Fascinated, I asked if we might meet and arranged a visit to the signal box. I was delighted to hear that somebody was tackling this much neglected subject and wondered how realistic his aims were. Upon arrival in Great Rocks Junction, a strong cup of tea was offered and then a phone call came from the Local Operations Manager; he was on his way for a box visit. I offered to make myself scarce but Alex reassured me that his LOM was a good guy and wouldn't mind, I just had to sit in the corner and keep out of the way! As the LOM arrived, Alex immediately started to explain who I was to which Anthony McIntyre exclaimed, "I know exactly who this is, this is Dr. Rhodes". Both Alex and I stood open mouthed as we had no idea how Anthony knew. The story then unfolded. Back in 1984, I had visited Denton Junction signal box on a dreary March day and taken a picture of the working gas lamps. The young signalman of the day was in his first post and I had offered to send an 8x10 inch print, which I duly did. The young signalman was none other than Anthony McIntyre! He had lost the print in a house move, but had never forgotten the photographer. More tea was served and I promised to send a digital copy of the image when I got home (much easier than an evening in the darkroom, followed by packaging up a print in a card envelope and a visit to the post office).

As we chatted I explained about the project I had done for Network Rail on the Norwich to Ely route and as a result, Anthony unlocked several doors which allowed me to record nearly all the boxes in the North West of England. Although semi-retired from 2013, work took me to both the North East and North West and further contacts were made. Just as sending images now takes just seconds via the internet, so contact is much easier through the various internet platforms and particular help was offered by Trevor Maxted, John Stocks, James Skoyles, James Wells, John Illingworth, & Craig Munday. One or two of these signalmen appear in many of my images as they both work or worked for Network Rail, but also had an interest in signalling nationwide.

As it became clear that the pace of resignalling was increasing, so the drive to record as many signal boxes as possible increased. As I began to realise that I had a collection of images of most of the surviving mechanical and heritage signal boxes around the country, the idea of a definitive illustrated encyclopaedia sprung to mind. It was then of course that I had to rely on the kindness and generosity of other photographers who dipped into their collection. Foremost amongst these was David Allen who generously filled many of the gaps in my collection, particularly with respect to those signal boxes that had closed between January 2000 and December 2016. Similarly my old colleague and fellow author, Paul Shannon helped with images. For the Southern Region Trevor Maxted, a lifelong signalman, Mark Jamieson, a LOM and Stuart Company all provided invaluable images. Other current and former Network Rail employees including FFP Media, Ivan Stewart, John Illingworth, Nick Allsop and Craig Munday were invaluable in filling many gaps. Thanks to the many people mentioned above, this encyclopaedia has finally taken shape under the ever patient eyes of Andrew Dyson and Sarah Gillott at Platform 5 Publishing. I hope the reader enjoys it.

Michael Rhodes - Attleborough, October 2019

A Brief History of Signalling

There are many learned histories about railway signalling and I can warmly recommend the three volume series published by the National Railway Museum entitled: "The History and Development of Railway Signalling in the British Isles". Another excellent work by Geoffrey Kitchenside and Alan Williams is "Two Centuries of Railway Signalling" published by the OPC. In producing this illustrated encyclopaedia of all the mechanical and heritage signal boxes in the UK since 2000, my aim has been to record the boxes for posterity, rather than delve deeply into the mechanics and science of signalling. I have however tried to provide a brief overview of how we came to abolish our Victorian signalling so late in the day.

Before the invention of the telegraph, trains operated on the interval principle whereby a train would leave a station and then after an accepted interval a second train would be allowed to leave, with the assumption that the train in front had continued to travel forwards without stopping and thereby obstructing the line. The flaws in this system are fairly obvious and it was as early as 1837 on the Manchester to Liverpool Railway that a prototype telegraph machine was shown to move a needle several miles away to indicate the passing of a train. As the first rudimentary telegraph machines were refined and improved, the Tyer's needle became the standard indicator across the UK railway network. Until 1889, the telegraph was simply a communication tool, rather than one which controlled access to sections of track. This all changed with the death of 78 people in the Armagh train crash and the system of absolute block was introduced on all lines.

Information was first passed to trains by hand signals by the "Bobby" or local policeman who doubled as a signalman. Diamonds or spheres were then used before the semaphore we know so well today became the standard indicator for trains. As the rail network became more complex, these semaphores were controlled from cabins or signal boxes and in 1860, Saxby & Farmer built the first interlocking signal box, designed to avoid conflicting movements or signals, essential as layouts at stations and yards became more complex. For the next seven decades, the mechanical signal box with interlocking was the standard control method throughout the UK.

In the early 1900s, experiments were undertaken to introduce electrical or pneumatic control of signals and points, avoiding the need for physical wires and rods between the signal box and the track. This led to the construction of dozens of miniature lever signal boxes by Westinghouse and other companies. The largest of these was built at Glasgow Central in 1908 and contained a staggering 374 miniature levers which controlled the station using electro-pneumatic power. Just two of these miniature lever boxes survive today at Maidstone East and Immingham Reception Sidings.

The next significant development in railway signalling was the fully electrical signal box, the first of which opened in York in 1952. The OCS (short for One Control Switch) panel there replaced 868 mechanical levers in eight older mechanical signal boxes. This became the model for future panel boxes where the NX (entrance/exit) switch was employed. Until the 1980s, most resignalling was based on the construction of NX panel boxes to control discreet areas around major stations or junctions. The next big change was solid state technology which allowed the large banks of electromechanical relays underneath NX panel signal boxes to be replaced by a small box with solid state relays. The control for 40 sets of points and 40 signals could now be housed in a small metal box just 2 feet across! With digital technology, the large "panels" used in the power signal boxes of the 1970s and '80s could be replaced by a VDU or computer monitor, further reducing the footprint needed to control large areas of track. These two final developments were the catalyst for the idea to control the whole UK network from just 12 Regional Operating Centres or ROCs. By the end of 2018 the twelve ROCs at Gillingham (Kent), Three Bridges, Basingstoke, Romford, Didcot, Cardiff, Derby, Rugby, Manchester, York, Edinburgh and Cowlairs were all open, although the degree to which they were fully operational varies greatly. The signalling centre at Saltley may yet become the 13th ROC whilst the RETB centres at Inverness and Banavie as well as the ETCS control room at Machynlleth will remain operational alongside the ROCs.

In view of these sweeping developments, it is remarkable to think that significant parts of today's railway network are still controlled by Victorian signalling dating back to the 1870s. Whilst motive power and rolling stock would be unrecognisable to our forefathers, hundreds of today's signal boxes are virtually unchanged since the time they were built in the 19th century. The application of digital technology and in particular the drive to introduce a Europe-wide signalling system, has led to the Network Rail strategy to replace all of the signal boxes in the UK and control the railway from a dozen Regional Operating Centres or ROCs mentioned above. In 2010 a document was produced by Network Rail, outlining the closure schedule for signal boxes and whilst this schedule is now nine years old and many changes have occurred, the direction of travel remains the same. The aim is to abolish mechanical signalling and older power signal boxes as soon as financially possible. This is evidenced by the closure of 161 signal boxes between 2000 and the end of 2010, an average of 15 per annum. This compares to increased closures after the introduction of the Network Rail 2010 plan with 225 signal boxes closing between January 2011 and December 2018, an average of nearly 28 per annum. This rate of closures has slowed as the massive burden of debt within Network Rail and new borrowing restrictions have reduced the flow of ready money to implement the plan. Matters have also not been helped by significant cost over-runs in most of the major resignalling schemes undertaken between 2010 and 2018, not to mention the high profile scaling back of both Great Western and Midland Main Line electrifications. In spite of these problems, a brief look at current projects suggests that many further signal box closures will follow.

At the time of writing, several major resignalling schemes have recently been completed. The line between Saltmarshe and Melton Lane has been resignalled with the closure of nine boxes and the downgrading of Goole Swing Bridge and Crabley Creek to crossing boxes with no role in controlling the passing traffic. The route is now controlled from the York ROC. The massive ROC in York has also taken over the work of Healey Mills and Huddersfield power signal boxes, and also the line between Mill Lane in Bradford and Milner Royd Junction (with closure of four signal boxes). The first stage of the North Wales resignalling was completed in 2018 with closure of seven boxes between Rockcliffe Hall and Llandudno Junction. Resignalling from Llandudno to Holyhead, which was to have been undertaken with the current resignalling of the eastern end of the North Wales Main Line, has now been postponed indefinitely. The new ROC at Ashburys in Manchester has taken over the routes controlled by Ashton Moss North Junction, Liverpool Lime Street, Allerton & Speke Junction, whilst in Scotland Dyce and Inverurie boxes are due to close with control handed to a new workstation in Inverness Signalling Centre. One final significant resignalling scheme is taking place along the Wherry lines with control of this area to be handed to Colchester power signal box and closure of eight signal boxes. The next 12 months looks like continuing the rate of closures set since the Network Rail plans for Control Periods 4 & 5 were published, with many more signal boxes projected to close.

Above:- Old and new combine in this view of Stockport No.2 signal box taken in December 2015. On duty that day were Andrew Law, who had started on the railway at the age of 16 working as a train recorder at Manchester Victoria, and Guy Henry, whose career as a signalman had started at Oldham Mumps and then ended up in Stockport No. 2 via a spell in Baguley Fold box. The business and size of the box demand that it is double manned, as is Stockport No. 1. Both boxes were originally to have been replaced by the new panel at Wilmslow, but the complexity of the track work and signalling means that a pocket of mechanical signalling survives between Heaton Norris and Edgeley No. 1 signal box. M. Rhodes

Signal Box Closures in the 21st Century

Introduction

Modernisation and improvement have been intrinsic to our railways since their inception. Nowhere more so than in methods of signalling trains. By the Second World War most lines were controlled by semaphore signals with some larger stations and junctions being controlled by electro-mechanical, rather than purely mechanical signal boxes. The first major impact on the humble Victorian signal box was the introduction from 1945 onwards of the new "panel box". The first two major schemes were between Liverpool Street and Shenfield in 1949 (linked to the route's electrification) and in York where the panel box boasted to contain the largest relay interlocking in the world.

Subsequent resignalling was envisaged in the 1955 Modernisation Plan. The total budget for modernisation was £1,240 million, of which £105 million was set aside for resignalling. The first route to benefit from this new investment was between Manchester and Crewe when this line was electrified in 1959. The entire WCML from London to Glasgow was eventually resignalled by 1974, with the later schemes benefitting from ever larger signal boxes. The signal boxes at Warrington, Preston and Motherwell were no longer "boxes" but large control centres. This pattern was repeated when the ECML was electrified in 1991 with the entire route from King's Cross to north of Newcastle controlled by just five signalling centres (King's Cross, Peterborough, Doncaster, York & Newcastle).

The next stage in modernisation came with microprocessors and Solid State Interlocking. This allowed the equipment needed to control a given area to shrink to less than a 10th of the size. This in turn led to the possibility of controlling much larger areas from a relatively small building when compared to the room needed for a traditional NX panel system. Add to this the use of a VDU to control train movements and the foundations for the modern ROC (Regional Operating Centre) have been laid. Of course, in between the headline schemes of the last four decades of the 20th century, resignalling has carried on in smaller ways, using the established NX panel. Schemes such as Plymouth, Exeter, Chester, Stoke-on-Trent and Lincoln have effectively closed dozens of manual signal boxes in smaller defined areas. For the first 12 years in the 21st century, closure of manual signal boxes was predominantly a result of small "panel box" schemes. Other closures occurred as a result of simple rationalisation to add a panel to a neighbouring manual signal box or due to enlargement of an established major IECC, like Liverpool Street. Everything changed in 2012 with the commissioning of the Norwich to Ely resignalling. Network Rail envisaged the project as a crucial testbed for a new modular signalling system which would allow the use of existing technologies but with a simplified design and future compatibility with ETCS Level 2. Signalling Solutions undertook the work between Norwich and Ely, whilst a similar scheme between Shrewsbury and Crewe was undertaken by Invensys. After teething problems and late delivery, both schemes were eventually fully functional by the end of 2013. The success of the new methodology is reflected in the acceleration of signal box closures from 2012 onwards. The days of the surviving manual signal boxes really are numbered as the Figures 1 & 2 illustrate.

The rest of this chapter allocates a section to each year of the 21st century. Each section contains a table listing the signal box closures of that year and also a short explanation of the reasons for the closures. There then follows a comprehensive illustrated section, showing the boxes that closed in that year. Between January 2000 and the end of 2018 a total of 386 signal boxes were closed, the majority of which were mechanically operated and heritage buildings. This section of the book provides a unique illustrated guide to these buildings.

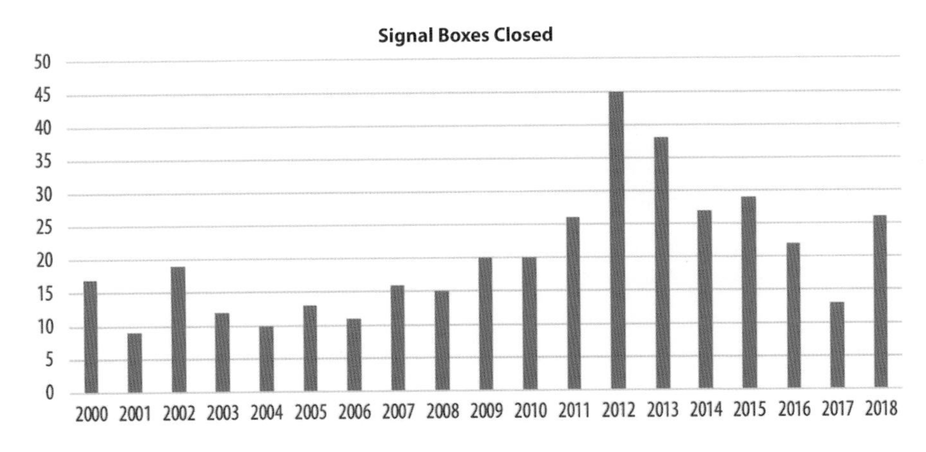

Figure 1

The rate of closure for manual and heritage signal boxes remained relatively constant for the first decade of the 21st century. The introduction of low-cost modular resignalling and the drive to concentrate control for the whole network in 12 Regional Operating Centres led to a marked acceleration in closures from 2012 onwards. Whether Network Rail budget cuts will lead to a slowing in the closure rate remains to be seen.

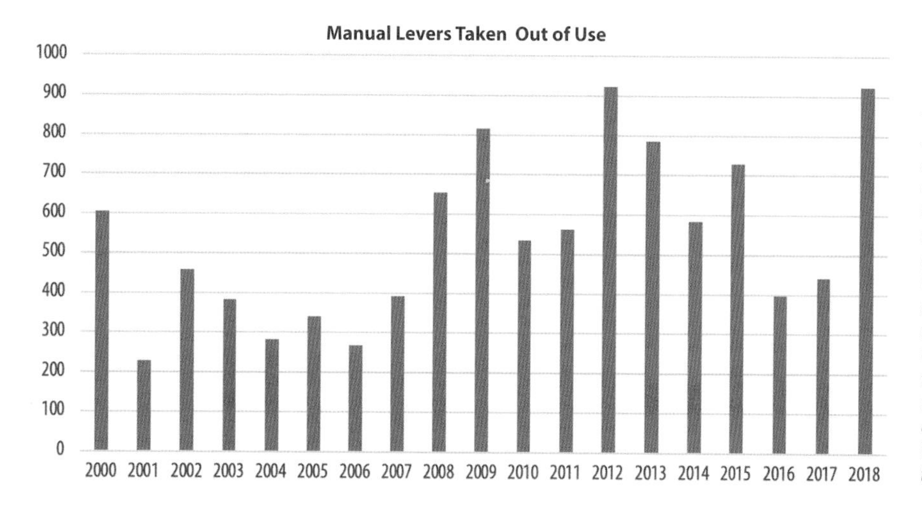

Figure 2

Another way of plotting the changes during the first part of the 21st century is to look at the loss of manual levers each year. Bearing in mind that the new York panel of 1952 led to the abolition of 868 levers, losses have been relatively small. The increase from 2012 onwards is less marked than might be expected because the modernisation of signalling since then has also involved the closure of many panel boxes and some larger signalling centres, also using the NX panel.

2000

Perhaps the most significant resignalling scheme of 2000 was that between Norwich and Cromer. This resulted in the closure of four signal boxes, with control of the line taken over by a new panel in Trowse Bridge SCC. The two large LMR lever boxes at Ditton were replaced by a new building containing an NX panel. Signalling at Seamer was rationalised by placing a new NX panel in Seamer East signal box and closing Seamer West and Filey boxes. The crossing at Cayton, between Seamer and Filey was also converted to automatic half barriers (AHB) controlled from Seamer East signal box. Similar minor changes were made in Nairn, with a small VDU and token machine in the station master's office replacing two small signal cabins. The old NX panels at Euston and Willesden Junction were decommissioned and control of this area taken over by the Wembley Mainline SCC. Simple rationalisation to reduce manpower costs or as a result of loss of traffic were responsible for the closure of Plumpton Junction (loss of the Glaxo branch).

Box	Type of Box & date opened	Date closed
Acton Lane Signal Frame	BR (LMR) - 30 levers - 1964	27/12
Cayton Gate Box	NER - 14 levers - 1908	26/6
Cheadle Hulme	LNWR - 36 levers - 1901	26/8
Christ's Hospital	LBSCR - 36 levers - 1902	16/2
Cromer	MGNR - 35 levers - 1914	23/6
Ditton Junction No. 1	BR (LMR) - 100 levers - 1956	10/12
Ditton Junction No. 2	BR (LMR) - 55 levers - 1960	10/12
Euston	BR (LMR) - NX panel - 1965	14/8
Filey	NER - 24 levers - 1911	26/6
Nairn East	HR - 13 levers - 1891	9/4

Box	Type of Box & date opened	Date closed
Nairn West	HR - 19 levers - 1891	9/4
North Walsham	GER- 35 levers - 1896	23/6
Plumpton Junction	FR - 65 levers - 1898	19/3
Seamer West	NER - 60 levers - 1906	10/4
Whitlingham Junction	GER - 34 levers - 1909	23/6
Willesden Junction	BR (LMR) - NX panel - 1965	27/12
Wroxham	GER - 50 levers - 1900	23/6
Closure of 15 mechanical boxes and 2 panel boxes		
Loss of 606 levers		

ACTON LANE

Right:- Acton Lane reception sidings lie to the west of the WCML between the overbridges for the North London Line and the freight route to Neasden. Entry to the small yard was controlled by Acton Lane shunting frame, built to a BR (LMR) design in 1964 and containing 30 levers. This image was taken in the early 1990s. FFP Media

CAYTON

Right:- The crossing box at Cayton disappeared because the crossing here was converted to automatic half barriers as part of the rationalisation of signalling at Seamer. The box dated from 1908 and was of an NER design. A McKenzie & Holland frame contained 14 levers. The NYMR had planned to remove it to Pickering. However, NR decreed there was no safe method of removal and it was demolished in December 2003. D. Allen

CHEADLE HULME

Left:- The 36-lever, 1901 vintage signal box at Cheadle Hulme closed in 2000 and was replaced by an IFS panel situated in a rather ugly temporary "double-decker portable building". This in turn closed in 2003 when control of the area passed to the Manchester South signalling centre. Here a light engine movement for the Stoke on Trent line pauses opposite the box to drop off two staff. D. Allen

CHRIST'S HOSPITAL

Left:- This view of Christ's Hospital signal box is taken well after closure, when the structure was falling down. The LBSCR-designed cabin contained 36 levers and dated from 1902. In April 1902 a new seven platform station was opened at Stammerham Junction to serve the new Christ's Hospital school. Regrettably, the station never justified the scale of development but it did somewhat take the pressure off Horsham by acting as an interchange for the branch lines to Guildford and Shoreham. Alas, both branches were casualties of the 1960s as were five of the platforms. The station was provided with two SBs; Christ's Hospital 'A' and 'B'. After the 'B' SB was abolished in 1968, the 'A' box was re-christened Christ's Hospital. The SB is seen following a disastrous fire in February 2000, after which it was immediately decommissioned. It had latterly been largely 'switched out of circuit'. Following this, the AB section was extended from Horsham to Pulborough until the closure of Horsham SB in 2005. D. Allen

CROMER

Left:- Class 153 No. 153309 approaches Cromer station with a Norwich to Sheringham service. To the left is the 1914 MGNR signal box with its 35 levers. In 2019 the signal box is the object of an ambitious renovation project which hopes to bring the box back to complete working order including refitting the original relays and electronics. M. Rhodes

DITTON JUNCTION NO. 1

Right:- In 1954, a member of the BR staff, W. Hardman, designed a very successful standard type of SB. Eventually over 150 were built over a 30 year period. Ditton Junction No. 1 was one of the earliest. It replaced a life-expired LNWR structure in 1956. In November 1960, during Stage 2 of the Crewe to Liverpool Lime Street resignalling, all the main running line signals were replaced by colour lights but the ground shunting signals remained mechanical. Railtrack North West eventually decommissioned Ditton No. 1 and nearby No. 2 in December 2000. They were replaced by a new Ditton SB with an eNtrance-eXit (NX) panel. At the time, it was planned the new SB would control most of the route into Liverpool under the so called 'Weaver-Wavertree Resignalling'. The paintwork is in need of repair on Ditton No. 1 signal box as Class 47 No. 47052 arrives to pick up a Freightliner service from the nearby Ditton container depot. The box was opened in 1956 and used to contain a 100-lever frame. The new Ditton NX panel was constructed on this side of the line, a couple of hundred yards to the west on the other side of the road overbridge. D. Allen

Left:- The splendid 1956 vintage 100-lever frame at Ditton No. 1 signal box is shown from lever No. 25 upwards in this view taken in October 1999, just before the box closed and was demolished. A.F. Bullimore

DITTON JUNCTION NO. 2

Left:- Ditton No. 2 was a smaller box, constructed later in 1960, but to the same design as No. 1 box. It contained 55 levers and was also replaced by the new Ditton NX panel. By 1960, BR realised it couldn't afford to re-signal the WCML by means of PSBs alone. Three purpose-built electro-mechanical SBs were built on the main line between Crewe and Liverpool Lime Street. Track Circuit Block working was used on the main line. Ditton No. 2 displays the features of this type well. It has the characteristic flat roof and pre-fabricated wooden panels for the operating floor; the brick base was common but some used wood. Note the extended locking room to house the relays. D. Allen

FILEY

Right:- The signal box at Filey closed when the level crossing here was placed under CCTV control from the new NX panel in Seamer East signal box. Built in 1911 to NER design, the box had 24 levers and not only controlled the crossing at Filey but also the entrance to the single-track section north to Seamer. Filey SB is seen on 19 April 1989. It was typical of many built at the time; similar survivors can be seen at Beverley and Seamer. The white screen on the side windows suggests the signalmen (sic) didn't like the prying eyes of passengers on the station! Also note, the staircase divided into two. One seems to lead to the rather isolated and basic "facilities". The SB closed in June 2000 following transfer of the line between Seamer and Hunmanby to Seamer SB. The level crossing gates were replaced by barriers controlled by means of CCTV. D. Allen

Left:- A close-up of the block shelf in Filey SB in November 1995. The LNER block instrument controlled the AB section to Hunmanby. It is a later version combining both "up" and "down" lines. Note the commuter has a rotating action and is turned in a clockwise direction when "Line Clear" and "Train on Line" are appropriate. The single line to Seamer was controlled by track circuits and direction levers. The identical instruments above the signaller's arm illustrate the prevailing situation. In this instance the "up" line is pointing to "Train in Section"; a train is approaching from Scarborough. D. Allen

NAIRN

Left & below:- The two small signal boxes at Nairn East and Nairn West opened in 1891 and closed together, with the block token machine for Nairn moving into the station master's office, along with a new VDU screen controlling traffic through the station. These two images show the smaller Nairn East box, preserved at the end of the platform, with its 13-lever frame. Nairn West box was slightly larger boasting 19 levers. M. Rhodes

NORTH WALSHAM

Left:- The signalman takes the token from an old-style Rail Head Treatment Train in the hands of Class 20s Nos. 20904 & 20903 back in July 1997. North Walsham box was a GER design dating from 1896 with a 35-lever frame of a much younger vintage, dating from 1944. M. Rhodes

PLUMPTON JUNCTION

Right:- The Furness Railway signal box at Plumpton Junction controlled the main line between Ulverston and Grange-over-Sands as well as the freight branch to the Glaxo works (now sadly closed). Dating from 1898 it had a 65-lever frame. By the time Railtrack North West abolished Plumpton Junction SB it had lost all of its advantages. The line towards Lakeside was last used by regular traffic in 1967. Likewise, freight traffic to the Glaxo works on the Priory branch, ceased in 1994. There had been a triangular layout serving some quarries and an iron works but that was also history. Because the SB was in a remote location, Railtrack decided to replace it with the more conveniently situated SB at Ulverston station, which had latterly been normally switched out of circuit. It seems, less than four days after the Plumpton Junction signaller directed the last train on 19 March 2000, the apparently solid SB was reduced to rubble in just two hours. D. Allen

SEAMER EAST

Left:- The lever frame at Seamer East was replaced by an NX panel in 2000 but the 1910-vintage NER building was retained and renamed simply Seamer. The panel initially took over control of Seamer East and West boxes but now controls Scarborough as well. In November 1992, an unidentified Class 158 unit is pausing with a Scarborough to York service. M. Rhodes

SEAMER WEST

Right:- In November 1992, Class 142 No. 142070 is seen passing Seamer West box with a Hull to Scarborough service. Seamer West signal box dated from 1906 and had a 60-lever frame. M. Rhodes

WHITLINGHAM JUNCTION

Left & below:- The Norwich to Yarmouth and Lowestoft lines have been famous for their motive power variety with everything from Deltics to this preserved Hastings unit being used to fill in on summer Saturdays and also more recently for motive power shortages. No. 1001 passes Whitlingham Junction signal box on a summer Saturday in August 1998 with a Yarmouth to Norwich extra. The box here was of classic GER design, dating from 1909 and with 34 levers. Our internal view, taken in 1991, shows the compact frame with the signalman on the phone. The route to Cromer curves away to the left in the background. Both M. Rhodes

WROXHAM

Right:- On a gloomy day in December 1995, Class 37 No. 37689 passes Wroxham box, surrendering the token for the single line section from North Walsham. The GER box here dated from 1900 and was the largest along the Cromer line with 50 levers, most of which were white or "out of use" by this date as the line to Lenwade had closed, as had the grain sidings in the background. M. Rhodes

2001

2001 was a very quiet year for signal box closures, with just six mechanical boxes closing. The GWR box at Kingswinford Junction South was damaged by fire and replaced with a portable building structure, whilst that at Bestwood Park had been out of use since the previous year as a result of colliery closures. The only planned work that had an impact on the remaining mechanical boxes on the network was the transfer of control from Hunmanby in the North East to the newly opened NX panel in Seamer signal box. The two boxes at Enfield Town and Seven Sisters had control migrated to the IECC at Liverpool Street whilst one final minor closure was at Lincoln Street Crossing where the manual crossing was converted to a CCTV-controlled automated crossing supervised by Trent power signal box.

2001		
Appleford Crossing	BR (WR) - no frame - 1952	27/5
Bestwood Park Junction	BR (LMR) - 55 levers - 1952	12/10
Dartford	BR (SR) - NX panel - 1970	17/4
Enfield Town	GER - 68 levers - 1890	25/11
Hackney Downs	BR (ER) - NX panel - 1960	28/5
Hunmanby	NER - 16 levers - 1875	5/3
Kingswinford Junction South	GWR - 77 levers - 1916	16/11
Lincoln Street	MR - 12 levers - 1916	12/10
Seven Sisters	GER - 48 levers - 1905	25/11
Closure of 6 mechanical boxes, 2 NX panel and 1 other		
Loss of 276 levers		

APPLEFORD CROSSING

Right::- The GWR box at Appleford dated from 1952 and actually had no frame but simply controlled the level crossing just north of Didcot on the Oxford line. Here, back in 1982, Class 47 No. 47121 approaches the crossing with 6A06, the Stoke Gifford to Banbury Road stone train. M. Rhodes

HUNMANBY

Left:- The 1875 NER box at Hunmanby was at the northern end of the single line section from Bridlington. It had a 16-lever frame and was the fringe box to the NX panel at Seamer, so was a logical candidate for closure with control taken over by Seamer. When photographed on 19 April 1989, Hunmanby SB controlled the northern end of the line to Bridlington Quay SB. This had been singled in January 1973 and was controlled by Tyers No. 6 Electric Token machines. When Bridlington Quay SB was decommissioned in February 1998, the method of working changed to TCB. Following the closure of Filey SB in 2000, AB working on the double track section to the north was replaced by TCB. Then in March 2001, Seamer SB assumed control and this delightful NER SB was redundant. D. Allen

ENFIELD TOWN

Right:- Built in 1890 to a GER design, Enfield Town box had a 68-lever frame which had been installed in 1959. The box is illustrated here shortly before closure. The box finally succumbed in November 2001 as part of the West Anglia Route Modernisation (WARM). Control of the new 4-aspect signalling being transferred to the Brimsdown workstation in Liverpool Street IECC. This GER structure was the third to supervise the suburban terminus. It witnessed the introduction of the so-called 'Jazz' trains in 1920 and the addition of a third platform. In 1934/35 the LNER resignalled between Bethnal Green and Enfield with automatic colour lights and 17 SBs were decommissioned. Enfield was retained to control the still largely semaphore signalled station and the route towards Seven Sisters via Bury Street Junction. Further changes followed in May 1960 when the area was electrified. All mechanical signalling at the terminus was dispensed with and a new panel installed above the lever frame. D. Allen

BESTWOOD PARK

Left:- Taken in 1985, the box, signals and yard at Bestwood Park form the backdrop for this view of Class 20 Nos. 20019 & 20004 hauling 6T71, a Hucknall to Toton Speedlink Coal trip working. The signal box was built in 1952 to BR (LMR) design and contained a 55-lever frame. M. Rhodes

KINGSWINFORD JUNCTION SOUTH

Above:- The 1916-vintage GWR box was on the freight line between Dudley and Stourbridge Junction, once busy with freights to the Birmingham steel industry and mixed traffic to and from Bescot Yard. The box also controlled access to the Brierley Hill steel terminal and the Pensnett branch. Not surprisingly it had a large 77-lever frame. Sadly in 2001 the box was damaged by fire attributed to vandalism and replaced with a portable building. In 1985 Class 45 No. 45016 has called into Brierley Hill Yard to pick up empty steel wagons on its way south with 6V70, the Cliffe Vale to Severn Tunnel Junction Speedlink service. M. Rhodes

LINCOLN STREET

Left:- The small crossing box at Lincoln Street dated from 1916 and was of classic Midland Railway design with 12 levers. Lincoln Street SB became a fringe to Trent PSB under Stage 3 of the Trent Resignalling in December 1969. Passenger services had only been restored for a few weeks when this view was taken on 31 July 1993. Ever since the withdrawal of passenger services to Mansfield, 29 years earlier, the line had been freight-only. The SB was a casualty of the Railtrack enabling works for the Nottingham Express Transit light rail system in October 2001. The new signalling and the CCTV-operated level crossing were controlled from a new panel installed in Trent PSB. Today, you can still stand on the former Midland Railway footbridge and compare the view. The site of the SB is occupied by a relocatable equipment building (REB) housing the control equipment for the CCTV crossing. The level crossing now also crosses the Nottingham Express Transit lines at David Lane station which, since September 2011, has been supervised by the Mansfield workstation in East Midlands SCC. D. Allen

SEVEN SISTERS

Above:- Seven Sisters and Enfield Town SBs were decommissioned by Railtrack East Anglia in November 2001. The routes from Rectory Road to Cheshunt (exclusive) and Enfield Town were resignalled and control transferred to Liverpool Street IECC. Completion of the so-called 'West Anglia' resignalling was completed by Network Rail in 2004. The signal box at Seven Sisters was built in 1905, and had a 48-lever Mackenzie & Holland frame. D. Allen

2002

Several signalling schemes in 2002 had a significant impact on box closures. The largest of these was the opening of the Stoke-on-Trent signalling centre which took over control from the old Stoke-on-Trent power box as well as boxes at Bradwell, Grange Junction, Kidsgrove, Longport, Meaford Crossing and Mow Cop. The IECC at Liverpool Street continued to widen its control area, leading to the closure of the boxes at Brimsdown, Chingford and Highams Park. The Tyneside IECC was extended to cover the Newcastle to Sunderland route with closures at Boldon, East Boldon, Monkwearmouth and Sunderland. In a similar way very significant changes occurred in the York IECC with control of the whole Leeds area moved to the facility. Whilst a very major signalling change, this expansion at York only led to the closure of one heritage signal box at Church Fenton. Smaller changes occurred when Seaford was closed with the area controlled by Newhaven Harbour box. A similar small rationalisation took place in Shropshire where Wellington box closed with Madeley Junction extending its area of influence.

2002		
Boldon Colliery	NER - NX panel - 1893	11/1
Bradwell Sidings	NSR - 35 levers - 1899	27/5
Brimsdown	LNER - 42 levers - 1944	27/8
Chingford	GER - 30 levers - 1920	24/6
Church Fenton	NER - IFS panel - 1904	21/4
East Boldon	NER - 26 levers - 1895	11/1
Grange Junction	BR (LMR) - 75 levers - 1966	27/5
Highams Park GB	LNER - no frame - 1938	24/6
Kidsgrove Central	BR (LMR) - 50 levers - 1965	27/5
Leeds	BR - NX panel - 1967	16/6

2002		
Longport Junction	LMS - 70 levers - 1939	27/5
Meaford Crossing	NSR - 26 levers - 1876	27/5
Monkwearmouth	NER - 30 levers - 1879	11/1
Mow Cop	NSR - no frame - 1890	27/5
Seaford	LBSCR - 24 levers - 1895	18/1
Stoke-on-Trent	BR (LMR) - NX panel - 1966	27/5
Stourton	BR (ER) - NX panel - 1981	28/7
Sunderland	BR (NER) - IFS panel - 1965	11/1
Wellington	BR (WR) - 71 levers - 1953	16/12
Closure of 11 mechanical boxes, 6 panels and 2 other		
Loss of 479 levers		

BOLDON COLLIERY

Above:- The NER signal box was opened in 1893 and named Brockley Whins. It wasn't until 1925 that the LNER re-christened the station and SB in the less-glamorous form; Boldon Colliery. Precisely a century after the SB was opened, the station regained its old name but the SB didn't! When this view was taken on 16 April 1987, Boldon Colliery SB worked TCB to Gateshead PSB and Tile Shed SB. By May 1985, when the new East Curve was commissioned, the lever frame had been replaced by a panel. The SB was eventually made redundant in January 2002 as part of the 'Sunderland Direct' Metro extension, the first example of a shared light/heavy rail scheme in the UK. Control was transferred to Tyneside IECC. A Class 31 is seen passing with the daily parcels service to the Brian Mills parcels depot on the Sunderland Docks branch line. D. Allen

BRADWELL SIDINGS

Left:- In 2002, with colour light signals all erected and ready to take over, this view shows Bradwell Sidings box, north of Longport. It was originally constructed in 1899 to a North Staffordshire Railway Type 2 design. At this stage it was fitted with a 45-lever frame. In 1965 the box was refurbished with a brick base and equipped with a 35-lever frame. D. Allen

BRIMSDOWN

Right:- The 42-lever 1944-constructed LNER box at Brimsdown was built to replace an earlier 1884-vintage GER box, which was destroyed in a bombing raid. By the time this image was taken, a second-hand NX panel had been installed (seen in the background where the signalman is at work). This took over the Temple Mills area and in order to install it, the frame was reduced to 37 levers. D. Allen

CHINGFORD

Above & right:- The signal cabin box at Chingford dates back to 1878 and at its largest had a 60-lever mechanical frame. This was reduced to just 30 levers in 1960 when an IFS panel was installed. This view shows the second SB to be built at Chingford. It opened in 1920 when its predecessor was demolished to accommodate platform extensions. A new intensive steam suburban service to the Capital (known popularly as The Jazz) had just been introduced. No longer just a gateway to Epping Forest, Chingford was becoming an important dormitory for London. In 1938, the LNER resignalled the branch with 3-aspect searchlight signals. Only the Chingford terminus retained semaphores. In March 1960, in preparation for electrification, all of Chingford's semaphores were replaced by 3-aspect searchlights. The panel mounted above the lever frame dates from this time. The SB became redundant in June 2002 when control was transferred to Liverpool Street IECC. Both D. Allen

CHURCH FENTON

Above:- The imposing 1904 NER signal box at Church Fenton is seen here in January 1989. The lever frame here was replaced by an IFS panel in 1968 at the same time as the semaphore signals were converted to colour lights. M. Rhodes

EAST BOLDON

Above:- On 20 August 1986, Class 56 No. 56099 passes East Boldon with 6J68, an empty MGR from Tyne Dock to Wearmouth Colliery. The NER signal box dated from 1895 and was fitted in 1956 with a 26-lever McKenzie & Holland mechanical frame. M. Rhodes

GRANGE JUNCTION

Right & below:- Before closure of the British Steel plant at Etruria (BSC Shelton), there were daily incoming steel slabs from Teeside and daily trains of beams and special-profile milled steel. Steel production at the site had ceased in 1978 and complete closure of the works came in 2000. Here on 17 June 1993, Class 56 No. 56069 departs with finished steel for Tees Dock. The 1966 vintage BR (LMR) signal box is seen on the left. As shown in the interior view, the cabin had a 75-lever frame, greatly simplified with many white levers after the closure of the steelworks in 2000, it closed completely in 2002. P. Shannon & N. Allsopp

KIDSGROVE CENTRAL

Below & bottom:- The signal box at Kidsgrove Central dated from 1965 and was constructed at the time of electrification of the line. It had a 50-lever frame which by the time of these images was largely reduced to white or out-of-use levers as a result of the closure of the goods yard at Kidsgrove in the late 1960s. Both D. Allen

LONGPORT JUNCTION

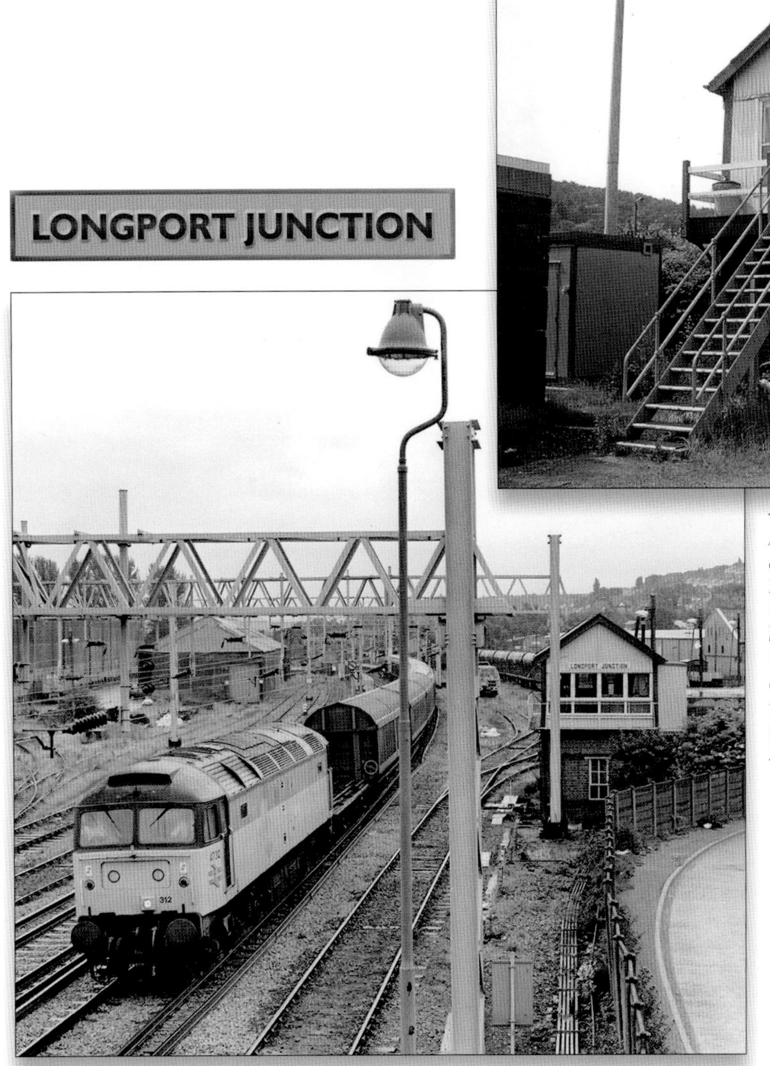

Above & left:- The box at Longport predates the electrification of the route in March 1967 and is of LMS design, dating from 1939 when the original 1870-built box was replaced. It had a 70-lever frame but this was replaced by a smaller 50-lever one in 1977. The strange windows which seem somewhat out of keeping were fitted in 1990. The black and white image shows Class 47 No. 47312 arriving with the Bescot–Longport Speedlink feeder service on 5 August 1991. *N. Allsopp & P. Shannon*

MEAFORD CROSSING

Left:- Meaford Crossing box (at Stone station) was of North Staffordshire Railway design. It dated back to 1876 and had a 26-lever frame. As part of the Stoke-on-Trent to Manchester resignalling of 1966/67 it had some IFS switches installed which were used on a temporary basis. In 1977 the gate wheel (gates locked by No. 26 lever) was removed and the gates had to be opened and closed manually by the signalman. *D. Allen*

MONKWEARMOUTH

Right:- Back in November 1983 a Metro-Cammell DMU passes Monkwearmouth box with a Newcastle to Sunderland service. This line is of course now operated by the Tyne & Wear Metro and the branch seen on the left of the image to Wearmouth Colliery is long gone. The signal box itself dates from 1879 and had a 30-lever frame. M. Rhodes

MOW COP

Right & below:- The tiny North Staffordshire Railway box at Mow Cop dated back to 1890. Originally it had a 14-lever frame. Lever No. 1 was for the gate wheel. In 1981 the barriers were replaced by manually-opened barriers and at the same time the mechanical frame was decommissioned to be replaced by two individual function switches. Both N. Allsopp

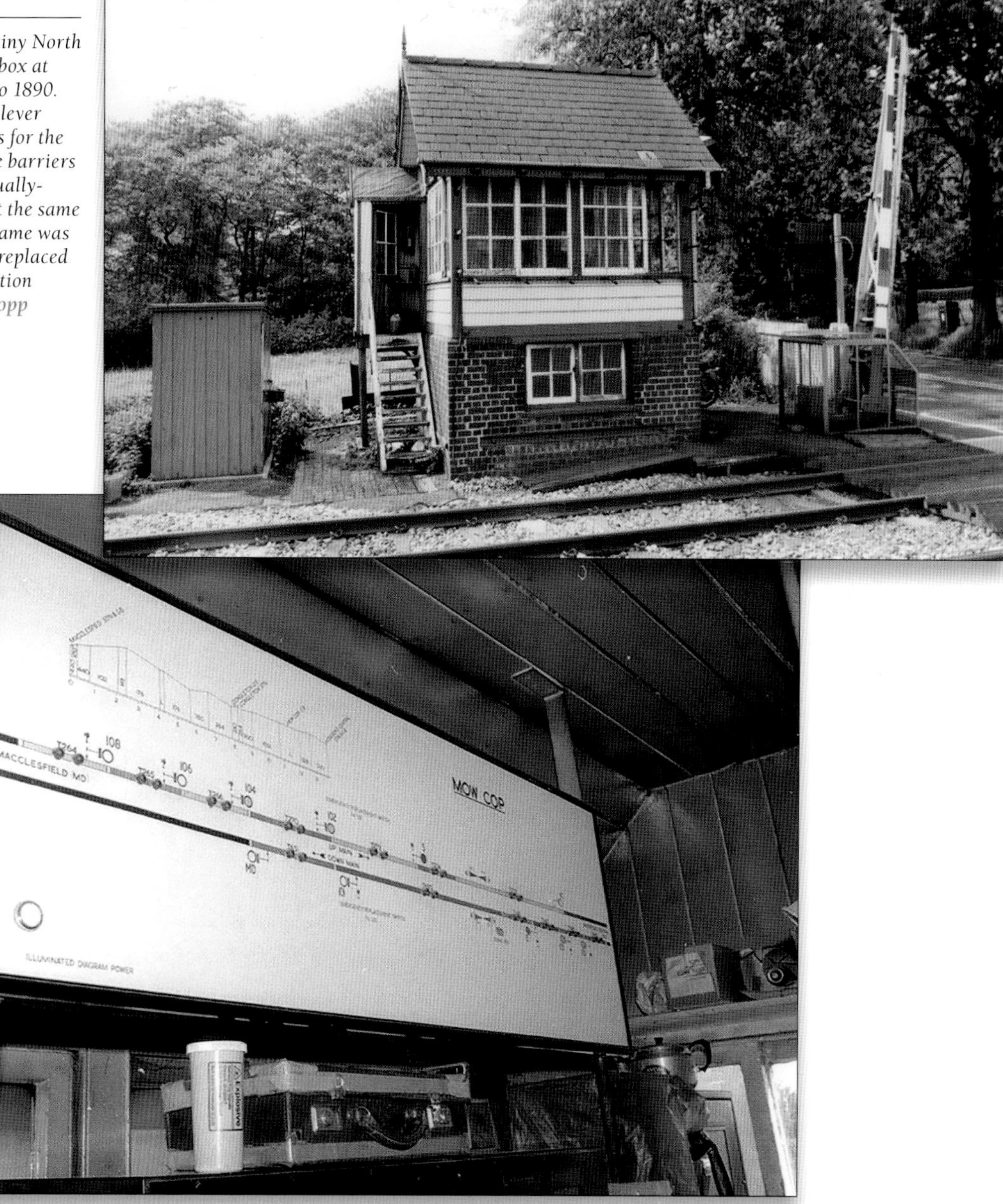

SEAFORD

Left:- The tiny 2-mile branch line from Newhaven Harbour to Seaford used to boast its own manual signal box. The 1895-vintage London, Brighton and South Coast Railway signal box had a 24-lever frame and closed in 2003. T. Maxted

STOKE-ON-TRENT

Right:- It is interesting to reflect that when the Stoke-on-Trent power signal box, illustrated here, closed in 2002, the large NX panel there was replaced by VDUs and workstations. The structure seen here was then renamed Stoke-on-Trent SCC. N. Allsopp

WELLINGTON

Left:- When Wellington No. 2 SB was opened by BR(WR) in 1953, with its 71-lever frame, there were four SBs in the vicinity. However, the SB numbering was a legacy of when the LNWR jointly operated the line with the GWR. This SB replaced an ageing structure previously located to the right. Aesthetically not very pleasing, it resembled the ARP (Air Raid Precaution) types constructed by the GWR during WWII. When seen on 19 August 1989, it was the last surviving of the Wellington SBs. Closing in December 2002, it was the first SB casualty for Network Rail. Madeley Junction SB assumed control of the newly-track-circuited and resignalled route to Shrewsbury Abbey Foregate. D. Allen

2003

The main changes in 2003 again related to expansion of the London Liverpool Street IECC with the boxes at Bishop's Stortford, Broxbourne, Cheshunt Junction, Harlow Mill, Hertford East, Roydon, St. Margarets, Spelbrook and Ware all being absorbed into the centre. Smaller changes occurred on the south coast as Bournemouth and Branksome boxes closed to be replaced by a new Bournemouth area signalling centre. Another heritage box on an isolated freight only railway, Garston Junction was destroyed by fire as the result of vandalism.

2003		
Bishop's Stortford	LNER - 45 levers - 1931	24/10
Bournemouth	SR - 60 levers - 1928	15/12
Branksome	LSWR - 30 levers - 1886	15/12
Broxbourne	BR (ER) - panel - 1960	24/5
Cheshunt Junction	GER - panel - 1891	24/5
Garston Junction	LNWR - 78 levers - 1908	27/7
Harlow Mill	BR (ER) - panel - 1960	24/10
Hertford East	GER - 45 levers - 1887	18/5
Roydon	GER - 27 levers - 1876	24/5
St. Margarets	GER - 56 levers - 1887	18/5
Spelbrook	GER - 24 levers - 1898	24/10
Ware	BR (ER) - 20 levers - 1960	24/5
Closure of 9 mechanical boxes & 3 panel boxes		
Loss of 385 levers		

BISHOP'S STORTFORD

Left:- There were originally two signal boxes controlling the station area at Bishop's Stortford. The South box dated from1870 and at its largest had a 65-lever frame. Changes related to suburban electrification in 1960 led to the installation of an IFS panel and more changes came in 1990 when an NX panel was installed to control the new Stansted Airport branch. Here in the late 1980s, an unidentified Class 47 pauses with a King's Lynn to Liverpool Street express. FFP Media

BOURNEMOUTH

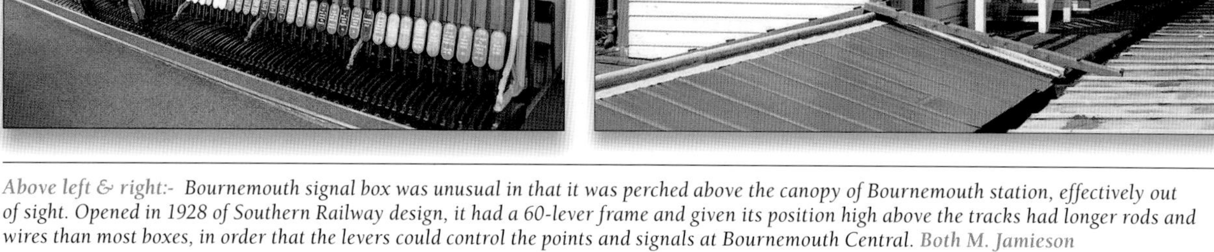

Above left & right:- Bournemouth signal box was unusual in that it was perched above the canopy of Bournemouth station, effectively out of sight. Opened in 1928 of Southern Railway design, it had a 60-lever frame and given its position high above the tracks had longer rods and wires than most boxes, in order that the levers could control the points and signals at Bournemouth Central. Both M. Jamieson

BRANKSOME

Left & below:- *Branksome signal box controlled the junction to Bournemouth Traction & Rolling Stock Maintenance Depot. It dated back to 1886 and had a 30-lever frame as shown here in the interior view.* Both M. Jamieson

BROXBOURNE

Below:- *Perhaps not strictly within the remit of this book is the 1960 panel box at Broxbourne. Built as part of the GE suburban electrification and a modern panel box, it closed in 2003 as the Liverpool Street IECC extended its sphere of influence. Its external design is typical of many smaller panel boxes of the era.* D. Allen

CHESHUNT JUNCTION

Below left:- *Cheshunt Junction SB dated from 1891 and was fitted with a 64-lever McKenzie & Holland lever frame. It was a time of great change at Cheshunt. The new Churchbury loop (known today as the Southbury loop) opened and the SB controlled the junction. In addition, the station was re-sited and provided with bays on both the "up" and "down" sides. Major changes accompanied electrification of the Southbury loop in 1960. All main running line semaphores at Cheshunt were replaced by searchlight colour light signals. Control of the Southbury loop was now shared between Cheshunt and Enfield Town SBs. The platform bays were retained to cater for terminating DMU services using the non-electrified Lea Valley to the south. When the Lea Valley was electrified in 1969, the "up" bay platform was taken out of use. However, it wasn't until December 1975, during further resignalling and remodelling, that the lever frame was removed and replaced by a small panel. It was decommissioned in May 2003.* D. Allen

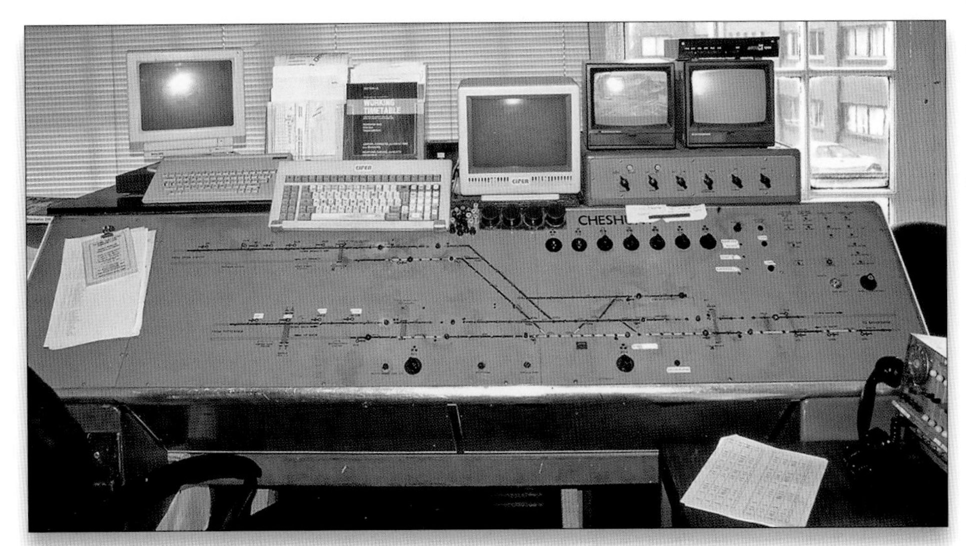

GARSTON JUNCTION

Right:- *The signal box at Garston Junction was not closed voluntarily, but destroyed by fire (and eventually demolished in 2006). Freight traffic to Garston Docks was in decline but the box might have survived for a few more years had it not been for the fire, which was almost certainly vandalism. The box dated back to 1908 and was of LNWR design with a 78-lever frame.* M. Rhodes

HARLOW MILL

Left:- *Another 1960-vintage panel box which disappeared in 2003 as a result of the expansion of the Liverpool Street IECC was at Harlow Mill. Class 317 No. 317668 passes with a Liverpool Street to Stansted Airport service.* D.Allen

HERTFORD EAST

Right- *With a Network SouthEast-branded nameboard, the box at Hertford East is seen here shortly before closure. Dating back to 1887 it had a 45-lever McKenzie & Holland frame.* D. Allen

ROYDON

Left:- The signal box at Roydon certainly wouldn't win any beauty contests! Suitably "modernised" it is hard to discern the GER 1876 origins of the structure. It contained a 27-lever frame and was closed as part of the expansion of the Liverpool Street IECC along the Cambridge line in 2003. D. Allen

SPELBROOK

Right:- The wooden box at Spelbrook dated back to 1898 and contained a 24-lever frame. D. Pearce

ST. MARGARETS

Below:- The 56-lever frame in St. Margarets signal box on the Hertford East branch can be glimpsed in this view. Dating back to 1887, the box closed as part of this year's London Liverpool Street IECC expansion. D. Allen

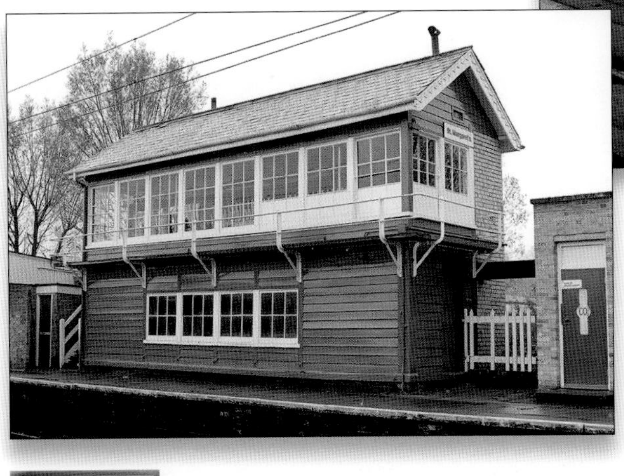

WARE

Right:- Ware signal box was unusual in that it was built in 1960, when the Hertford East branch was electrified, but it had a lever frame rather than a panel like the boxes at Broxbourne and Harlow Mill. Originally it had a 33-lever frame in the old 1881 GER signal box, but the new 1960 construction seen here was fitted with a 20-lever frame which survived until closure. D. Allen

2004

The main resignalling event of 2004 was the Marston Vale scheme and the opening of the new Marston Vale signalling control centre, located at Ridgmont on the Bedford to Bletchley line. This led to the closure of the signal boxes at Bedford St. Johns No. 1, Fenny Stratford, Forders Siding, Millbrook Station, Ridgmont and Woburn Sands. Leamington power box, opened in 1985 as a replacement for the 121-lever GWR box, also extended its coverage by taking over Fenny Compton signal box. Lastly the Stoke-on-Trent signalling centre was extended with the closure of Betley Road, Madeley and Norton Bridge.

2004		
Bedford St. Johns No. 1	BR (LMR) - 34 levers - 1977	6/9
Betley Road	LNWR - 23 levers - 1875	28/6
Fenny Compton	BR (WR) - 77 levers - 1960	4/5
Fenny Stratford	LNWR - 22 levers - 1883	6/9
Forders Siding	LMS - 40 levers - 1931	6/9
Madeley	LMS - 40 levers - 1930	28/6
Millbrook Station	LNWR - 10 levers - 1870	6/9
Norton Bridge	BR (LMR) - NX panel - 1961	28/6
Ridgmont	LMS - 12 levers - 1934	6/9
Woburn Sands	LNWR - 25 levers - 1904	6/9
Closure of 9 mechanical boxes and 1 NX panel		
Loss of 283 levers		

BEDFORD ST. JOHNS

Right:- In 2004, when the Bedford to Bletchley line was resignalled, the dreaded palisade fencing was already beginning to appear around the network. Bedford St. Johns signal box is seen here, a relatively modern 1977 construction, necessitated when the original LNWR box was severely damaged by fire. It had a 34-lever frame and was replaced along with all the other boxes along the line by the Marston Vale SCC. D. Allen

BETLEY ROAD

Above:- The diminutive Betley Road SB opened in 1875 when the LNWR widened the route from two to four tracks between Stafford and Crewe and opened a station; the latter closing in 1945. In 1961, as part of preparation for electrification, the SB was converted to electro-mechanical operation with a 23-lever frame, and all semaphores replaced by colour lights. It was decommissioned in June 2004 when control was transferred to the Norton Bridge workstation in Stoke-on-Trent SCC. Since March 2016, the route has been the responsibility of Rugby ROC Stafford workstation. D. Allen

FENNY COMPTON

Right:- On 11 February 1983, Class 56 No. 56096 passes Fenny Compton signal box with 6V57, a Barrow Hill to Didcot MGR service. The author's first car, a dilapidated Renault 7, stands in the foreground. Fenny Compton dated from 1960 and was of BR (WR) design with 77 levers. M. Rhodes

FENNY STRATFORD

Left:- A somewhat constricted view of the box at Fenny Stratford – which was built in 1883 by the LNWR and had 22 levers. The box opened when block working was first introduced along the route. In June 1965 it became a fringe to Bletchley PSB. The signals on the Bletchley side of the SB were replaced with colour lights and Fenny Stratford controlled the junction with the newly-built flyover lines. This conventional double-track junction was singled in stages during 1972. Then in February 1976, half a mile of the route through the station was singled leaving all traffic to use the former "up" platform. AB working to Woburn Sands SB continued until September 2004 when Fenny Stratford and all SBs on the Bedford to Bletchley line were replaced by Marston Vale SCC. D. Allen

FORDERS SIDINGS

Right:- Back in summer 1986 signalling alterations were under way to the semaphores at Forders Sidings as a Bedford to Bletchley service passes with an incorrect destination blind. The box dated from 1931 and had 40 levers. P. Shannon

MADELEY

Above left & right:- Most of the 40-lever frame of Madeley box is shown in this superb internal night view. The box itself dated from 1930 and was built by the LMS. The expansion of the Stoke-on-Trent SCC along the main line led to the closure of this box as well as Betley Road and Norton Bridge in 2004. Both FFP Media

MILLBROOK STATION

Right:- The small hut on the right of this image dated back to 1870 and was the LNWR signal box at Millbrook. The lever frame, which controlled the approaches to the station and the manually-operated crossing here, can be seen outside to the left of the box. The original 11-lever frame was replaced in 1990 by a frame containing 10 levers. P. Shannon

NORTON BRIDGE

Right & below:- Another WCML electrification signal box which perhaps is neither heritage nor mechanical is illustrated here, thanks to the amazing collection of David Allen. Norton Bridge PSB was commissioned in October 1961 as part of the Euston Main Line Electrification Scheme. Besides initially replacing six mechanical SBs, the station was reduced to a single island platform and the junction with the Stoke-on-Trent line simplified. The PSB was decommissioned by Network Rail in June 2004 when control was transferred to Stoke-on-Trent SCC's Norton Bridge workstation. From then, the station was out of use but was not officially closed until December 2017. In March 2016, the former junction for Stoke-on-Trent was severed and a grade-separated junction (flyover) commissioned connecting the slow lines with the line towards Stoke-on-Trent. In March 2016, control was transferred to the Rugby ROC Stafford workstation. Both D. Allen

RIDGMONT

Right:- The arrangement of levers 'exposed to the elements' on Ridgmont's station platform, though very unusual, wasn't unique. For some reason, the Railway Inspectorate gave approval for this cheap arrangement to exist. The block instruments were housed in the station building allowing a porter/signalman to operate them. Note that both distant signals (levers 1 and 12) are mechanically worked semaphores and both section signals (levers 3 and 10) have a white band indicating Line Clear Release (LCR). This view taken on 14 May 2004 shows work under way for the Marston Vale resignalling the following September, with the 12-lever frame dating from 1934 in a sorry state.

This pattern of external frame survives on several minor lines like the York to Harrogate route and the Barton-on-Humber branch, where lever frames are housed outside, with the signalman expected to pop out from the station, into the elements, to change the points. D. Allen

WOBURN SANDS

Above:- Typical motive power for the Bedford to Bletchley service was a single-car DMU, as seen here on 6 August 1993 at Woburn Sands station. The signal box dated from 1904 and had a 25-lever frame. P. Shannon

2005

Two signal boxes which had been out of use for many years were finally demolished in 2005; Saxby Junction on the Peterborough to Leicester line and Snowdon Colliery signal box in Kent. The 1959 box at Sandbach was also removed from service. Elsewhere, the Stoke area resignalling continued, with closure of the box at Colwich. The area controlled by the Chester power signal box was also extended to include lines formerly controlled by Mold Junction and Sandycroft mechanical boxes. A new gabled structure was built at Allington Junction with an NX panel to take over the work of the former Allington Junction mechanical box and also the box at Barkston East Junction. Two other small changes in the form of single box closures took place when New Hythe box was closed and taken over by Aylesford. Similarly Horsham box was closed with control ceded to Three Bridges area signalling centre.

2005		
Allington Junction	GNR - 22 levers - 1875	3/10
Barkston East Junction	GNR - 29 levers - 1882	3/10
Colwich	BR (LMR) - 40 levers - 1961	12/6
Horsham	SR - 90 levers - 1938	30/8
Mold Junction	LNWR - 60 levers - 1902	24/1
New Hythe	SR - 20 levers - 1939	7/11
Sandbach	BR (LMR) - OCS panel - 1959	10/12
Sandycroft	LNWR - 60 levers - 1900	24/1
Saxby Junction	MR - 63 levers - 1893	6/2
Snowdon Colliery	BR (SR) - 18 levers - 1953	28/2
Warnham	LBSCR - 20 levers - 1877	22/8
Willesden Suburban	BR (LMR) - NX panel - 1965	18/7
Wilmslow	BR (LMR) - OCS panel - 1959	10/12
Closure of 10 mechanical boxes and 3 panel boxes		
Loss of 422 levers		

ALLINGTON JUNCTION

Right:- The 1875 GNR signal box at Allington Junction was closed and demolished in 2005 and replaced by a Network Rail standard gable-roofed modern construction. This was situated roughly where the 15 mph sign is in this view. The new box contained a small NX panel which took over the work of the 22-lever frame here and also the tracks controlled from neighbouring Barkston East Junction box. D. Allen

BARKSTON EAST JUNCTION

Left:- Summer Saturday traffic to Skegness was heavy during the 1980s and one of several services from the East Midlands is seen here passing Barkston East Junction on 16 July 1983 behind Class 45 No. 45007. The single-line chord to the East Coast Main Line was removed during the 2005 resignalling. The box here dated back to 1882 and had a 29-lever frame. P. Shannon

COLWICH

Right:- The 1961 box at Colwich, built at the time of electrification and resignalling of the WCML, closed and the work of its 40 levers was added to the Stoke-on-Trent SCC. FFP Media

HORSHAM

Below:- The imposing signal box at Horsham was built in 1938 and had a 90-lever frame. Its work was moved to the Three Bridges signalling centre, which later morphed into the Three Bridges ROC. D. Allen

MOLD JUNCTION

Below:- Mold Junction SB – formerly Mold Junction No. 1 – was one of four SBs controlling this location. In common with other SBs on the North Wales coast, it was opened when the route was quadrupled. When Stage 2 of the commissioning of Chester PSB was implemented in May 1984, Mold Junction SB became the fringe on the North Wales Main Line. When this view was taken in June 1994, it also controlled Absolute Block working to Sandycroft. By the time the box at Mold Junction closed in 2005, the intricate trackwork and extensive marshalling yards in the area had all been closed. The 1902 box had 60 levers and once controlled access to extensive marshalling yards at Mold Junction as well as a short branch to a slate tip. Upon closure the new fringe box for Chester PSB became Rockcliffe Hall. D. Allen

NEW HYTHE

Right:- The thick concrete roof of New Hythe box is typical of several designs built during and just after the Second World War. The small 1939 box had a 20-lever frame and closed when a new IFS panel was installed at neighbouring Aylesford. During the autumn of 2005, Network Rail (South) carried out a programme of signalling changes to the so-called Medway Valley Line. Most significant was the complete removal of mechanical signalling. Between Cuxton and Wateringbury, AB working was retained and New Hythe SB was the only SB casualty. It wasn't really required since the level crossing had been replaced by a bridge in 1995 and the new AB section between Aylesford and Snodland was only 2 miles. It was a relatively simple matter to install a ground frame to access the Brookgate Siding. Following the closure of Snodland SB in June 2013, the line between Cuxton and Aylesford was converted to Track Circuit Block. D. Allen

SANDBACH

Right:- An early example of Modernisation Plan investment was the 1959 box at Sandbach with its red LMR sign boards looking somewhat out of place on what was considered a sleek modern building at the time. A.F. Bullimore Collection

SANDYCROFT

Above:- Having paused for a signal check, Class 47 No. 47364 accelerates past Sandycroft on 14 August 1986 with 4D58, the Lawley Street to Holyhead freightliner service. The box at Sandycroft dated from 1900 and had a 60-lever frame. P. Shannon

SAXBY JUNCTION

Right:- Saxby Junction was something of an anachronism, in that the junction it controlled disappeared in the 1960s when the Midland line to Little Bytham closed. The fine 1893-vintage Midland Railway box had been out of use for several years before its demolition in 2005. Trains along the Leicester to Peterborough line were controlled by Melton Mowbray and Whissendine signal boxes along this stretch, with closure of Saxby Junction simply leading to longer sections on this piece of line. D. Allen

SNOWDON COLLIERY

Left:- The second signal box at Snowdon burnt down in 1950 and was replaced by a 4-lever ground frame. The SB illustrated here was the third and last to be built on the site. It opened in March 1953 to serve the Kent coalfield mine of the same name and had an 18-lever frame. Though the mine closed in 1987, the SB survived until February 2005. It is shown proudly proclaiming its ownership by Railfreight; a short-lived period when BR was preparing for Privatisation and infrastructure became the responsibility of the Sectors. All the other SBs on the route were the responsibility of Network SouthEast. D. Allen

WARNHAM

Right:- The small, Saxby & Farmer-designed box at Warnham was built in 1877 and had a 20-lever frame. Its closure was part of the Horsham resignalling scheme with control taken over by the Three Bridges signalling centre. T. Maxted

2006

The major new construction in 2006 was at Ferrybridge where a new NX panel was installed, allowing the closure of the old Ferrybridge box which had dated from 1956 and also Knottingley cabin. A new Westcad VDU at Madeley Junction took control of the areas formerly signalled by the boxes at Codsall, Cosford and Lightmoor Junction. Similar small schemes led to the closure of Hinckley and Narborough boxes with a new Westcad VDU installed in Croft signal box and also the closure of Mouldsworth box with the area controlled by Mickle Trafford cabin. Once again a signal box was lost to fire and vandalism when Northampton Bridge Street closed. The signal box at Stanton Gate closed after many years out of use, as did Wennington Junction which had last been regularly manned as long ago as 1992.

2006		
Codsall	GWR - 25 levers - 1929	23/10
Cosford	GWR - 39 levers - 1939	23/10
Ferrybridge	BR (NER) - panel - 1956	18/4
Hinckley	LNWR - 20 levers - 1894	31/7
Knottingley	BR (NER) - panel - 1967	29/8
Lightmoor Junction	BR (WR) - 31 levers - 1951	23/10
Mouldsworth	CLC - 34 levers - 1903	22/5
Narborough	LNWR - 23 levers - 1875	31/7
Northampton Bridge Street	LNWR - 19 levers - 1907	15/4
Stanton Gate	BR (LMR) - 50 levers - 1969	24/6
Wennington Junction	MR - 27 levers - 1890	14/1
Closure of 9 mechanical boxes and 2 panel boxes		
Loss of 268 levers		

CODSALL

Left:- A Shrewsbury to Birmingham service passes Codsall signal box on 20 August 1993. The 1929 GWR structure contained a 25-lever frame which was replaced by a new VDU in Madeley Junction covering the line from there to Wolverhampton. M. Rhodes

COSFORD

Right:- A Littleton Colliery to Ironbridge Power Station MGR service passes Cosford behind Class 58 No. 58008. The 39-lever frame in this 1939-vintage GWR box had controlled LMS upper quadrant signals towards the end of its life. M. Rhodes

FERRYBRIDGE

Right:- The flat-roofed box at Ferrybridge was constructed in 1956 to a BR (NER) design and had a small panel installed in 1981, replacing the mechanical frame. Here, Class 56 No. 56005 passes the box in June 1986 with 6K95, an empty MGR from Ferrybridge Power Station to Goldthorpe Colliery. M. Rhodes

HINCKLEY

Above & right:- Two images taken in July 2005, just before it closed, show the 1894 box at Hinckley. The lever frame has already seen the loss of some levers in the central section, with just 20 still in place located at either end of the box. Both N. Allsop

KNOTTINGLEY

Left:- The rather shabby-looking former box at Knottingley closed in 1965 when control was transferred to the new Ferrybridge signal box. The new box, opened in 1967 to a BR (NER) design, was constructed on the rebuilt brick base of its predecessor. The new box contained a small panel. Class 66 No. 66555 is seen here passing with an empty MGR from Drax Power Station on 30 April 2004. M. Rhodes

LIGHTMOOR JUNCTION

Right:- The replacement Lightmoor Junction SB opened in 1951 with a 31-lever frame. Though not built to a common style, BR(WR) did commission a similar and larger example at Wellington No. 2 in 1953. They are rather uninspiring 'box-like' structures with flat roofs. Note also the internal staircase; very much a GWR/BR(WR) feature. The SB witnessed the end of passenger services between Wellington and Craven Arms and later Much Wenlock; it survived the closure of the Dawley branch in 1981. Even after the opening of the Ironbridge coal-fired power station in 1969, the single line to Madeley Junction was controlled by Electric Token Block (ETB). In October 2006, the SB was decommissioned and the branch to the power station became the responsibility of Madeley Junction SB. D. Allen

MOULDSWORTH

Left:- One of just a handful of surviving Cheshire Lines Committee (CLC) signal boxes closed in 2006 at Mouldsworth Junction. The box is seen here in 2002; it was built in 1903 with a 34-lever frame. P. Shannon

NARBOROUGH

Left & above:- Both Narborough and Hinckley signal boxes closed with control passing to Croft signal box (which itself closed just five years later). The signal cabin at Narborough dated back to 1875 and had been equipped with a 23-lever frame which, as the internal view shows, had been replaced with a small panel during the 1990s. D. Allen & N. Allsop

NORTHAMPTON BRIDGE STREET

Right:- Situated on a rarely-used freight-only line, the signal box at Northampton Bridge Street was burnt down in 2006. Built in 1907 it had a 19-lever frame. In 1982 Class 25 No. 25288 is seen passing with 9T26, a trip freight from Northampton Yard to Bridge Street Sidings made up of engineering wagons. M. Rhodes

STANTON GATE

Left:- The large tracts of waste land around the signal box at Stanton Gate bear witness to the large marshalling yards that used to operate here. The 1969-built signal box had a 50-lever frame. Class 31 No. 31218 passes in July 1984 with empty steel wagons used to carry continuously-welded rails. M. Rhodes

WENNINGTON JUNCTION

Right:- The classic Midland Railway box at Wennington Junction had only seen occasional use during the previous 14 years and finally closed in 2006. A lengthy Leeds to Morecambe service (doubled in size for summer Saturday traffic to the coast) passes the 1890-vintage box with is 27-lever frame in July 1983. M. Rhodes

2007

2007 was characterised by a number of small schemes where a single box was closed with traffic control taken over by an adjacent signal box, usually by the addition of a small panel or extension to an existing panel. The first of these was at Cliff House, south of Hartlepool where control was transferred to Greatham box. In Wakefield, Oakenshaw box closed with its signals then controlled from Wakefield Kirkgate signal box, which itself was newly built with an NX panel in 2007 to replace an older 1982-vintage portable building. This in turn had replaced the original Wakefield Kirkgate signal box which dated back to 1901. Larbert Junction box was closed with trains controlled from Larbert North, just a couple of hundred yards away. Further south in Lancashire, Rainhill box was closed and control passed to Huyton signal box. Two signal boxes that had been out of use for some time in the North West were demolished at Chorley Level Crossing and Carterhouse Junction near Runcorn.

In the Ebbw Vale, Lime Kiln Sidings closed, with Park Junction, just north of Newport, assuming control of this section of track. In South Wales again, Pencoed Crossing closed with supervision of the crossing passing to Port Talbot power box. In the East Midlands, Pinxton closed when the route was added to the panel at Trent power signal box, which also took over the track through Sleights East. Then at Hademore Crossing the box was closed and the gates supervised from Lichfield Trent Valley box. The heritage structure at Stallingborough closed to be replaced by a new gabled building with an NX panel inside. The poor old building at Stallingborough was listing so badly that signalmen used to race marbles down the slope for entertainment! The one major new build project was the Havant area signalling centre which led to the closure of signal boxes at Havant itself as well as Portsmouth and Portsmouth Harbour.

2007		
Carterhouse Junction	LNWR - 30 levers - 1896	14/4
Chorley Level Crossing	L&Y - 4 levers - 1879	20/8
Cliff House	BR (NER) - 70 levers - 1958	9/7
Coventry	BR (LMR) - NX panel - 1962	29/8
Hademore Crossing	LNWR - 15 levers - 1899	18/3
Havant	LBSCR - 63 levers - 1876	29/10
Larbert Junction	CR - 40 levers - 1881	14/5
Lime Kiln Sidings	GWR - 29 levers - 1887	30/11
Oakenshaw	LMS - panel - 1928	27/12
Pencoed Crossing	GWR - 38 levers - 1905	13/4
Pinxton	MR - 28 levers - 1897	6/8
Portsmouth	BR (SR) - NX panel - 1968	
Portsmouth Harbour	SR - IFS panel - 1946	29/10
Rainhill	LNWR - 25 levers - 1895	26/3
Sleights East	MR - IFS panel - 1892	6/8
Stallingborough	MS&LR - 20 levers - 1884	1/10
Wakefield Kirkgate	BR (ER) - panel - 1982	27/12
Closure of 11 mechanical boxes and 6 panel boxes		
Loss of 362 levers		

Above:- By 2007, the Fiddlers Ferry branch line had been controlled from Ditton and Fidlers Ferry (note the different spelling of the box name!) signal boxes for many years, with Carterhouse Junction "switched out". The 1896 LNWR box with its 30-lever frame, was finally demolished in 2007. D. Allen

CHORLEY LEVEL CROSSING

Right:- The signal box at Chorley Level Crossing was rendered redundant when the crossing at the south end of the station was replaced by an underpass in the 1990s. Dating back to 1879, it contained just four mechanical levers. It was finally demolished in 2007. Here, in April 1984, Class 47 No. 47497 passes with an Edinburgh & Glasgow to Manchester service. P. Shannon

CLIFF HOUSE

Right:- The once extensive sidings at Cliff House, south of Hartlepool, were rusty and disused by the time this image was taken of the signal box here. Opened in 1958 and with a 70-lever frame, the box was to have been at the centre of a new Modernisation Plan marshalling yard. In the end the new yard was never built and the colliery traffic controlled by the box had dwindled to almost nothing by the early 1980s. D. Allen

HADEMORE CROSSING

Left:- Hademore Crossing signal box controlled the Fisherwick Road level crossing between Tamworth and Lichfield on the Trent Valley Line. Dating from 1899 it originally had a 15-lever frame but this was replaced in the late 1970s by individual function switches (IFS). The box lives on having been donated to the Chasewater Railway and placed on a new brick base. D. Allen

HAVANT

Left:- At the time of writing the signal box at Havant is still standing, albeit having been closed for more than a decade. Built in 1876, it contained a 63-lever frame. T. Maxted

LARBERT JUNCTION

Above:- The 1881-built former Caledonian Railway signal box at Larbert Junction was situated on an intensively-signalled stretch of railway between Larbert, Polmont and Greenhill. The closure of its 40-lever frame was made possible by the installation of colour light signals and motorised points, controlled from Larbert North box. Both D. Allen

LIME KILN SIDINGS

Left:- Resignalling in conjunction with the reopening of the Ebbw Vale Line to passenger services in February 2008, led to the closure of Lime Kiln Sidings signal box; built in 1887, it contained a 29-lever frame. Control of this area and indeed the whole valley became centred in Park Junction signal box. Here in 1979, Class 37 No. 37158 heads up the valley "engine & van" from Ebbw Junction depot to Celynen South Colliery. M. Rhodes

OAKENSHAW

Left:- Oakenshaw North Junction box was opened in 1928 and from 1965 the lever frame here was replaced by a panel. Back in June 1986, Class 47 No. 47340 passes along the former Midland Main Line from Leeds to Sheffield with 1V88, a Leeds to Plymouth parcels train. Once the Midland Main Line closed, only the tracks to the right of this view were left and by the 21st century the once busy junction served only as the entrance to a single-track freight route to Monk Bretton glassworks. M. Rhodes

PENCOED CROSSING

Right:- Pencoed Crossing, between Bridgend and Port Talbot on the South Wales Main Line, was controlled by a 1905-vintage GWR signal box shown here. In September 1965, stage 4 of the Port Talbot Extension Multiple Aspect Scheme was brought into use. Eight SBs between Pyle and Pencoed on the South Wales Main Line were decommissioned and one, Cowbridge Road, was replaced. Pencoed East SB, renamed Pencoed Crossing ground frame was retained as a gate box with a 38-lever frame. The external condition leaves a lot to be desired but the grilles over the windows are regrettably often a necessary precaution. It was decommissioned in April 2007, when the level crossing was fitted with CCTV controlled from Port Talbot PSB. D. Allen

PINXTON

Left:- Pinxton box, in the shadow of the M1 motorway, dated back to 1897 and had a 28-lever frame. Here, on 2 January 1990, Class 58 No. 58048 restarts 6Z92, a Shirebrook to Toton MGR, having been assisted over the slippery rails by fellow Class 58 No. 58044 because it was the first train over Kirkby summit since before Christmas 1989. M. Rhodes

PORTSMOUTH HARBOUR

Right:- The original Portsmouth Harbour box was built in 1876, but that wooden structure was replaced by the 1946 building illustrated here. This contained a 47-lever Westinghouse 'L' miniature lever frame which was replaced in 1968 by an IFS panel. T. Maxted

RAINHILL

Right:- Rainhill box, on the site of the famous Rainhill trials, opened in 1895 and had 25 levers. Rainhill SB became a fringe to the newly-opened Warrington PSB on the Chat Moss lines towards Liverpool in September 1972. It closed in March 2007 when Absolute Block working to Huyton was replaced by Track Circuit Block and Huyton SB assumed control. D. Allen

SLEIGHTS EAST

Below:- Opened in 1892, the Midland Railway box at Sleights East enjoyed a 'makeover' in 2003 and after only four years of operational life on Network Rail, the SB looks very nice considering it was celebrating its 111th birthday. It is displaying the characteristic features of former Midland Railway SBs, although at least one finial is missing. Sleights East SB became a fringe to Trent PSB in October 1969. Later, in 1980, a panel replaced the lever frame when the last semaphores were removed and the level crossing gates were replaced by lifting barriers. It continued to work AB to Pinxton SB until both SBs were dispensed with with under Part 1 of the East Midlands Resignalling Scheme in August 2007. Control was transferred to the Erewash workstation, which was temporarily housed in Trent PSB. Twelve months later, the workstation was moved to East Midlands SCC. The signal box was saved by a local businessman and is now at Bolton Abbey. D. Allen

STALLINGBOROUGH

Left:- The Manchester Sheffield and Lincolnshire Railway signal box at Stallingborough was already leaning significantly when this image was taken in 1996. Indeed, the signalman on duty demonstrated the speed of marbles running down the sloping floor when I visited!. Built in 1884 and with a 20-lever frame, its closure came as a result of structural instability. It was replaced by a Network Rail gabled brick building which itself closed at the end of 2015 when the line from Scunthorpe to Cleethorpes came under the control of York ROC. M. Rhodes

2008

The major signalling event of 2008 was the August Bank Holiday possession at Lincoln with the removal of the fine semaphores in the city. The Lincoln signalling centre, located out at West Holmes, took over the work of four boxes at Pelham Street Junction, High Street (Lincoln), East Holmes and West Holmes. Another solitary box closure occurred at Abercynon, where a new building made up of two portable buildings replaced the GWR-era signal box and housed a new IFS panel and VDUs. On the Southern Region, Barnham box closed with control passing to the new Barnham signalling centre which housed an NX panel under a gabled roof. In the West Midlands, Bentley Heath Crossing, Lichfield Trent Valley and Tamworth Low Level boxes all closed as the West Midlands signalling centre and the Rugby signalling control centre extended their respective reaches. Finally, Stanlow & Thornton box, which had been out of use for a couple of years, was demolished, although the frame from the box was saved for use on The Embsay & Bolton Abbey Steam Railway.

2008		
Abercynon	GWR - 35 levers - 1932	30/5
Barnham	LBSCR - 75 levers - 1911	10/11
Bentley Heath Crossing	GWR - 49 levers - 1932	18/2
Cemetery North Junction	NER - 20 levers - 1905	20/12
East Holmes	GNR - 35 levers - 1873	1/9
Glasgow Central SC	BR (ScR) - NX panel - 1961	27/12
High Street (Lincoln)	GNR - 36 levers - 1883	1/9
Lichfield Trent Valley	LNWR - 80 levers - 1911	29/5
Nuneaton	BR (LMR) - NX panel - 1963	8/9
Pelham Street Junction	GNR - 100 levers - 1883	1/9
Plean Junction	CR - 26 levers - 1870	30/6
Rosyth Dockyard	NBR - 45 levers - 1917	6/7
Stanlow & Thornton	LMS - 50 levers - 1941	11/2
Tamworth Low Level	LNWR - 35 levers - 1910	8/9
West Holmes	GER - 69 levers - 1882	1/9
Closure of 13 mechanical boxes and 2 panel boxes		
Loss of 655 levers		

ABERCYNON

Right & below:- Two views of Abercynon signal box taken in the 1990s. The external view shows Class 66 No. 66026 passing with an empty MGR from Barry to Tower Colliery. The signalman walks back to the box having given the token to the train driver for the single-line section to Abercwmboi. Opened in 1932, the GWR box replaced two older cabins at Abercynon North & South. Originally it had 93 levers, but by 1999 when this image was taken, the frame had been reduced to 35 levers. A new panel was added in 1977 when the box at Stormstown to the south was closed. Further panels were added in 1989 and 2001 arising from the new passenger service to Aberdare. The interior view shows signalman Mr J. Morgan filling in the train register book after the train has passed. The 35-lever frame can be seen behind him and the 1977 panel in the distance. Both M. Rhodes

BARNHAM

Right & below:- The 75-lever frame at Barnham was built in 1911 by the London Brighton and South Coast Railway. Barnham was the junction for the Bognor Regis branch and also had a few carriage sidings as our external view of the box illustrates. Both T. Maxted

BENTLEY HEATH CROSSING

Right:- Bentley Heath Crossing replaced an earlier SB in 1932, when the GWR main line was quadrupled between Lapworth and Olton. It was reduced to a gate box in 1969, when control passed to Saltley PSB. In 1973 the gates were replaced by barriers. Control of the signalling and level crossing became the responsibility of the West Midlands SC when the Leamington Corridor Resignalling was commissioned in February 2008. Regrettably, rationalisation of the route was started in 1968 when the relief lines north of Bentley Heath were lifted. To the south, loops were retained as far Dorridge. When this photograph was taken on 21 August 1996, the SB was in a good external condition. A peculiarity of the GWR was to include 'Signal Box' on the iron name boards. D. Allen

CEMETERY NORTH JUNCTION

Left:- On a dismal day in August 1986, Class 37 No. 37239 arrives at Cemetery North Junction with 6P62, the daily limestone train from Thrislington Quarry. The box, which opened in 1905, had by this time had its frame reduced to just 20 levers. M. Rhodes

EAST HOLMES

Right:- Using a newly-acquired (and rapidly sold!) 500mm mirror lens, this view shows Lincoln East Holmes signal box with an unidentified Class 31 in the goods yard behind the box, taken from the footbridge at Lincoln High Street. East Holmes controlled a manual gate crossing, was built in 1873 and had a 35-lever frame. M. Rhodes

HIGH STREET (LINCOLN)

Left:- In 1996, Class 153 No. 153364 arrives at Lincoln with a local service from Newark. High Street signal box was built in 1883 and had a 36-lever frame and was busy controlling the road crossing to the west of Lincoln Central station. East Holmes signal box can be seen to the left, in the background. M. Rhodes

LICHFIELD TRENT VALLEY

Right:- In summer 1984, Class 86 No. 86218 passes Lichfield Trent Valley No. 1 signal box. Built in 1911 by the LNWR, it contained 80 levers. M. Rhodes

PELHAM STREET JUNCTION

Above:- The 1883 GNR signal box at Pelham Street Junction was a member of the signalling "100" club with its 100 levers. The view of the frame was taken during a visit in July 1996. The box was located below the flyover of the main road through Lincoln and was difficult to photograph with a train in the view. The external view, taken in 1984, shows the eastern half of the box as Class 114 DMU No. 53015 & 54017 arrives with a Peterborough to Doncaster passenger service. In the background is Sincil Bank signal box which had closed at the start of 1984; the automated barriers which replaced the previously manually-operated ones can be seen half raised. Both M. Rhodes

PLEAN JUNCTION

Right:- Plean Junction SB, dating back to the early 1870s, is another survivor from the introduction of block working. It was tall to enable the signalman to see over the road bridge. The trackbed on either side of the main line was formerly occupied by loops serving three colliery branch lines and a quarry, the last of which closed in 1964. However, in 1974 a totally new connection was laid into the Scottish Timber Products plant. The closure of Plean SB took place in June 2008 during Stage 2 of the resignalling. All pointwork leading to the siding was removed and AB working was replaced by TCB between Larbert North and Stirling Middle SBs. D. Allen

ROSYTH DOCKYARD

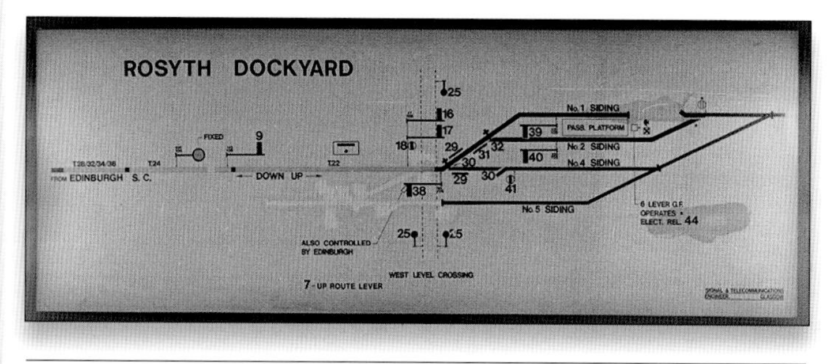

Right & above:- The 45-lever-framed, 1917-vintage NBR signal box in Rosyth Dockyard was rarely photographed because it was within the MOD security perimeter. I was fortunate in 1990 to ride on the 6G07 trip freight from Thornton Yard to Rosyth via Crombie and a run-round at Townhill Junction. I was invited into the signal box to record the box diagram, before trundling back to Thornton Yard in the cab of Class 20 No. 20137. Both M. Rhodes

STANLOW & THORNTON

Left:- The signal box at Stanlow & Thornton dated back to 1941 and had a 50-lever signal frame. It controlled access to the yard at Stanlow Oil Refinery but after the decision by Shell in 1998 to cease all rail traffic from the oil refinery (even though it was one of the biggest producers in the UK), the box spent much of the subsequent decade switched out. Here, back in 1986, Class 25 No. 25907 passes with an Arpley to Ellesmere Port Speedlink service. P. Shannon

TAMWORTH LOW LEVEL

Left:- The final of three signal boxes to close as a result of the Trent Valley resignalling was Tamworth Low Level. Seen here in 2001, the box was opened in 1910 and had a 35-lever frame. Class 66 No. 66506 is seen passing with 6Z25, an extra freight from Dagenham Dock to Basford Hall Yard. I. Stewart

WEST HOLMES

Right & below:- West Holmes was the fourth of the Lincoln boxes to close during the resignalling of the area over the August bank holiday. The area had been earmarked for a new hump yard during the Modernisation Plan and the 1882-built, 69-lever box would have been pivotal to the eastern access to the yard. In the event the yard was never built and what sidings there were in Lincoln were eventually removed to build the new Lincoln University. The external view shows the box and associated semaphore signals, looking west from East Holmes Yard in 1986, whilst the interior view was taken a decade later in 1996. Both M. Rhodes

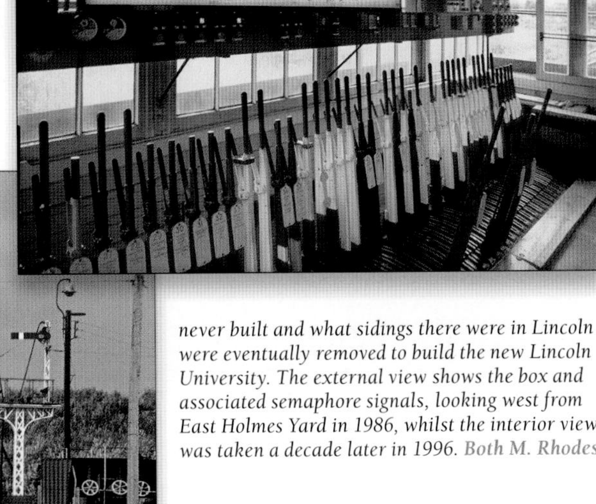

2009

There were no major building or resignalling schemes in 2009, but nevertheless small changes to existing signalling centres led to 19 mechanical boxes closing. The resignalling of the Nuneaton to Coventry line saw the closure of the signal boxes at Hawkesbury Lane, Three Spires Junction and Coundon Road. The northern half of this line is now signalled from the Rugby signalling centre, whilst the southern half is controlled by the West Midlands signalling centre. New facilities at the Colchester area signalling centre saw boxes at East Gate Junction, Frinton and Thorpe-le-Soken close. Thorpe-le-Soken was destined for preservation on the Chappel and Wakes Colne Railway, whilst East Gate Junction was kept standing as it is situated in a preservation area.

Work to extend Manchester Metrolink led to closure of Oldham Mumps and Shaw Station boxes. Resignalling between Mirfield and Sowerby Bridge saw control of this line taken on by Healey Mills power box and the signal boxes at Elland and Greetland closing. Three signal boxes closed after fire damage or long periods of disuse. Ollerton Colliery was vandalised and burnt down, whilst the boxes at Betteshanger Colliery and Church Stretton had long been out of use. The iconic signal box under the A52 at Stapleford & Sandiacre closed as the Toton area was resignalled to be controlled from the East Midlands signalling centre. This also led to the closure of Lock Lane Crossing signal box.

Three small local schemes saw Axminster close, to be controlled by Chard Junction and Harringay Park Junction was closed with control taken over by Tottenham signal box. The third local scheme saw Haltwhistle have a portable building replace the striking 19th century NER signal box, which fortunately has been preserved for other uses. Finally one change which didn't lead to the closure of the signal box, but abolition of a fine array of semaphores, was the installation of a new NX panel at Croes Newydd North Fork, just south of Wrexham. Fortunately the 1905 GWR signal cabin has survived, albeit without its 83-lever frame.

2009		
Axminster	BR (WR) - IFS panel - 1973	6/12
Betteshanger Colliery	SR - 16 levers - 1923	24/4
Church Stretton	S&H - 25 levers - 1872	14/3
Coundon Road	LNWR - 23 levers - 1876	26/5
East Gate Junction	LNER - 35 levers - 1924	2/3
Elland	BR (NER) - 60 levers - 1958	27/7
Frinton	LNER - 15 levers - 1936	4/5
Greetland	LMS - 55 levers - 1942	27/7
Haltwhistle	NER - IFS panel - 1915	20/4
Harringay Park Junction	BR (ER) - 25 levers - 1957	16/11
Hawkesbury Lane	LNWR - 26 levers - 1896	23/5
Lock Lane Crossing	BR (LMR) - 20 levers - 1955	27/12
Low Row	NER - 29 levers - 1874	6/4
Oldham Mumps	BR (LMR) - 50 levers - 1967	5/10
Ollerton Colliery	LNER - 30 levers - 1926	23/3
Shaw Station	BR (LMR) - 24 levers - 1940	5/10
Stapleford & Sandiacre	BR (LMR) - 115 levers - 1949	17/10
Thorpe-le-Soken	GER - IFS panel - 1882	4/5
Three Spires Junction	LNWR - 53 levers - 1914	26/5
Closure of 16 mechanical boxes and 3 panel boxes		
Loss of 601 levers		

AXMINSTER

Right:- Not listed in most records as a "signal box", the small panel and traditional signal box diagram at Axminster were located within the station building. A traditional desk with train register book was also present. The facility closed as part of the Salisbury to Exeter line resignalling. M. Jamieson

BETTESHANGER COLLIERY

Left:- Betteshanger was the largest colliery in the Kent Coalfield. The SB opened at the same time as the mine in 1923 and although the mine closed in 1989, the SB lingered on for another 20 years. When photographed in August 2001, the SB had been switched out of circuit for many years and boarded up. The appropriate signals were 'off' but all the facing crossovers and the trailing connection into the former colliery had been removed. Official closure was in April 2009 when all signals except the "down" distant were removed. The 3-aspect "down" distant also functioned as Deal SB's section signal. It was replaced by a 2-aspect LED. D. Allen

CHURCH STRETTON

Right:- Opening in 1872, Church Stretton SB dated from the introduction of block working on the Shrewsbury to Hereford line. When photographed in August 1988, Church Stretton box was only usually open for one shift (Monday–Friday) and subsequently it wasn't manned at all. Fortunately, neighbouring SBs at Dorrington and Marsh Brook survived and are now 145 years old. These very old SBs are extremely solid and have hipped roofs. Marsh Brook SB was retained because it is only three miles away and controls a level crossing. Church Stretton SB was never officially closed; it was just slowly demolished in March 2009. D. Allen

COUNDON ROAD

Above:- When these views were taken on 23 July 1998, Coundon Road SB was in a generally good condition. It dated from 1876, when the LNWR had just begun to use gable roofs. The brick base is obviously not original and there aren't any locking room windows. Needless to say, the steel staircase is not Victorian either! In contrast, the woodwork is in good order. An attempt has been made to paint out 'Station' and unfortunately, some of the letters are missing. The brick relay room alongside the SB dates from when Coundon Road SB became a fringe to the new Coventry PSB in April 1962. In the end, Coundon Road SB outlived Coventry PSB by 2 years. It closed in May 2009, when control was transferred to the West Midlands SC Coventry workstation. Both D. Allen

EAST GATE JUNCTION

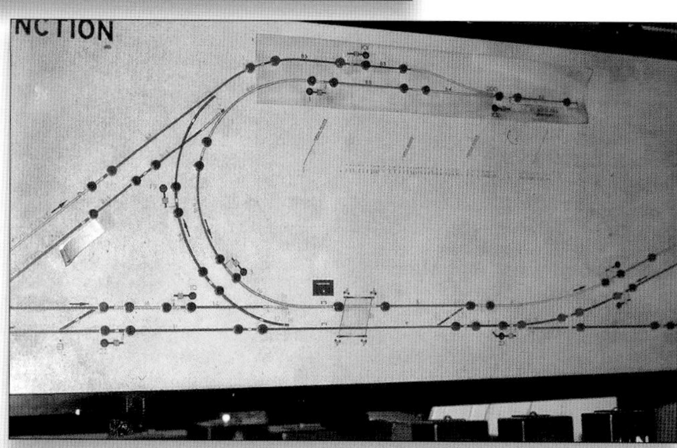

Above & right:- *The LNER SB at East Gate Junction opened in 1924. It amalgamated the roles of the former eponymous structure and the nearby Colne Junction. Complete control of the triangular layout was achieved in 1958 when Hythe Junction SB closed in the resignalling prior to electrification. Following the closure of Colchester Junction SB, it became a fringe to the new Colchester PSB in 1962. This PSB was replaced in 1983, but East Gate Junction SB remained a fringe. Earlier the same year, a panel was installed to replace St. Botolphs SB. East Gate Junction SB was decommissioned in March 2009, when the East Gate workstation in Colchester PSB assumed control.* Both D. Allen

ELLAND

Left:- *Elland SB, a BR (North Eastern Region) design, was commissioned in 1958 to replace the former L&Y East and West SBs. They opened in 1894 when the station was enlarged and the route widened. At the time, John Aspinall envisaged major improvements to the Calder Valley Line or the 'Line to Europe'. In July 2009, as part of a £6M resignalling scheme, Network Rail closed Greetland and Elland SBs. Pending transfer of control to Healey Mills SB, a temporary panel was established in the relay room at Greetland.* D. Allen

FRINTON

Right:- *The 1936 box at Frinton, with its 15 levers, was very unusual in that full size semaphores survived the 1959 Great Eastern electrification to Walton-on-the-Naze. Indeed it wasn't until Frinton gate box was decommissioned in April 2009, that they were replaced by 2-aspect LED signals. At the same time, control of signalling and the CCTV level crossing was transferred to the Thorpe-le-Soken workstation in Colchester ASC. A passing loop was installed by the LNER in 1938, but taken out of use by BR(ER) in 1974. During this period Frinton SB could switch out of circuit and all trains use the "up" platform. However, when the SB was 'switched in', the interlocking required all "down" trains use the "down" platform. This wasn't favoured unless trains were required to pass.* D. Allen

GREETLAND

Left:- Greetland No. 2 SB dates from 1942. The familiar air raid precaution (ARP) features are a give away. H.E. Morgan designed a standard SB that would withstand a bomb blast or direct hit by a 1kg incendiary bomb. It seems the 3-storey structure it replaced was too much of a risk. Note, someone has tastefully removed the 'No. 2' from the nameboard. It was photographed on 24 July 1990 and was, as usual, switched out of circuit. Though the SB controlled a junction, there was no regular traffic towards Halifax. This all changed in May 2000 when a passenger service was restored. The SB eventually closed in July 2009 and control transferred to Healey Mills SB. D. Allen

HALTWHISTLE

Left:- A classic design and Grade II listed (along with Wylam and Hexham signal boxes), the cabin at Haltwhistle remains preserved by Network Rail. Originally opened in 1915 and with an 80-lever frame, it is seen here in 1989 as a Newcastle to Carlisle service approaches Haltwhistle station. The lever frame of the box was reduced to 61 levers in 1976 when the Alston branch closed, then removed altogether in 1993 when the semaphore signals at Haltwhisltle were replaced by colour light signals. The new IFS panel installed in 1993 was located on the opposite platform; at the time there was the view that it might eventually return to the original signal box (which was retained as staff accommodation). In the event this never happened, although the Grade II listed box has been renovated by Network Rail. In 2009 a new portable building was erected to house the IFS panel at Haltwhistle. M. Rhodes

HARRINGAY PARK JUNCTION

Right:- The signal box at Harringay Park Junction was opened in 1957. Standing in front of the 25-lever frame is the North London Line signalling inspector, Mr Dave Littlechild. FFP Media

LOCK LANE CROSSING

Right & below:- Situated just south of Long Eaton but on the Castle Donnington line, the crossing box at Lock Lane was built in 1955 and originally had a 20-lever frame. With the introduction of colour light signalling controlled from Trent power box, the frame was reduced as our internal view shows, with just three operational levers to control the crossing. Both N. Allsop

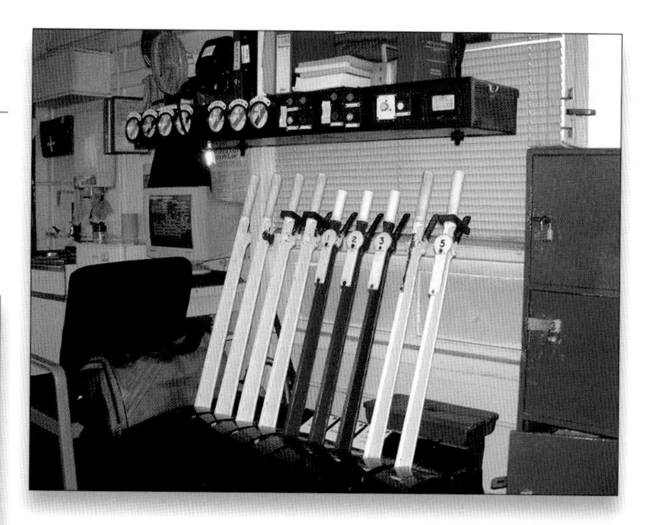

HAWKESBURY LANE

Right:- The LNWR signal box at Hawkesbury Lane dated back to 1896 and contained a 26-lever frame. Along with the boxes at Coundon Road and Three Spires it disappeared as the Coventry to Nuneaton line was resignalled. Here in 1984, Class 47 No.47233 passes the box with 7E88, an empty oil train from Bedworth oil depot to Humber Oil Refinery in Immingham. M.Rhodes

LOW ROW

Right:- Class 156 No. 156435 passes the 1874 NER signal box at Low Row with a Glasgow to Newcastle service on 22 April 1989. The 29-lever box was in poor structural condition and was therefore replaced by a Network Rail gabled structure and a small panel on retirement of the semaphore signals. M. Rhodes

OLDHAM MUMPS

Left:- As long ago as 1983, when this image was taken, Oldham Mumps signal box looked in a sorry state, surrounded by derelict land as the goods yard and sidings at Oldham had been removed. The 1967 structure, with its 50-lever frame, limped on until it closed in 2009 when the route through Oldham was closed for conversion to a tramway by Greater Manchester PTE. P. Shannon

OLLERTON COLLIERY

Left:- The GCR-designed box at Ollerton, dating from 1926, was seriously damaged by fire in April 2006, thought to be the result of an arson attack. Control of the area was assumed by Thoresby Colliery Junction signal box and the remains of the box cleared away before official closure was announced in 2009. Back in 1990, Class 56 No. 56007 passes the box, signalled onto the former main line from Lincoln by the 30-lever frame, with 7Z93, an extra MGR from Ollerton Colliery to Ratcliffe Power Station. M. Rhodes

SHAW STATION

Right:- The so-called Oldham Loop was closed, as was Shaw SB, on 5 October 2009 when the land was transferred to GMPTE (Greater Manchester Passenger Transport Executive) for conversion to a light rail system – Manchester Metrolink. Shaw Station SB was originally Shaw South when commissioned during WWII. The ex-L&Y operating floor contrasts with the breeze blocks below! When viewed in April 1993, Shaw SB worked AB to Oldham Mumps and TCB to Rochdale along the single line. This method of working began in July 1980, when the level crossing gates were replaced by lifting barriers and new colour lights installed. D. Allen

STAPLEFORD & SANDIACRE

Left:- The iconic BR(LMR) signal box at Stapleford and Sandiacre had been reduced to a shunt frame by the time it closed in 2009. Built in 1949 to the war-time brick and concrete design it contained 115 levers. In 1993, Class 60 No. 60079 passes with an MGR bound for Ratcliffe Power Station whilst another Class 60, No. 60082 is just passing under the bridge in the background with a Peak Forest to Washwood Heath stone train. M. Rhodes

THREE SPIRES JUNCTION

Above & right- Three Spires Junction was built by the LNWR in 1914 and had a 53-lever frame. The signal box was located to the south of the junction itself and our general view is looking north and shows Class 58 No. 58015 winding out of Three Spires Colliery with 7V44, an MGR service to Didcot Power Station. When this image was taken in 1986, the tiny LNWR signal box at Bedlam Crossing was still intact and can be seen above the 4th and 5th wagons of the train. It dated back to 1886 and had a small 6-lever frame controlling the manual crossing gates. Both M. Rhodes

THORPE-LE-SOKEN

Above:- Before its demise in May 2009, Thorpe-le-Soken SB witnessed many changes. It dated from 1882, when the branch to Clacton opened. Doubling of the line from Colchester was carried out in 1890 but onwards to Clacton didn't take place until the end of WWII, at which time the SB was extended. During 1958/59, further resignalling was in hand prior to electrification and all of Thorpe-le-Soken's semaphores were replaced with 3 or 4-aspect searchlight signals. However, it wasn't until 1989 that the lever frame was replaced by a panel. This coincided with resignalling of the Walton-on-the-Naze line. Conventional 3-aspect colour lights replaced the 'searchlights' and all traffic became concentrated on the former island "down" platforms. D. Allen

2010

Two local projects had a major impact in 2010, none more so than the resignalling of the lines to Stratford-upon-Avon, known as the North Warwickshire Resignalling Scheme. The West Midlands signalling centre took over the work of the three mechanical boxes at Bearley West Junction, Henley-in-Arden and Shirley. Further north, along the Durham Coast, a new workstation was added to the 40-lever signal box at Ryhope Grange, controlling down the coast beyond Hartlepool. The boxes at Clarence Road, Dawdon, Hall Dene and Stranton closed as a result.

The policy of marginal gains by the closure of a small neighbouring boxes continued with several examples of this type of rationalisation. Perhaps more surprising was the closure of Falsgrave box in Scarborough with its 120 levers, replaced by a small workstation in Seamer signal box. The wonderful signal gantry here was preserved and can be seen in action at Grosmont on the North Yorkshire Moors Railway. Other similar "neighbourhood takeovers" occurred with Parton box closing and control ceded to Bransty in Whitehaven, and Montrose South and Usan closing, to be controlled from Montrose North. Finally, Dalston Junction and Camden Road Junction boxes closed with Upminster IECC taking over their routes.

As always there was at least one signal box destroyed by fire and vandalism. East Usk was burnt down, forcing the transfer of control to the South Wales signalling centre in Cardiff. The signal box in Ashington, hidden under the main shopping street in the town, finally closed, surplus to requirements on the pared down Blyth & Tyne network. A modern box which closed, but was of huge significance, was at Tinsley Yard. The closure of the route into the former Tinsley complex from the east rendered the box redundant and the last remnant of the once mighty hump yard control system was removed, even if the derelict control tower would live on for a few more years.

2010		
Ashington	NER - 20 levers - 1896	14/2
Basingstoke Old ASC	BR (SR) - NX panel - 1966	6/4
Bearley West Junction	GWR - 30 levers - 1907	1/11
Camden Road Junction	NLR - NX panel - 1896	19/12
Clarence Road	NER - 36 levers - 1904	15/11
Dalston Junction	NLR - NX panel - 1891	19/12
Dawdon	NER - IFS panel - 1905	15/11
East Usk	BR (WR) - 39 levers - 1961	4/1
Falsgrave	NER - 120 levers - 1908	1/11
Hall Dene	NER - 21 levers - 1905	6/11
Henley-in-Arden	GWR - 57 levers - 1907	1/11
Millerhill Yard	BR (ScR) - IFS panel - 1988	11/2
Montrose South	NBR - 42 levers - 1881	1/2
Oxley	BR (LMR) - 60 levers - 1969	29/11
Parton	LNWR - 28 levers - 1879	31/5
Reading	BR (WR) - NX panel - 1965	30/12
Shirley	GWR - 31 levers - 1907	1/11
Stranton	NER - 30 levers - 1911	15/11
Tinsley Yard	BR (ER) - NX panel - 1965	19/6
Usan	NBR - 16 levers - 1906	1/2
Closure of 13 mechanical boxes and 7 panel boxes		
Loss of 530 levers		

ASHINGTON

Right:- The 1886, 20-lever NER signal box at Ashington was at the north end of the passenger station, almost under the main shopping street in Ashington. Originally fitted with a 25-lever frame, this was reduced to 20 levers near the end of its working life. The box is seen here behind the rear of 6B13, the lunchtime trip from Blyth Alcan to the Lynemouth smelter, hauled by Class 37 No. 37145. The signal box closed in 2010 with the former Lynemouth branch reduced to a long siding. M. Rhodes

BEARLEY WEST JUNCTION

Right & below:- Bearley West Junction SB and the line to Tyseley opened in 1907 when the GWR was creating an alternative route from Birmingham to the West Country via Honeybourne. Sadly, through passenger services ceased in 1968 and the southern end of the route was taken out of use in 1977. Bearley West Junction SB became a fringe to Saltley PSB via the north and south curves at Hatton during Stage 3A of the resignalling in 1969. At the same time, AB working was still in place to Henley-in-Arden and Stratford-upon-Avon SBs on the North Warwickshire line. Following the closure of Stratford-upon-Avon SB in 1998, a panel was added in Bearley West Junction SB. The SB closed in November 2010 when the West Midlands SC assumed control of the North Warwickshire Line. Both D. Allen

CAMDEN ROAD JUNCTION

Right:- Class 47 No. 47086 passes Camden Road Junction with a Temple Mills to Eastleigh mixed freight on 13 February 1981. The signal box here dated back to 1896 and still had a 45-lever frame when this photograph was taken. The frame was replaced by a panel in 1987. M. Rhodes

CLARENCE ROAD

Left:- Clarence Road signal box was just north of Hartlepool station. By the time of closure its frame had been reduced to 36 levers as the freight sidings north of Hartlepool station had long been removed. In 1987, Class 37 No. 37219 is seen passing the box with 6P07, the afternoon trip from Hartlepool Docks to Tees Yard transporting imported pulp from Scandinavia for paper making. M. Rhodes

DALSTON JUNCTION

Left:- Fred (Fitzherbert) Cumberbatch, who sadly passed away shortly after retiring in 2000, is seen operating the NX panel in Dalston Junction signal box. The cabin was built for the North London Railway in 1891 and had the NX panel installed in 1987. FFP Media

DAWDON

Right:- Taken in May 1997, this view shows the 1905-vintage NER signal box at Dawdon. Originally it was fitted with a 46-lever frame but this was replaced by an IFS panel in 1987 as can be seen in this view. The signal levers are conspicuous by their absence. A. Walker

EAST USK

Left & below:- East Usk was another unfortunate victim of arson. It was severely damaged by fire in April 2009 and declared officially closed in 2010. The box was built in 1961 at the time of the South Wales resignalling and controlled the sidings at East Usk as well as access to the Uskmouth branch. The internal view shows the 39-lever frame and the external view, taken in July 2001, shows Class 66 No. 66104 winding past the box with an MGR from East Usk Yard to the newly re-commissioned Uskmouth Power Station. Both M. Rhodes

FALSGRAVE

Above & above right:- Two views of the 1908 NER signal box at Falsgrave, which is situated on the end of the platform at Scarborough station. The first dates from 1984, before the box was refurbished and shows Class 31 No. 31406 shunting empty coaching stock past the 120-lever box; both the signal box and gantry were Grade II listed and in 2007 the box was fully refurbished. The second view, taken in August 2010, shows preserved LMS Class 8P, 'Princess Elizabeth', reversing past the refurbished box into the carriage sidings with the 'Scarborough Spa Express'. The gantry was removed after closure and reinstalled at the north end of Grosmont station. Both M. Rhodes

HALL DENE

Right:- In June 1990, Class 31 No. 31305 shunts an engineering special related to track removal in the former Vane Tempest Colliery. In the background is the 1905-vintage Hall Dene signal box with its 21-lever frame. M. Rhodes

HENLEY-IN-ARDEN

Left:- The signalman leans out of the box window at Henley-in-Arden with what was a green flag, which seems strange as the signal is "off" for this arrival from Birmingham. The 1907 box here had 57 levers and closed as part of the North Warwickshire resignalling scheme. A DMU headed by No. 53060 passes with a Birmingham to Stratford-upon-Avon train on 9 April 1985. M. Rhodes

MONTROSE SOUTH

Above & right:- Two views of Montrose South signal box are included to illustrate the drastic visual changes that "refurbishment" of heritage signal boxes can have. In July 1988, Class 47 No. 47004 passes the 1881, 42-lever signal box with a northbound engineers' train. In 2010, as Class 170 No. 170417 leaves with an Aberdeen to Glasgow passenger train, the box has a new roof and windows on the brick base and is almost unrecognisable. Both M. Rhodes

OXLEY

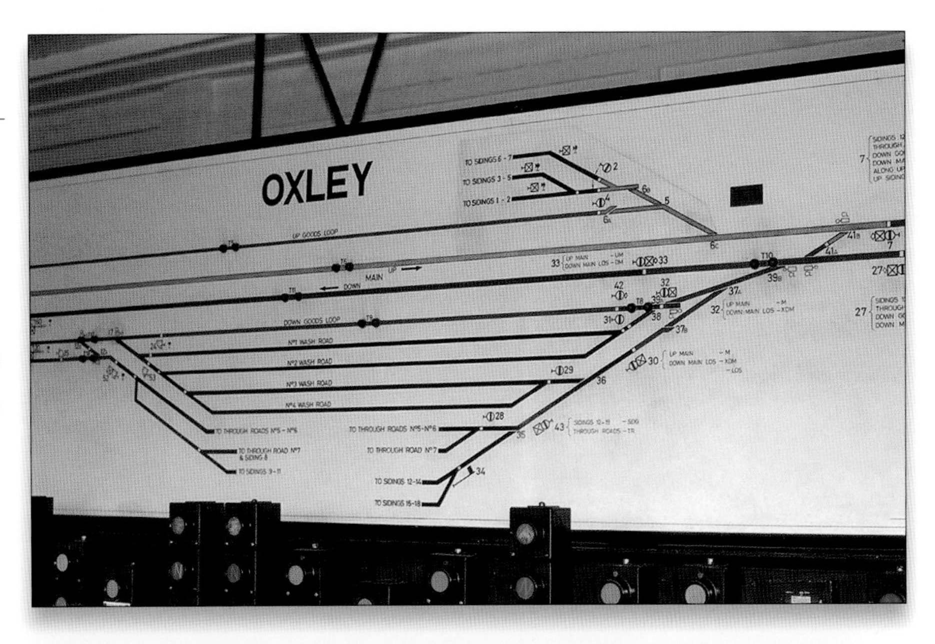

Right:- When this view was taken on 19 August 1996, Oxley SB, besides being responsible for the connections into the depot, was a fringe to Wolverhampton PSB and worked Absolute Block to Codsall. After the closure of Codsall SB in October 2006, Track Circuit Block working was introduced to Madeley Junction SB. Oxley SB was decommissioned in November 2010 when control was transferred to the West Midlands SC. Built to a BR (LMR) design, the box had opened in 1969 and contained a 60-lever frame. D. Allen

PARTON

Left:- The signal box at Parton dated back to 1879 and was originally fitted with a 36-lever frame which was reduced to 28 levers by the time of closure. It was often switched out during the 1990s and first part of the 21st century, so closure was no surprise. Here in July 1983, Class 25 No. 25191 passes, running light engine from Workington stabling point to Corkickle Yard, where it will pick up the evening chemical train to Oakleigh Yard in Northwich. M. Rhodes

SHIRLEY

Right:- Shirley SB became a fringe to Saltley PSB when Hall Green SB was closed in August 1984. Shirley succumbed on 31 October 2010 when Phase 2 of the Leamington resignalling was implemented. At the same time the surviving SBs at Henley-in-Arden and Bearley Junction also closed. Control was transferred to the West Midands signalling centre. Built in 1907 by the GWR, it had a 31-lever frame. D. Allen

STRANTON

Left:- With the cranes of Hartlepool Docks in the background, Class 37 Nos. 37003 & 37250 pass Stranton signal box with an Easington to York MGR carrying coal from the North East to blend with lower quality coal from the new Selby Drift Mine. The signal box dated back to 1911 and at the time of closure had a 30-lever frame, which had been reduced in size when the sidings associated with Hartlepool locomotive depot were removed in the early 1970s. M. Rhodes

TINSLEY YARD

Above:- Whilst strictly speaking neither heritage, nor mechanical, the signal box at Tinsley Yard was a significant closure in 2010. It was one of the last signal boxes to control one of Britain's Modernisation Plan marshalling yards. Like so many victims of vandalism it was isolated on a rarely-used freight-only line and was burnt down. Control of the rarely-used access into Tinsley from the east was assumed by Woodhouse Junction signal box. Here the signalman explains the residual responsibilities of the box during an official visit in 1985. The large blank area below his hand had been the reception sidings for the once mighty yard. M. Rhodes

USAN

Left:- At the same time as Montrose North took over responsibility for Montrose South signal box, it also assumed control of the tracks to the south of Montrose viaduct which had been in the hands of the 1906 NBR signal box at Usan, which had just 16 levers. In May 2006 an Aberdeen to Glasgow express is seen passing the box. M. Rhodes

2011

The largest signalling scheme of 2011 was the opening of the East Kent signalling centre, situated adjacent to the station at Gillingham in Kent. This led to the closure of the signal boxes at Canterbury East, Faversham, Margate, Ramsgate, Shepherds Well and Teynham Crossing. Perhaps the strategically most important project of the whole decade was however the introduction of ERTMS along the Cambrian Coast Line from Shrewsbury to Aberystwyth and Pwllheli. ERTMS is the European Rail Traffic Management System which is made up of ETCS which is the signalling system and GSM-R which is the global satellite communication system used for relaying signals to the train driver's cab. The RETB signalling along the Cambrian lines was nearing life expiry and so the line was the first UK test bed for the new pan-European system. For ERTMS to be introduced all mileages had to be converted to kilometres. Along the 215 km route 96 axle-counters and 346 "Eurobalises" were installed, which transmit information to passing trains and also receive information from trains, allowing their position and speed to be determined. The immediate impact of this revolutionary technology was the closure of Caersws and Machynlleth signal boxes.

Control of the North London Line was passed to the IECC at Upminster with the signal boxes at Gospel Oak and Willesden High Level Junction closing. In similar fashion the reach of the IECC at York extended along the former Midland Main Line with closure of the boxes at Hickleton and Moorthorpe. The East Midlands signalling centre (which became the East Midlands ROC), took over control of Croft signal box, which had itself, just six years earlier, taken over control from neighbouring boxes at Hinckley and Narborough. Interestingly one of the 1980s modernisation power boxes at Leicester also closed and was migrated into the East Midlands ROC. The closure of large power boxes with their extensive NX panels was set to increase from 2011 onwards, as integration of their interlocking and relays into the new ROCs became more straightforward. In Manchester, the new Manchester East signalling centre (located on the old Edgeley locomotive depot, south of Stockport), took over much of the Hatfield and Glossop branch line with closure of Ashburys and Guide Bridge boxes.

Smaller localised changes occurred in Scotland where Annat closed and was merged into Banavie signalling centre. Similarly Carmuirs West Junction signal box closed and the area was signalled from the neighbouring Carmuirs East box. In East Anglia, Kennett box closed and neighbouring Bury St. Edmunds then controlled as far as Chippenham Junction. In Rochdale, the signal box closed and control was relocated to the oddly named Rochdale West signal box - odd because the box is actually opposite Castleton East signal cabin! Two other closures were simply because the signal boxes concerned were no longer required. Blackpool North No. 1 was surplus to requirement as the carriage sidings at Blackpool were downsized and operated by a ground frame and hand points. At Watery Lane (near Tipton in the West Midlands), the crossing box never officially closed but it was demolished in 2011.

2011		
Annat	BR (ScR) - 16 levers - 1964	23/10
Ashburys	GCR - NX panel - 1906	19/9
Blackpool North No. 1	BR (LMR) - 65 levers - 1959	24/1
Caersws	CamR - 18 levers - 1891	19/3
Canterbury East	SECR - 28 levers - 1911	28/12
Carmuirs West Junction	CR - 20 levers - 1882	11/7
Croft	LNWR - Westcad VDU - 1901	31/12
Faversham	BR (SR) - NX panel - 1959	28/12
Gospel Oak	BR (ER) - IFS panel - 1985	7/2
Guide Bridge	GCR - NX panel - 1906	4/12
Hickleton	LMS - 50 levers - 1931	31/5
Kennett	GER - 17 levers - 1880	12/11
Kirkby Summit	RT - NX panel - 1995	12/9
Leicester SC	BR (LMR) - NX panel - 1986	31/12
Longbridge East	MR - 36 levers - 1917	8/5
Machynlleth	BR (WR) - 50 levers - 1960	19/3
Margate	SECR - 80 levers - 1913	28/12
Moorthorpe	MR - 36 levers - 1908	31/5
Paisley SC	BR (ScR) - NX panel - 1985	27/12
Ramsgate	SR - 88 levers - 1926	28/12
Rochdale	L&Y - 30 levers - 1889	30/8
Shepherds Well	LCDR - 23 levers - 1878	28/12
Slough IECC	BR (WR) - VDUs - 1992	27/12
Teynham Crossing	BR (SR) - 5 levers - 1970	28/12
Watery Lane Shunt Frame	LMS - IFS panel - 1942	12/12
Willesden High Level Junction	LMS - NX panel - 1930	27/2
Closure of 15 mechanical boxes and 11 panel boxes		
Loss of 562 levers		

Left:- Annat SB opened in 1964 in connection with the new Corpach paper mill and had a 16-lever frame. It was certainly non-standard and probably second hand. Not long after this photo was taken in August 1984, the flat roof was replaced by a pitched one; certainly more appropriate for the west coast of Scotland! When RETB was introduced in December 1987, Annat was reduced in status to a gate box and retained semaphores to protect the two level crossings. The new RETB section was Mallaig Junction to Loch Eil Outward Bound supervised from Banavie SC. Annat gate box was decommissioned in October 2011, when the level crossings were fitted with CCTV and controlled from Banavie SC. Needless to say, the semaphores were replaced by 2-aspect LED signals. D. Allen

ASHBURYS

Right:- The signal box at Ashburys had originally been called Ashburys East Junction and was constructed by the Great Central in 1906. It was fitted with a 52-lever frame which was still in place when this view was taken in November 1983. Class 40 No. 40174 arrives light engine at Ashburys Yard, which by this stage had become the main Speedlink yard for the whole of Greater Manchester. Shortly after this view, in 1984, an NX panel was fitted in the box and the mechanical frame removed. M. Rhodes

Left:- Blackpool North No. 1, with its 65-levers, dated from 1959 when it replaced an earlier structure. Though not really required, it lingered on until January 2011, four years after it had been switched out of circuit. Access to the carriage sidings was simplified by eliminating the facing crossover and providing a ground frame released by Blackpool No. 2 SB. Pride of place on the block shelf are a pair of L&Y block instruments controlling the sections to Carleton Crossing and Blackpool North No. 2. I like to think they were moved from the old SB into the new one. D. Allen

Right:- The SB at Caersws has witnessed two recent signalling revolutions. In October 1988 it was reduced to a gate box when Stage 1 of the Cambrian Lines RETB (Radio Electronic Token Block) was implemented. However, since January 1987, when the loop was taken out of use, its role became limited. After the introduction of RETB, Caersws continued to supervise conventional fixed signals. It finally closed in March 2011, as part of the Cambrian Lines ERTMS Signalling Stage 2. Needless to say, the use of cab signalling removed the need for fixed signals. D. Allen

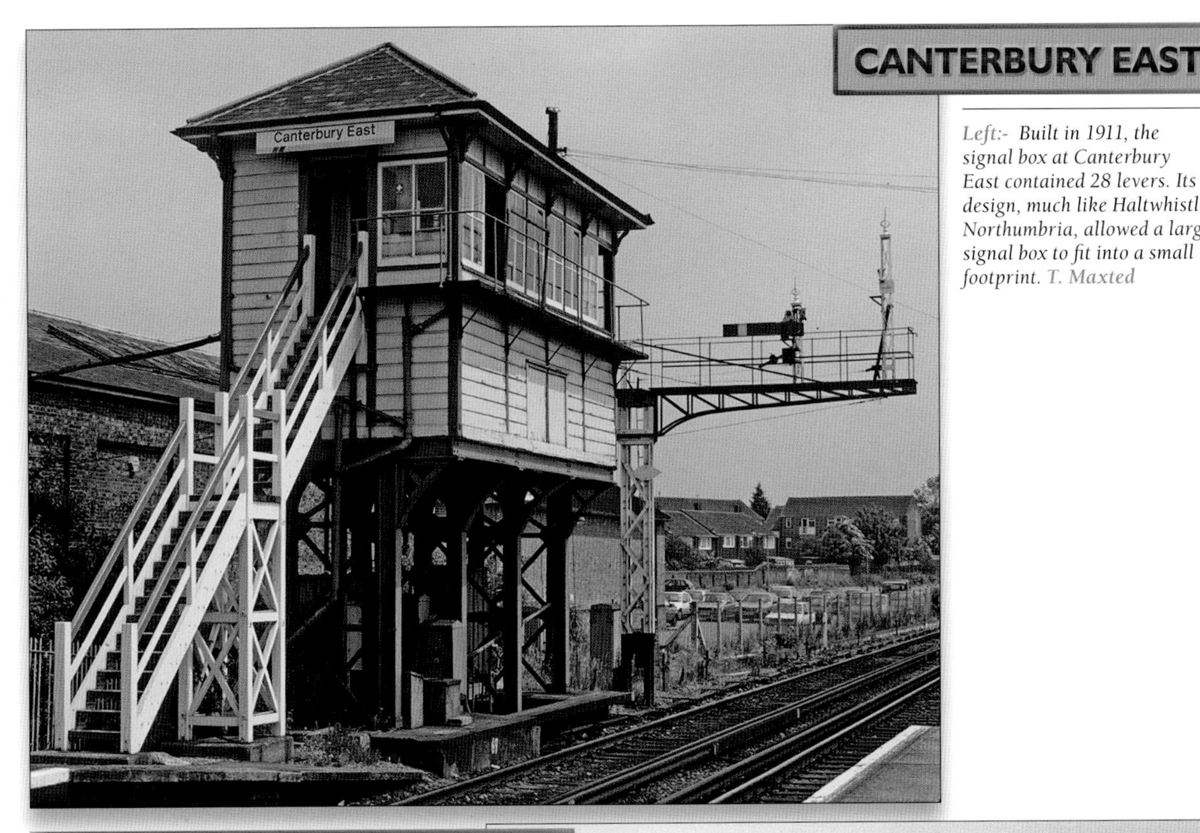

CANTERBURY EAST

Left:- Built in 1911, the signal box at Canterbury East contained 28 levers. Its design, much like Haltwhistle in Northumbria, allowed a large signal box to fit into a small footprint. T. Maxted

CARMUIRS WEST JUNCTION

Right:- This 1989 view shows a stopping service from Edinburgh to Glasgow passing Carmuirs West Junction. It is on the line from Grangemouth, whilst the lines on the left of the image are the main line from Glasgow to Stirling. Off to the left of the image is Larbert Junction. The box was opened in 1882 with a 30-lever frame. This was reduced to 20 levers in 1979. M. Rhodes

CROFT

Left:- The industrial shunter at Croft Quarry shuttles past the signal box at Croft with sand. The box here had taken over control of virtually the whole Leicester to Nuneaton line. Built in 1901, it had originally contained a 22-lever frame. By the time this view was taken in April 2012, shortly after the box closed, it had been equipped with Westcad VDUs, which had been introduced during the 2006 resignalling of the Leicester to Nuneaton line. Sadly, regular freight traffic from the quarry ceased in 2017. M. Rhodes

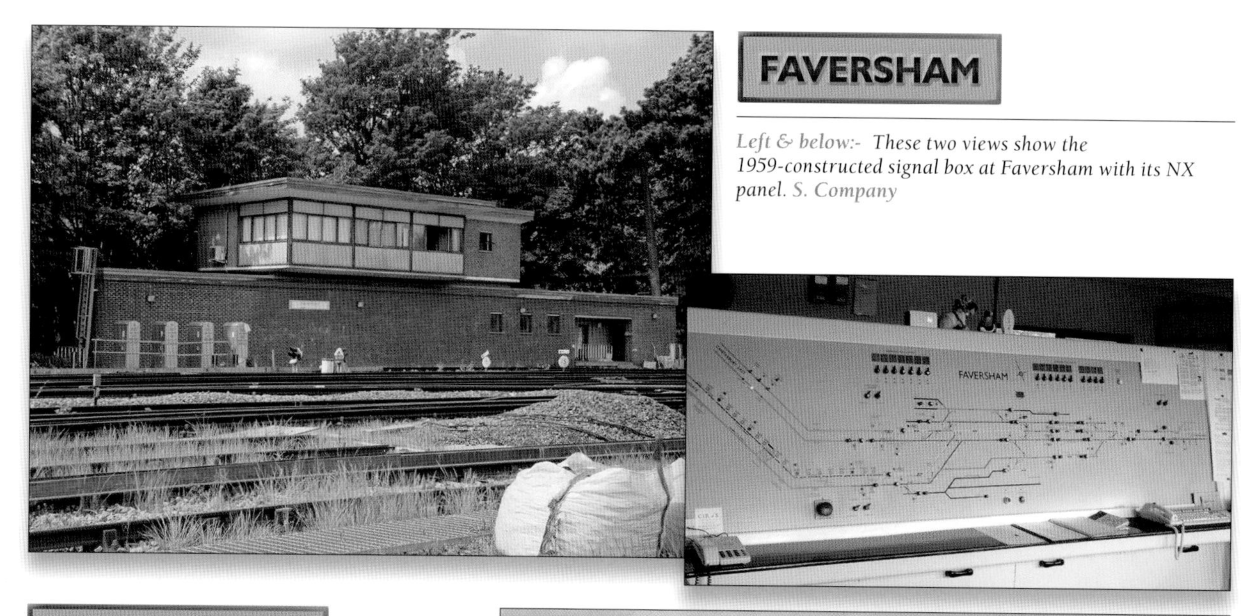

FAVERSHAM

Left & below:- These two views show the 1959-constructed signal box at Faversham with its NX panel. S. Company

GUIDE BRIDGE

Right:- In 1906 the GCR resignalled between Ardwick and Hyde Junction. Then named Ashton Junction, Guide Bridge SB was one of 14 new SBs fitted with low-pressure pneumatic miniature lever frames. The new signalling accompanied the widening to four tracks and many other improvements. The longevity of the SBs was a testament to their success. Most succumbed during a major track rationalisation in 1984, when Ashton Junction SB was renamed Guide Bridge and fitted with a panel. It was finally decommissioned in December 2011 when control was transferred to Manchester East SC. D. Allen

HICKLETON

Below:- Hickleton SB continues to display its original full name; Hickleton Main Colliery Sidings. It was opened in 1931, with a 50-lever frame, when the LMS reduced the number of SBs at the location. Interestingly, the MR-style window corner pieces were still being used, but not for long. In complete contrast to the earlier MR SBs on the route, this structure features a gabled roof. It succumbed at the same time as its neighbour at Moorthorpe. The official notice NR/LNE No. 23 unusually mentioned 'the existing Hickleton and Moorthorpe SBs will be closed and demolished'!. D. Allen

KENNETT

Left & below:- In March 2011, signaller Katrina contemplates the frame of her soon-to-close box. Kennett was opened in 1880 and had a 17-lever frame. It was fully refurbished in 2006 with new uPVC windows. The external view shows Katrina on the box balcony as Class 66 No. 66540 passes with the afternoon Felixstowe to Doncaster freightliner service.Both M. Rhodes

LONGBRIDGE EAST

Left:- During May 2011, Network Rail removed the connections to the Longbridge car terminal and thereby closed the branch. Most of the route had closed in 1964; this stub was retained to serve the BMC (British Motor Corporation) site. It seems Longbridge East SB was reduced to a shunt frame when Saltley PSB was commissioned. Interestingly, though Network Rail effectively closed the branch, they didn't decommission the SB. This is not unique;. Canning Street North is still officially a SB despite being burnt out and derelict. In addition, the unusable route into the Birkenhead docks area remains officially open. D. Allen

MACHYNLLETH

Right:- Machynlleth SB dated from 1960 when it replaced the former East and West SBs. It was not a glamorous structure; an example of a type irreverently known as 'plywood wonders'. It was retained in 1988, when Radio Electronic Token Block (RETB) was introduced between Shrewsbury and Aberystwyth/Pwhelli. As an economy measure, the existing TCB working to Dovey Junction and the mainly mechanical signals at Machynlleth were retained and operated from the 50-lever frame! The SB was replaced by Machynlleth SC in March 2011 when the method of working for the Cambrian network changed to the European Train Control System (ETCS). D. Allen

MARGATE

Left & below:- Margate was a significant signal cabin, built in 1913, with an 80-lever frame. These two views give an excellent idea of the building and its mechanical frame. Both S. Company

MOORTHORPE

Left:- Moorthorpe SB was photographed on 2 April 1991. Formerly Moorthorpe South, it still proudly displayed the nameboard on the front despite the demise of the other two MR SBs on the so-called 'Swinton & Knottingley' line at this location. The window corner pieces are a tell-tale feature of Midland Railway SBs. Similarly, with very few exceptions, they were wholly wooden structures. The hipped roof and finials are also distinctive. I wonder if the roof received any attention before the box was decommissioned in May 2011, when the Leeds Ardsley workstation in York IECC assumed control and the goods loops on either side of the main lines were upgraded to passenger loops. When opened in 1908 the box was equipped with a 36-lever frame. D. Allen

RAMSGATE

Right & below:- A second large mechanical signal box to close in the North Kent Resignalling Scheme was at Ramsgate. These two views show the 1926-constructed, 88-lever-framed box just before closure. Both S. Company.

ROCHDALE

Right:- Rochdale signal box is seen in the distance in this view of a Manchester Victoria to Rochdale local service formed of Class 142 No. 142 012. The signal box originally stood in the goods yard at Rochdale and was called Rochdale Goods Yard signal box. The goods yard disappeared in the early 1970s and the lever frame was reduced to 30 levers to reflect this in 1976. P. Shannon

SHEPHERDS WELL

Right & below:- Shepherds Well signal box opened in 1878 and remained remarkably unaltered until closure, with a 23-lever frame dating back to the time of opening. The top of the box was to be preserved and moved to the East Kent Railway. Both S. Company

WATERY LANE SHUNT FRAME

Right:- In August 1965, when Wolverhampton PSB was commissioned, Watery Lane SB, built by the LMS in 1942, was reduced in status to a shunt frame. Following the closure of Tipton Station Shunt Frame in May 1977, Watery Lane became responsible for controlling Owen Street level crossing remotely by CCTV. Watery Lane Shunt Frame was made redundant when the busy Owen Street level crossing was replaced by a road underpass in October 2009. D. Allen

WILLESDEN HIGH LEVEL JUNCTION

Left:- With the West Coast Main Line filling most of the foreground, this 1981 view shows Class 47 No. 47018 with an empty oil train bound for Thames Haven Oil Refinery. When this view was taken the semaphore signals were still in place and the 1930 box still had a lever frame. This was replaced in 1985 with an NX panel and colour light signals. M. Rhodes

2012

Signal box closures reached their peak in 2012 and it was a seminal year because of the introduction of a new modular resignalling method. The line between Norwich and Ely was used as a test-bed for the modular system which aimed to replace like for like, but using easy to maintain colour light signals and automated crossing gates with obstacle detectors (rather than the more common CCTV monitoring). Produced by Intergo and installed by Signalling Solutions, the project was to have been completed by November 2011. It eventually went live in December 2012. A similar project undertaken by Invensys was also under way along the line between Shrewsbury and Crewe, but this ran even further behind schedule, so the manual boxes along that route survived into 2013. The boxes at Attleborough, Brandon, Eccles Road, Harling Road, Lakenheath, Shippea Hill, Spooner Row, Thetford and Wymondham South all closed as a result of the Norwich–Ely resignalling, as did the manned gates at Poplar Crossing. The line was unusual in that all boxes, except Thetford and Wymondham, also had an associated crossing keeping the signalmen pretty fit, except of course at Brandon where the gates were automated.

Two other lengthy stretches of line were resignalled, from Stourbridge Junction to just short of Droitwich and from Gillingham to Exmouth Junction. In the West Midlands the boxes at Blakedown, Hartlebury, Kidderminster Junction and Stourbridge Junction closed as well as the makeshift double-deck portable building at Kingswinford Junction South (installed just a decade earlier when the original GWR box here burnt down). The West Midlands signalling centre also took over the work of the last remaining Midland Railway box at the once vast marshalling yards at Washwood Heath, Washwood Heath No. 1 signal box. Down in the West Country, Feniton, Gillingham, Honiton, Templecombe and Yeovil Junction all closed, with control, of the western end of the Waterloo to Exeter route handed to the Basingstoke area signalling centre.

The pattern of several small local projects continued, bringing marginal savings on manpower. The Manchester East signalling centre took over from Stalybridge box which closed. Preston power signal box took over the work of Bare Lane box on the Morecambe branch. Bollo Lane Junction and Kew East Junction were subsumed by Acton Wells Junction, whilst Horsforth and Rigton were controlled by a new workstation in Harrogate signal box. Prescot closed with work transferred to St. Helens box and the small signal cabin at Crosfields, in the former Persil factory at Warrington, closed with the gates controlled from Monks Siding a few hundred yards down the line towards Liverpool.

Several crossing boxes disappeared at Caldicot, Lydney and Causeway on the western region whilst elsewhere one crossing hut was upgraded. The small crossing hut at Gosberton, classified MGH (manual gate hut) was upgraded to an MCB (manual crossing box) because the nearby box at Gosberton was closed due to structural problems. An interesting move as within a couple of years the whole of the former Joint Line was completely resignalled! Two derelict boxes finally bit the dust at Whitchurch and Seymour Junction where observers noted that after demolition of the superstructure, thieves stole much of the brick base. Last but by no means least, the former Great Central electro-pneumatic signal box at Immingham East Junction was closed and a new portable building erected to take over its work, but situated outside the Port of Immingham on Network Rail land. This left just one example of this electro-pneumatic design in existence at Immingham Reception.

2012		
Attleborough	GER - 36 levers - 1883	3/12
Bare Lane	LMS - 32 levers - 1937	10/12
Blakedown	GWR - IFS panel - 1888	28/8
Bletchley	BR (LMR) - NX panel - 1965	27/12
Bollo Lane Juncton	LSWR - NX panel - 1878	4/6
Brandon	LNER - 40 levers - 1931	20/8
Butterwell Bunker	BR (ER) - IFS panel - 1977	3/9
Caldicot Crossing	BR (WR) - 10 levers - 1979	29/10
Causeway Crossing	BR (WR) - IFS panel - 1975	15/4
Chard Junction	BR (WR) - NX panel - 1982	12/3
Crosfields	LNWR - 16 levers - 1906	9/7
Eccles Road	GER - 21 levers - 1883	3/12
Feniton	BR (WR) - IFS panel - 1974	26/3
Gillingham	BR (SR) - 30 levers - 1957	26/3
Gosberton	GER - 30 levers - 1882	19/3

2012		
Harling Road	GER - 25 levers - 1883	3/12
Hartlebury	GWR - IFS panel - 1876	28/8
Honiton	BR (SR) - 24 levers - 1957	26/3
Hornsey Carriage Sidings	BR (ER) - IFS panel - 1976	16/7
Horsforth	NER - 15 levers - 1873	29/10
Immingham East Junction	GCR - 60 levers - 1913	2/12
Kew East Junction	NLR - 50 levers - 1900	4/6
Kidderminster Junction	BR (WR) - 66 levers - 1953	28/8
Kingswinford Junction South	NR - 14 levers - 2003	28/8
Lakenheath	GER - 25 levers - 1883	20/8
Lydney Crossing	GWR - IFS panel - 1918	29/10
Madeley Junction	BR (LMR) Westcad VDUs - 1969	19/11

2012		
Millerhill	BR (ScR) - NX panel - 1988	25/11
Newport	BR (WR) - NX panel - 1962	29/10
Polmont	BR (ScR) - NX panel - 1979	25/11
Prescot	BR (LMR) - 30 levers - 1954	24/9
Rigton	NER - 6 levers - 1873	29/10
Rugby PSB	BR (LMR) - Westcad VDU - 1964	5/6
Seymour Junction	BR (ER) - 25 levers - 1963	1/1
Shippea Hill	GER - 30 levers - 1883	20/8
Spooner Row	GER - 15 levers - 1881	3/12
Stalybridge	MS&LR - 70 levers - 1886	4/11
Stourbridge Junction	GWR - NX panel - 1901	28/8
Swindon B	BR (WR) - IECC - 1993	27/12
Templecombe	SR - 16 levers - 1938	27/2
Thetford	GER - 33 levers - 1883	20/8
Washwood Heath No. 1	MR - 60 levers - 1899	10/4
Whitchurch	LNWR - 55 levers - 1897	5/8
Wymondham South	GER - 42 levers - 1877	3/12
Yeovil Junction	LSWR - 45 levers - 1909	12/3
Closure of 28 mechanical boxes and 17 panel boxes		
Loss of 921 levers		

ATTLEBOROUGH

Below (2 images):- The night view of Attleborough was taken just a fortnight before closure in December 2012. The newly-designed LIDAR detector can be seen standing proud in the "six foot". Opened in 1883, the box had a 36-lever frame dating from 1912. Originally the box only needed a 20-lever frame but as the goods yard in Attleborough grew, so the frame was expanded three times to reach its final size. Steve Ashling, the West Anglia operations manager, is seen chatting with the signalman during one of the weeks when he covered annual leave for the Local Operations Manager for the line. Both M. Rhodes

BARE LANE

Right:- The last signal box left on the Morecambe and Heysham branch lines closed in 2012. Bare Lane was opened in 1937 and had a 32-lever frame. Here, the Lancaster–Morecambe shuttle is in the hands of Class 142 No. 142065, seen passing the box in June 2012. P. Metcalfe

BLAKEDOWN

Right:- Churchill & Blakedown SB was opened by the GWR in 1888. After the station was renamed in 1968, so was the SB. We should be thankful that the cast iron name board wasn't replaced, but painting out the unwanted part has not been carried out very tastefully. When photographed in August 1991, it is otherwise in a delightful condition. At the end of 1980, the signalling was simplified. The lever frame was removed in favour of a small panel, the back of which can be seen through the operating floor windows. In August 2012, the West Midlands SC Stourbridge Junction workstation assumed control of the route. Fortunately, the redundant structure was donated to a local community association for use as a meeting room. D. Allen

BOLLO LANE JUNCTION

Left:- Bollo Lane Junction box was located on the Richmond branch, south of Acton. The box dated back to 1878 but had its lever frame removed in 1983 to be replaced by an NX panel. Seen here in the 1990s, with Fred Cumberbatch leaning out of the window for the photographer, it was fitted with a crossing observation extension. This was removed after 2000 and the box was fully restored to its original condition in 2007. FFP Media

BRANDON

Above & left:- On 12 July 2012, Class 66 No. 66054 passes Brandon signal box with the daily Peak Forest to Norwich Trowse stone train. The box was opened by the LNER in 1931 and replaced an older wooden structure. It had a 40-lever frame which is shown being worked by signalman Derek Holland, known to all as Dutchy. Dutchy started in Brandon in 1974 and spent a total of 27 years working the box, much of it as a relief. With advancing years and arthritis in his knees, he returned to Brandon as a resident signalman because the crossing gates were automated and he didn't have to race up and down the box steps to open and close the crossing! Both M. Rhodes

CHARD JUNCTION

Left & below:- The signal box at Chard Junction looks more like a garden shed than a signal box! Opened in 1982, it contained an NX panel and replaced an earlier mechanical signal box with a 15-lever frame, dating from 1874. Both M. Jamieson

CROSFIELDS

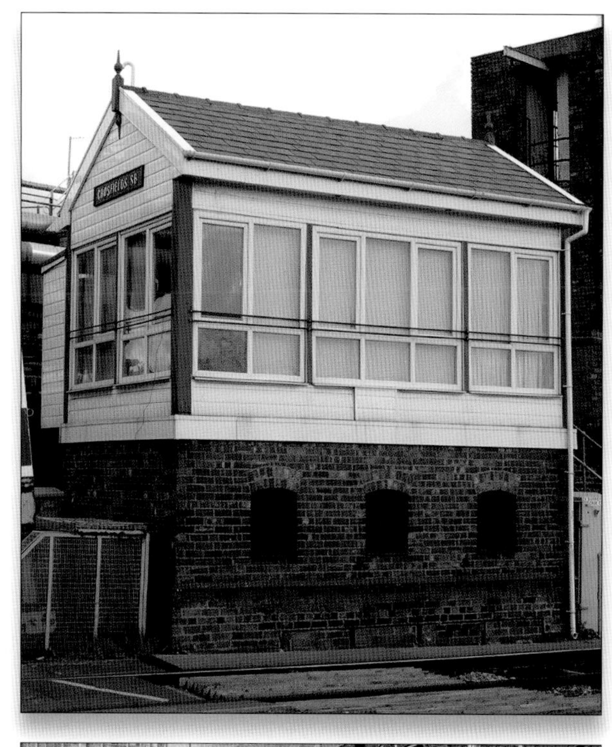

Left, below left & below:- Crosfields signal box nestled beneath the Lever Brothers factory in Warrington on the low level line to Fiddlers Ferry Power Station. Class 60 No. 60045 is seen passing the box in April 2012 with an empty coal train from Fiddlers Ferry back to Liverpool Gladstone Dock. The automated crossing here is now controlled from nearby Monks Siding signal box. Our internal view (J. Illingworth) shows the 18-lever frame, which by the time of closure had been reduced to 16 levers, all but four of which were white or unused. M. Rhodes (2) & J. Illingworth

ECCLES ROAD

Above & Left:- *Class 58 No. 58008 approaches Eccles Road crossing on 27 November 1997 with 6Z20, a Norwich to Calvert spoil train. These services ran as the old goods yards at Norwich were cleared to make way for the Riverside development. Eccles Road box dated from 1883 and had a 21-lever frame. Our internal view shows newly-qualified signalman Owen Bushell at the start of his night shift in August 2011. Owen was the last signaller recruited to the line before closure of the signal boxes a year later.* Both M. Rhodes

FENITON

Below & right:- *Resignalling of the route between Salisbury and Exeter took place in 2012 with the line now controlled from the Basingstoke ROC. Amongst the small and unusual signal boxes to close was Feniton. Originally the box here had 5 levers and when first opened in 1959 was called Sidmouth Junction Crossing ground frame. In 1974 a new structure was opened as a station office and fitted with a small panel.* Both M. Jamieson

GILLINGHAM

Below:- The original signal box at Gillingham in Dorset was opened in 1875 with a 16-lever frame. It was replaced in 1957 by this box which had a 30-lever frame fitted. Back in "Network SouthEast" days an unidentified Class 47 pauses with a Waterloo to Exeter express. FFP Media

GOSBERTON

Below:- It was structural instability that caused the slightly premature demise of the signal box at Gosberton. Opened in 1882 and with a 30-lever frame, by the time of my visit in August 2011, metal steps and support beams had been fitted to prevent the box falling down. A short-term solution was to install an NX panel in the crossing box just a couple of hundred yards north of the main signal box until the line was fully resignalled in 2014. Both M. Rhodes

HARLING ROAD

Right & below:- Harling Road signal box dated from 1883 and had a 25-lever frame, which by the time of our 2011 internal view had half its levers unused. Back in November 1997, a Saturday Norwich to Calvert spoil train is seen passing the signal box behind the unlikely combination of Class 37 Nos. 37686 & 37013 with Class 60 No. 60029 in tow. The Class 60 had failed just short of the crossing at Harling Road, completely blocking the "up" line for three hours before the Class 37s could be summoned from March to rescue the train. A relieved signalman looks on as the train finally passes the box. Both M. Rhodes

HARTLEBURY

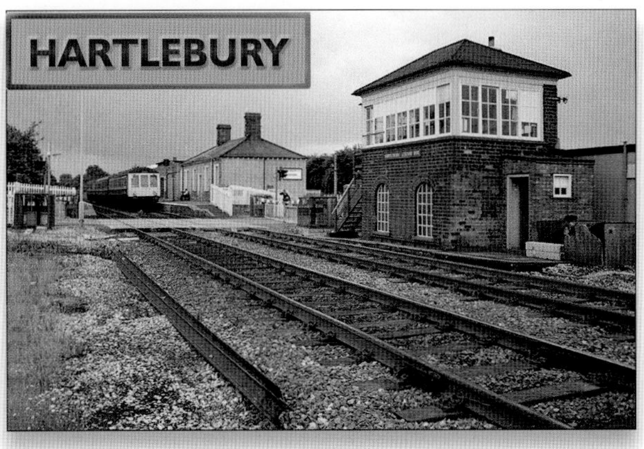

Above:- Extension of the reach of the West Midlands signalling centre at Saltley during 2012 saw the line from Stourbridge Junction to Hartlebury resignalled. The signal box at Hartlebury was opened in 1876 and had contained a 30-lever frame. By the time this picture was taken in 1985, the frame had been replaced by an IFS panel. A DMU headed by No. 53871 pauses at the station with a Worcester to Birmingham New Street service. M. Rhodes

HONITON

Below:- These two views show the 24-lever frame and the brick signal box at Honiton. The original signal box at Honiton dated back to 1875 and had a 17-lever frame. The Salisbury to Exeter line was modernised in 1957 when this new brick signal box with its 24-lever frame (similar to that at Gillingham) was opened. Both M. Jamieson

HORSFORTH

Right:- A Leeds to York (via Harrogate) passenger service heads north out of Horsforth on 11 May 2012. To the left is the 1873-vintage NER signal box which by this date had a reduced 15-lever frame. M. Rhodes

IMMINGHAM EAST JUNCTION

Left, below left & bottom:- At the time of its closure, Immingham East Junction was one of three surviving GCR signal boxes built in 1913 in conjunction with the opening of the Port of Immingham. The internal view of the signal box shows local Freightliner manager, James Skoyles, chatting with the signalman on a sunny evening in July 2012. The 60-lever electro-pneumatic frame is seen on the left and above the signalman's head is the generator to power the signal frame. The box also contained a small IFS panel installed in 1981 to control private sidings along the line to Grimsby. The box was replaced by a small portable building, outside the dock perimeter and on Network Rail land. This had a small panel and the incongruous installation of the original block token instruments for the single line section to Pyewipe Junction.

In the overall view of Immingham East Junction, taken in July 1989, Class 47 No. 47314 departs with 6D58, the evening Immingham to Doncaster Speedlink service. All M. Rhodes

KEW EAST JUNCTION

Right:- The cabin at Kew East Junction dated back to about 1900 and was of North London Railway heritage. It contained a 50-lever frame. Control of the freight lines at Kew East Junction was assumed by Acton Wells Junction signal box in 2012. T. Maxted

KIDDERMINSTER JUNCTION

Right:- The setting winter sun highlights the signalman and part of the frame at Kidderminster Junction in 1996. The box dated from 1953 and contained a 66-lever frame. Most levers were disused by this time as the Severn Valley Railway had taken over the former goods yards to the right of this view, decades earlier. A Birmingham New Street to Worcester service heads south in the hands of Class 150 No. 150012. M. Rhodes

LAKENHEATH

Below:- Signalman Anthony Pedersen opens the gates at Lakenheath in August 2012, just weeks before the box closed. Built in 1883, the box contained a 25-lever Saxby & Farmer frame. Both M. Rhodes

LYDNEY CROSSING

Right:- Lydney Crossing ground frame was originally called Lydney West when it opened in 1918, replacing an older 1879 box on the same site. It contained a 25-lever frame but this was replaced by an IFS panel in 1969, at which time the box changed its name. I. Stewart

MADELEY JUNCTION

Left:- Madeley Junction signal box was opened in 1969 and originally had a 40-lever frame. In 2002 and 2006, as it took over work from neighbouring boxes at Wellington, Lightmoor Junction, Codsall and Cosford, new Westcad VDUs were introduced. Upon closure these were transferred to the Saltley ROC. Here, in August 1993, Class 58 No. 58013 passes the box with 6T82, an empty MGR from Ironbridge Power Station to Littleton Colliery. M. Rhodes

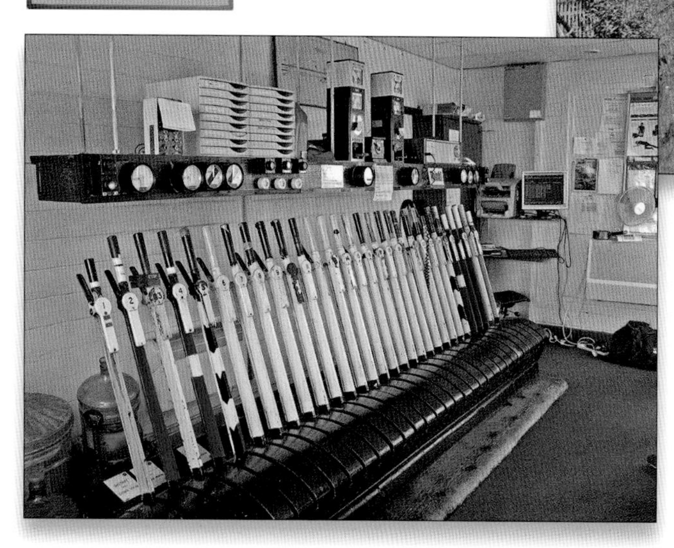

Above & left:- External and internal views of the 1954 signal box at Prescot. It appears older than its years and this may be because it was constructed from older LNWR parts on a new brick base. The frame contained 30 levers, which as our interior view shows were virtually all redundant by 2012. Both J. Illingworth

RIGTON

Left & below:- The tiny gate box at Rigton, between Leeds and Harrogate, was opened in 1873 and had just 6 levers. It also contained a gate wheel for the crossing there. Control of this box and crossing was taken on by Harrogate box. Both M. Rhodes

SEYMOUR JUNCTION

Right & below:- Opened in 1963, Seymour Junction signal box replaced an earlier 1929 construction which had rotted due to repeated flooding in the area. The modern box contained a 95-lever frame controlling points and signals for the large associated yard. The 1981 image (below) shows Class 20 Nos. 20023 & 20001 leaving the yard with a trip freight to Barrow Hill Yard. Our second image was taken from a similar location, in 1985, by which time major rationalisation had taken place. The signal box had by this time been reduced to 25 levers (Nos. 71–95) and all the semaphore signals had gone. Class 58 No. 58024 passes the box with a Markham Colliery to Barrow Hill MGR (bound eventually for Didcot Power Station). Decline in the local coal industry led to the box being effectively out of use from 2006 and like so many isolated signal boxes on freight only lines, it succumbed to fire damage and was finally declared closed in 2012. P. Shannon & M. Rhodes

SHIPPEA HILL

Above & right:- These late-2012 external and internal views of the 1883 Shippea Hill signal box show the crossing (which was regularly afflicted by mud spray from sugar beet lorries) and the 30-lever frame, also dating from 1883. Demolition of the signal box here was delayed (and still is) because it was found that a rare colony of bats had made their home in the eaves. Both M. Rhodes

SPOONER ROW

Left & below:- Back in 1999, Class 60 No. 60015 passes Spooner Row signal box and station with an empty aggregates train from Norwich to Mountsorrel. The box dated from 1881 and had 15 levers. The internal view shows signalman Alan Norman, who typifies the traditional railwayman. He had joined the railway at the age of 14 as a messenger boy at Norwich Thorpe, tasked with cycling out to drivers and guards when needed for unexpected duty. After passing out as a signalman in 1975 he worked at Cantley, Trowse Upper Junction, Acle, Wroxham and finally, when that box closed in 2000, Spooner Row. He took his retirement when the box closed at the end of 2012. Both M. Rhodes

STALYBRIDGE

Left:- Stalybridge SB dates from 1886, when the station was rebuilt by the Manchester, Sheffield and Lincolnshire Railway (MS&LR). It was the former Stalybridge No. 2; the space at the end of the nameboard shows something is missing! Until the mid 1960s, Stalybridge required four SBs – Two of MS&LR (later GCR) origin and two LNWR. This box was decommissioned when the station was resignalled and remodelled with two new platforms in November 2012. Control was transferred to Manchester East SCC. Sadly, the old SB was the subject of an arson attack not long after closure. D. Allen

STOURBRIDGE JUNCTION

Right:- Stourbridge Junction signal box was opened by the GWR in 1901 and originally had a 91-lever frame. A new panel was installed in 1990 but accounts vary as to how much of the frame, if any, remained in situ. This view, taken shortly before closure, suggests that 40 levers remained in the box. M. Jamieson

Left & below:- Opened in 1938, the signal box at Templecombe originally had a 60-lever frame. By the time of these images, taken in 2008, this had been reduced to just 16 levers. This rationalisation came in 1967 and left a rather small mechanical frame "rattling around" in a large and impressive signal box. Both M. Jamieson

THETFORD

Left & above:- Opened in 1883, Thetford signal box is seen in the external view in the days of "one" and its colourful liveries. A Norwich to Cambridge service passes in July 2008. The internal view shows the 33-lever frame with relief signalman Chris Brown awaiting his 1400 relief. Both M. Rhodes

WASHWOOD HEATH NO. 1

Right:- By the time the yards at Washwood Heath reached their maximum extent in 1935, eight SBs were needed to supervise movements. Washwood Heath Sidings No. 1 was one of two that controlled traffic on the main lines. It opened in 1899 when the sidings were confined to the "down" side (towards Birmingham). The "up" sidings dated from 1918. A new lever frame was installed by the LMS in 1924 and was placed at the rear of the operating floor. Later, as a result of Stage 2 of the Saltley resignalling in August 1969, control was transferred to Saltley PSB and all surviving Washwood Heath SBs were reduced to shunt frames. However, the SB still looked in good condition when photographed on 11 August 1991, at which time it still had 60 levers in the frame. It closed in April 2012 when all slotting arrangements for the sidings were taken out of use under Phase 2 of the Water Orton Corridor Resignalling. Control was transferred to the Washwood Heath workstation in the West Midlands SC. D. Allen

WHITCHURCH

Right:- The 1897 LNWR signal box at Whitchurch had been out of use since 2007 and fully boarded up by Network Rail, but it didn't officially close until 2012. Here the 55-lever box is seen in a sorry state in April 2012 as Class 175 No. 175104 passes with a Cardiff to Manchester express. M. Rhodes

WYMONDHAM SOUTH

Left & below:- *The internal view of the 1877-vintage 42-lever signal box at Wymondham South shows two life-long friends, Steve Ashling and Ollie Robinson, chatting and I'm afraid to say anticipating a bag of doughnuts that Steve (the West Anglia OM) had brought for tea! It was under the guidance of Steve that Ollie became a signalman, but under the guidance of Ollie that Steve's model railway prospered. The external view captures a rare event with Class 60 No. 60033 shunting the Peak Forest to Norwich limestone in the "down" loops, whilst Class 20 Nos. 20314 & 20311 pass with the 2005 season "leaf buster".* *Both M. Rhodes*

YEOVIL JUNCTION

Above & right:- *Two views of Yeovil Junction signal box. Originally called Yeovil Junction East, it opened in 1909 and had a 60-lever frame. Rationalisation in 1967 reduced the frame to 45 levers (as seen here in this 2012 view).* *Both M. Janieson*

2013

2013 is probably when the ROCs or Regional Operating Centres started to "flex their muscles" with three of them extending their coverage very significantly during the year. The biggest changes took place in the South Wales ROC, a large complex built on the site of the old goods shed opposite Cardiff Canton Traction Maintenance Depot. In the Cardiff valleys, the ROC took over control of the Rhymney Valley with closure of Bargoed, Heath Junction and Ystrad Mynach South. Heath Junction was itself a replacement for the old GWR box, which was demolished back in 1984 in order to release valuable land for housing development. Elsewhere in South Wales, the Vale of Glamorgan route migrated into the ROC with the box at Aberthaw closing and the crossing box at Cowbridge Road also redundant. The largest stretch of line to migrate to the Cardiff ROC was, however, that between Shrewsbury and Crewe which was the second modular resignalling project, this time running nearly two years late. The signal boxes at Harlescott Crossing, Nantwich, Prees, Shrewsbury Crewe Bank, Wem and Wrenbury all closed during October of this year.

The West Midlands signalling centre, sometimes called the Saltley ROC, took control of the route from Bescot to Rugeley with closure of the mechanical signal boxes at Bloxwich, Brereton Sidings and Hednesford, but also the power boxes at Bescot Down Tower and Walsall. Interestingly, Bescot Down Tower was under consideration for Grade II listed status; sadly nobody seems to have told Network Rail who demolished the box shortly after it's closure. It was the last British marshalling yard panel in use and typical of 1960s-era British Railways modernisation buildings. The East Midlands ROC at Derby extended its sphere of control along the Nottingham to Grantham line as far a Bingham, with the closure of Netherfield Junction, Rectory Junction and Sneinton Crossing boxes. A second major panel scheme, this time from the 1960s, at Trent was closed and its work migrated to the Derby ROC.

Three other signalling centres expanded their coverage. The new Lincoln signalling centre took over the line towards Gainsborough with closure of the boxes at Saxilby and Stow Park as well as the manual crossing at Sykes Lane. The work was controlled from a new VDU installed in the Lincoln building. The Manchester Piccadilly signalling control centre had a new VDU workstation put into the large room housing the Piccadilly station NX panel. This workstation took over control of the Manchester to Wigan and Manchester to Chorley routes with subsequent closure of Atherton Goods Yard, Blackrod Junction, Crow Nest Junction and Walkden boxes. On the Southern Region the Woking area signalling centre extended with the closure of Aldershot, Ash Vale Junction and Farnham signal boxes.

Several crossing boxes closed. Hest Bank crossing became CCTV-controlled from Preston as did Thorpe Gates from Selby, Snodland from Aylesford and England Lane from Ferrybridge. One crossing box closure was because of closure of the footpath at Seaham and replacement with an underpass. Thus the last box along the Durham Coast Line disappeared well before its planned closure date of 2044! The whole Durham Coast Line from south of Sunderland to Greatham on Teeside is controlled from Ryhope Grange signal box.

2013		
Aberthaw	Barry - 53 levers - 1897	11/3
Aldershot	LSWR - 24 levers - 1900	27/8
Ash Vale Junction	LSWR - IFS panel - 1879	27/8
Atherton Goods Yard	BR (LMR) - 35 levers - 1956	29/7
Bargoed	BR (WR) - 51 levers - 1970	9/9
Bescot Down Tower	BR (LMR) - NX panel - 1965	27/8
Blackrod Junction	L&Y - 37 levers - 1881	11/2
Bloxwich	BR (LMR) - 30 levers - 1959	27/8
Brereton Sidings	LNWR - 20 levers - 1908	27/8
Cathcart	BR (ScR) - OCS panel - 1961	2/4
Cowbridge Road	BR (WR) - IFS panel - 1965	11/3
Cowlairs SC	RT - NX panel - 1998	6/10
Crow Nest Junction	BR (LMR) - 25 levers - 1972	29/7
Farnham	LSWR - 35 levers - 1901	27/8

2013		
Harlescott Crossing	LNWR - 38 levers - 1882	14/10
Havensmouth	RT - IFS panel - 1999	26/9
Heath Junction	BR (WR) - OCS panel - 1984	9/9
Hednesford	LNWR - 38 levers - 1877	27/8
Hest Bank	BR (LMR) - IFS panel - 1958	28/4
Hooton	BR (LMR) - NX panel - 1985	11/11
Nantwich	LMS - 30 levers - 1948	14/10
Netherfield Junction	BR (ER) - 40 levers - 1960	29/7
Prees	LNWR - 25 levers - 1881	14/10
Rectory Junction	GNR - 42 levers - 1888	29/7
Saxilby	LNER - 30 levers - 1939	21/12
Seaham	NER - 23 levers - 1905	13/9
Shrewsbury Crewe Bank	LMS - 45 levers - 1943	14/10

2013		
Sneinton Crossing	MR - 10 levers - 1914	20/7
Snodland	SER - IFS panel - 1870	24/6
Stow Park	GNR - 32 levers - 1877	21/12
Thorpe Gates	NER - IFS panel - 1873	21/10
Trent	BR (LMR) - NX panel - 1969	20/7
Walkden	L&Y - 19 levers - 1888	29/7
Walsall	BR (LMR) - NX panel - 1965	27/8

2013		
Wem	LNWR - 35 levers - 1883	14/10
West Burton	BR (ER) - IFS panel - 1964	23/9
Wrenbury	LNWR - 17 levers - 1882	14/10
Ystrad Mynach South	Rhymney - 45 levers - 1886	9/9
Closure of 24 mechanical boxes and 14 Panel boxes		
Loss of 779 levers		

ABERTHAW

Above & below:- The general view of Aberthaw box and its signals was taken in 1982. Class 47 No. 47233 leaves with 6C33, the afternoon freight to Radyr Yard, whilst 47230 is working as the power station pilot shuttling MGR trains from the yard to the power station loop. The signal box dated from 1897 and was a Barry Railway design. The frame contained 53 levers and in 2005 an NX panel was added to control the Vale of Glamorgan route as far as Cowbridge Road box in Bridgend. M. Rhodes & J. Illingworth (2)

ALDERSHOT

Left & above:- Signalman Barry Treadwell puts levers back into the frame at Aldershot box in June 2013, just weeks before closure. The box was built in 1900 and contained a 24-lever frame. It was originally known as Aldershot East, then renamed as Aldershot 'A' in 1957 and finally simply Aldershot in 1977. Both M. Rhodes

ASH VALE JUNCTION

Right & below:- The signal box at Ash Vale Junction was opened in 1879, at which time it was called North Camp Junction. It was renamed Ash Vale Junction in 1925 and had contained a 19-lever frame. This was replaced by an IFS panel, seen beneath the box diagram in our internal view of signalman Winston Thompson working the box in its last few weeks. Both M. Rhodes

ATHERTON GOODS YARD

Right, below right & below:- *Back in 1984 an eight-car DMU formation passes Atherton Goods Yard with a Manchester to Southport train, no doubt longer than usual to cater for Saturday traffic to the beach. The box opened in 1956 and contained a 35-lever frame, most of which was surplus to requirement once the goods yard here closed. The second and third images, taken shortly before closure, show the box in a rather dilapidated state and with just five levers still in use.* P. Shannon & J. Illingworth

BARGOED

Above & right:- *The signal box at Bargoed was erected here in 1970, but was originally built in 1960 at Cymmer Afan. In the external view of the box, Class 37 No. 37023 slows with the 0740 Rhymney to Cardiff service, as the signalman collects the single line token. The box also inherited the 51-lever frame from Cymmer Afan but intially operated with just 41 levers with Nos. 42–51 boarded over. Then in 1976, when Bargoed Pits signal box closed, the extra 10 levers were reinstalled and the frame remained at 51 slots until closure, as the interior view from 2013 shows.* M. Rhodes & J. Illingworth

BESCOT DOWN TOWER

Right:- Bescot Down Tower was opened in 1965 in conjunction with the modernisation of the yard and installation of a Dowty hump. This view, in 1985, 12 months after the retarders had been removed, shows the NX panel in operation. The box remained in use controlling freight until 2013 when it became the last hump yard signal box to close. It had been put forward for Grade II listing but nobody informed the contractors who demolished it shortly after closure. M. Rhodes

BLACKROD JUNCTION

Right:- When this view of Blackrod Junction was taken on 21 April 1993, the SB boasted maroon and cream paintwork and a vitreous enamel nameboard. By the time it was decommissioned in February 2013, the woodwork had been replaced by plastic and the windows by uPVC. Not a historian's delight but probably a better working environment for the signaller! It became a fringe to Preston PSB during Stage 1 of the Preston Resignalling in October 1972. Then in January 1990, Manchester Piccadilly PSB was extended to fringe with Blackrod. The SB then survived a further 23 years as a 'buffer' between two technologies that couldn't communicate. The problem was at last solved in February 2013, when Manchester Piccadilly PSB assumed control. D. Allen

BLOXWICH

Right:- Dating from 1959, Bloxwich was a typical example of the successful standard SB favoured by BR(LMR) at the time. The surviving maroon enamel nameboard is a particularly pleasant feature. It became a fringe to Walsall PSB during Stage 2B of the resignalling work in 1967. When this view was taken on 11 August 1991, it also worked AB to Hednesford. Though fitted with a lever frame which was used to control the main line and local ground signals, it acquired a small panel in 1981 to control entry to Essington Wood British Coal Sidings. This had a short life as the connections were clipped out of use in 1995. It was decommissioned in August 2013 when control of the Cannock lines was transferred to West Midlands SC Walsall workstation. D. Allen

BRERETON SIDINGS

Above & above right:- Two views of Brereton Sidings; the first shows Class 66 No. 66957 passing the semaphores with an empty coal train from Rugeley Power Station to Stoke Gifford Yard, having delivered imported coal from Avonmouth. Looking the other way, the coal train passes a Birmingham to Rugeley passenger service and the 1908 LNWR signal box at Brereton with its 20-lever frame. Both M. Rhodes

COWBRIDGE ROAD

Right:- It's amazing that the 12 x 8 foot timber shed at Cowbridge Road survived as long as it did! Opened in 1965, it contained a small IFS panel and replaced the much larger 75-lever Cowbridge Road Junction signal box. J. Illingworth

CROW NEST JUNCTION

Left & below:- These internal and external views of Crow Nest Junction signal box were taken just six months before closure and show the 1972 BR (LMR) box with its 25-lever frame. Both J. Illingworth

FARNHAM

Left & below:- Signalman Darren Whittenham-Gray fills in the TRB at Farnham signal box with most of the 35-lever frame visible. The box opened in 1901 and closed a few weeks after this image was taken, at which point Darren moved to work in Woking. Both M. Rhodes

HARLESCOTT CROSSING

Right & below:- The LNWR signal box at Harlescott Crossing, just outside Shrewsbury, opened in 1882 and had a 38-lever frame at the time of closure. This was smaller than the original frame but not by much; as the interior view taken in 2012 shows, there wasn't much room to accommodate more levers. Both M. Rhodes

HEDNESFORD

Below:- Resignalling of the line from Bescot to Rugeley involved closure of five boxes, including the panels at Bescot and Walsall. One of three mechanical boxes to close was at Hednesford, where the 1877-vintage box with its 38-lever frame had controlled the extensive colliery sidings for Cannock Colliery. By 1986 when this view of Class 20 Nos. 20178 and 20158 working an empty MGR from Rugeley Power Station was taken, the sidings had long since been removed. P. Shannon

HEST BANK

Left:- Hest Bank opened in 1958 and originally had a 30-lever frame. This was replaced in 1982 by an IFS panel. This view was taken in summer 1997 and shows Class 156 No. 156427 with a Barrow to Manchester service. M. Rhodes

NANTWICH

Above:- Although simply called Nantwich by the time this picture was taken in 2012, the box diagram still retains the original name of Nantwich Station. The box was opened in 1948 but the 30-lever frame was second-hand, having previously operated Wem North signal box. M. Rhodes

NETHERFIELD JUNCTION

Below (3 images):- As well as a 40-lever frame, the 1960-vintage Netherfield Junction signal box had several CCTV-controlled crossing barriers. Signalman Barry Adams fills in the TRB whilst regaling me with tales of how he came to own a part share in D1048, 'Western Lady'. The external view shows Colas Class 66 No. 66846 passing the box with a Washwood Heath to Boston Docks steel train in 2012. All M. Rhodes

PREES

Right (2 images):- A Shrewsbury to Crewe stopping service approaches Prees station on 16 April 2012. The signal box here dated from 1881 and had a 25-lever frame. Both M. Rhodes

RECTORY JUNCTION

Right & below right:- By the time of my visit to Rectory Junction in May 2013, the windows of the 1888 box had all been "modernised" somewhat spoiling the appearance of the old box. The interior view shows the reduced 42-lever frame numbered 43 to 84, and for the eagle-eyed the disused levers numbered 1 to 23 (just to the left of the chair back). The changes made in the early 1970s, after closure of the yard at Colwick, were aimed at providing a locker room for the signalmen and reducing the heating bills. Thus levers 24-42 were removed to build a partition wall which is behind the blue box/seat. Both M. Rhodes

SAXILBY

Below & below right:- The internal view of Saxilby box was taken in 2011 and shows relief signalman Tam Rennie looking over the manual crossing gates, before closing them for an approaching train. The signal box with its 30-lever frame was opened in 1939, replacing a 1922 structure which itself was built to replace the original 1875 signal box. The external view shows Saxilby box, looking south from the station as Class 66 No. 66742 passes with 4E33, a Felixstowe to Doncaster intermodal service. Both M. Rhodes

SEAHAM

Left:- The signal box at Seaham was retained even though the rest of the Durham Coast Line had been resignalled in 2010. This was because of the busy footcrossing south of the station. This was converted to an underpass in 2013 with control of the area taken over by Ryhope Grange. Here in 1988, Class 56 No. 56122 passes the 1905 box with a Sunderland South Dock to Dawdon empty MGR service. The box dated back to 1905 and had a 23-lever frame at the time. M. Rhodes

SNEINTON CROSSING

Right & below:- The small crossing box at Sneinton, just east of Nottingham, opened in 1914 and had 10 levers. These internal and external views were taken in May 2013. Both M. Rhodes

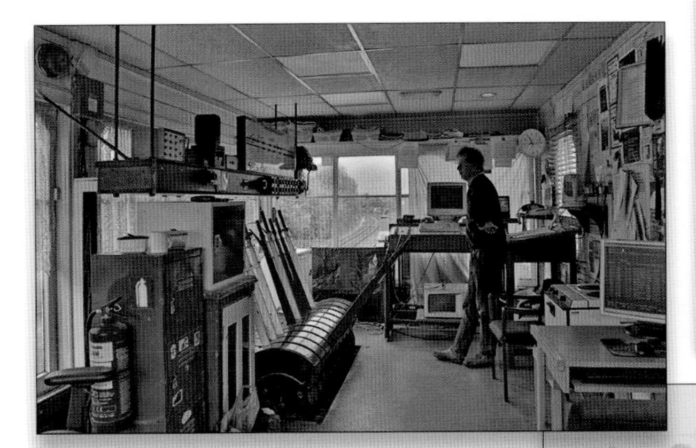

SHREWSBURY CREWE BANK

Right:- This view shows Shrewsbury Crewe Bank signal box, looking from the northern end of the platform at Shrewsbury station. It is unusual in that both upper and lower quadrant semaphores are in use, marking the boundary between London Midland and Western Region influences. The box was built during WWII in 1943 and the reinforced concrete roof was typical of this era. It contained a 45-lever frame but was usually switched out during the last few years of its existence, as indeed it is in this view of a Cardiff to Manchester train and a local Crewe to Shrewsbury service. M. Rhodes

SNODLAND

Right:- A Maidstone to London train passes the box at Snodland which opened in the early 1870s. It contained a 26-lever frame which was replaced (along with the associated semaphore signals) in 2005 by an IFS panel. Well after it opened a "greenhouse" style extension was constructed to allow better observation of the level crossing here whilst protected from the elements. Such extensions were generally added as motor traffic on level crossings increased. T. Maxted

STOW PARK

Left & below:- Signalman John Merriman can just be glimpsed through the door of the 1877-vintage GNR signal box at Stow Park. Class 153 No. 153352 passes with the morning Peterborough to Doncaster service. The box here had a 32-lever frame and a manually wound gate wheel. Both M. Rhodes

THORPE GATES

Below:- In May 1974, resignalling between Selby and Gascoigne Wood resulted in the reduction of Thorpe Gates SB to a gate box. New colour light signals were installed and Absolute Block was replaced by Track Circuit Block working. In March 1979, the nearby Thorpe Hall gate box was closed and the gates replaced by barriers controlled by Thorpe Gates. Though located more than 300 yards away, the crossing keeper checked to see if the crossing was clear by direct sight. In October 2013, Thorpe Gates gate box was decommissioned, the level crossings at both Thorpe Gates and Thorpe Hall being converted to MCB-OD supervised from Selby. At the time of closure the 1873-vintage box had an IFS panel installed which dated back to 1973. D. Allen

TRENT

Right:- Perhaps not strictly within the remit of this book, Trent power signal box closed in 2013 and this superb overall view taken by John Illingworth shows this early power box scheme just weeks before closure. The tracks controlled from here are now controlled by the East Midlands ROC at Derby. Whilst closure of mechanical and heritage signal boxes has predominantly yielded savings on operational expenditure or salaries, closure of panel boxes with transfer of control to the new ROCs may potentially save even more money by reducing traffic delays and their consequent penalties to Network Rail. J. Illingworth

WALKDEN

Right & below:- By the time of it's closure, the small L&Y signal box at Walkden, which dated from 1888, was hardly recognisable with new steel steps, new cladding and new uPVC windows. Internally however, the 24-lever frame was largely unchanged since construction, even if 5 levers had been removed to allow a modern train reporting screen to be installed. Both J. Illingworth

WEM

Right & below:- The 1883 signal box at Wem controlled a particularly complex level crossing with five roads funnelling into the crossing north of the station. It was one of the crossings that caused significant problems for the new "object detection" design of automated crossing used on the Crewe to Shrewsbury line and the Norwich to Ely route. In the event, closure of the box was at least 12 months behind the original plans, a matter that the signalman and MOM were discussing in this interior view showing the 35-lever frame back in April 2012. Both M. Rhodes

WEST BURTON

Right & below:- Another iconic signal box which closed in 2013 was that at West Burton. Its historical significance lay in the fact it was the first signal box supplied to British Railways by ML Engineering who became one of the "big three" providers of signalling equipment in the modern era. There had been a small 17-lever mechanical signal box controlling this stretch of track since the 1880s but historians disagree whether it was at West Burton or nearby Sturton. With construction of the new power station at West Burton, this new panel box was constructed in 1964 to control the main line but also the unloading loops in the power station. Both D. Allen

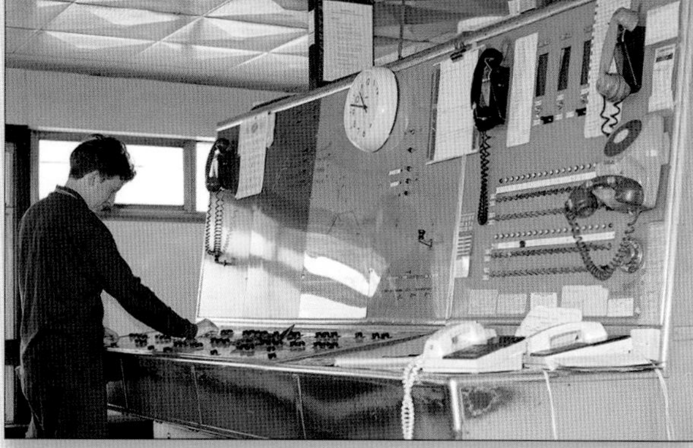

WRENBURY

Right:- Dating from 1882, the signal box at Wrenbury had just 17 operational levers left by the 21st century, although it had originally had a 64-lever frame. M. Rhodes

YSTRAD MYNACH SOUTH

Right & below:- Back in 1994, signalman Edward A Evans strikes a pose as he returns a lever to the frame at Ystrad Mynach South signal box. The imposing 1886 structure had a 1938-vintage 46-lever frame (reduced to 45 levers by time of closure). Class 150 No. 150261 is seen with a Penarth to Rhymney service, interestingly with the wrong destination board displayed. The external view also shows the unique decking which had to be installed to get point rodding and signal wires from the box down to track level. Both M. Rhodes

2014

By far the largest project of 2014 was the completion of resignalling the Joint Line from Peterborough through to Gainsborough Lea Road. New workstations in the Lincoln signalling centre took over from the signal boxes at Blankney, Blotoft, Gainsborough Lea Road (which had been out of use due to fire damage since 2009), Gosberton Crossing, Littleworth, Mill Green, St. James Deeping, Scopwick, Sleaford North, Sleaford South, and Spalding. The aim was to allow the Joint Line to open 24 hours a day instead of single shift operation between 0700 and 1630 on the section between Spalding and Sleaford. One factor which had prevented freight traffic using the route was the number of manual-gated crossings along the section between Spalding and Sleaford, ten in total. Even opening this stretch of line for a second shift would have meant significant manpower expenditure which would be hard to justify for half a dozen trains each day. The crossings at Bearty Fen, Blue Gowts, Brewery Lane, Cheal Road, Church Lane, Flax Mill, Golden High Hedges, Park Road (illustrated as an example in this chapter), Rowston No. 273 and Water Drove were all converted to either user-operated crossings controlled by phone from Lincoln, or barrier crossings with CCTV controls in the Lincoln signalling centre.

Two stretches of line on the Southern Region were resignalled. The route between Horsham and Arundel came under the control of the Three Bridges ROC with closure of the delightful mechanical boxes at Amberley, Billingshurst and Pulborough. In Dorset, the Poole to Dorchester route came under the care of Basingstoke ROC with closure of the boxes at Poole, Hamworthy, Wareham and Wool. In addition, the manual-gated crossing at Stoke No. 32 Gates was fitted with object detectors and controlled from the Basingstoke ROC.

The new Thames Valley ROC at Didcot took over control of Minety Crossing on the GW Main Line by means of the Swindon workstation. In a similar fashion a small change was made in the new Manchester ROC at Ashburys, in that the Liverpool workstation there assumed control of the area previously controlled by Huyton signal box. The crossing boxes at Brierfield and Huncoat stations were closed and the barriers controlled from Preston power signal box, both sets being fitted with object detectors. In Yorkshire, the boxes at Burn Lane and Henwick Hall closed with control taken over by Selby signal box, whilst Ferrybridge signal box extended its reach with the closure of Heck Lane, Hensall Station, High Eggborough and Sudforth Lane boxes. One final local rationalisation was the closure of Smithy Bridge signal box north of Rochdale, with control transferred to the new Rochdale West box.

2014		
Amberley	BR (SR) - 14 levers - 1950	17/3
Barry	Barry - 77 levers - 1896	30/6
Billingshurst	LBSCR - 19 levers - 1872	17/3
Blankney	LNER - 30 levers - 1928	14/4
Blotoft	GER - 16 levers - 1882	11/8
Brierfield Station	L&Y - IFS panel - 1876	15/9
Gainsborough Lea Road	GNR - 35 levers - 1877	2/1
Hamworthy	LSWR - 59 levers - 1893	19/5
Hensall Station	L&Y - 8 levers - 1875	27/5
Henwick Hall	NER - IFS panel - 1912	25/1
Huncoat Station	L&Y - 8 levers - 1902	24/11
Huyton	LNWR - 36 levers - 1899	14/7
Littleworth	GNR - 30 levers - 1875	3/11
Mill Green	GER - 21 levers - 1882	11/8
Minety Crossing	RT - IFS panel - 2000	23/8
Poole	LSWR - 51 levers - 1897	19/5
Pulborough	LBSCR - 30 levers - 1878	17/3
St. James Deeping	GNR - 32 levers - 1876	3/11
Scopwick	LNER - 25 levers - 1937	14/4
Sleaford North	GER - 18 levers - 1882	14/4
Sleaford South	BR (ER) - 25 levers - 1957	14/4
Smithy Bridge	L&Y - IFS panel - 1903	19/1
Spalding	GNR - IFS panel - 1921	3/11
Sudforth Lane	BR (NER) - IFS panel - 1961	27/5
Wareham	SR - 30 levers - 1928	19/5
Watford Junction	BR (LMR) - NX panel - 1964	29/12
Wool	LSWR - 19 levers - 1889	19/5
Closure of 20 mechanical boxes and 7 panel boxes. Loss of 583 levers		

AMBERLEY

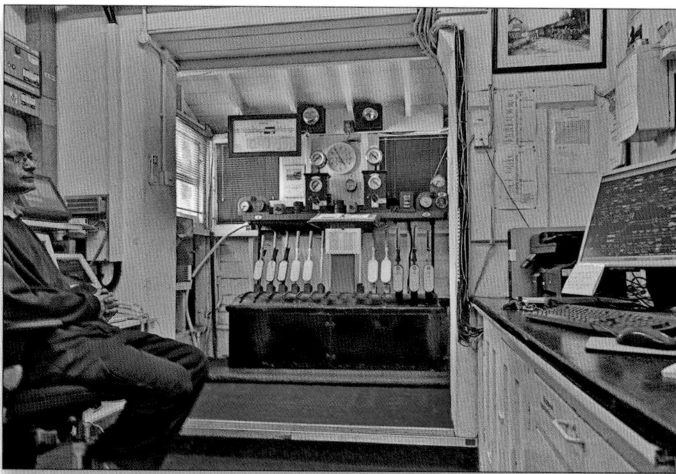

Left & below:- The small wooden signal cabin at Amberley was opened on the station platform in the 1950s replacing an older 1934 signal box. The 'knee' frame is seen with its 14 levers in our internal view with signalman Jason Greenfield, who was normally resident at Amberley but after closure went as a resident to Arundel. The signal box was unusual in that it had a hatch through which the signalman could sell tickets and receive Post Office deliveries. Both M. Rhodes

BARRY

Above & right:- The last surviving Barry Railway signal box, at Barry station closed in 2014. Opened in 1896, it originally contained a 115-lever frame. This was reduced to 101 levers in 1959 and further reduced in the early 1970s to 77 levers. Our external view, taken in 1994, shows Class 150 No. 150265 passing with a Barry Island to Merthyr Tydfil service. The interior view, showing most of the 77-lever frame was taken in 2013, just a year before closure. M. Rhodes & J. Illingworth

BILLINGSHURST

Below (2 images):- Billingshurst was the oldest signal box along the Three Bridges to Arundel line, dating from 1872. In the interior view, showing the 19-lever frame, signalman Paul Charman explains the track diagram. Both M. Rhodes

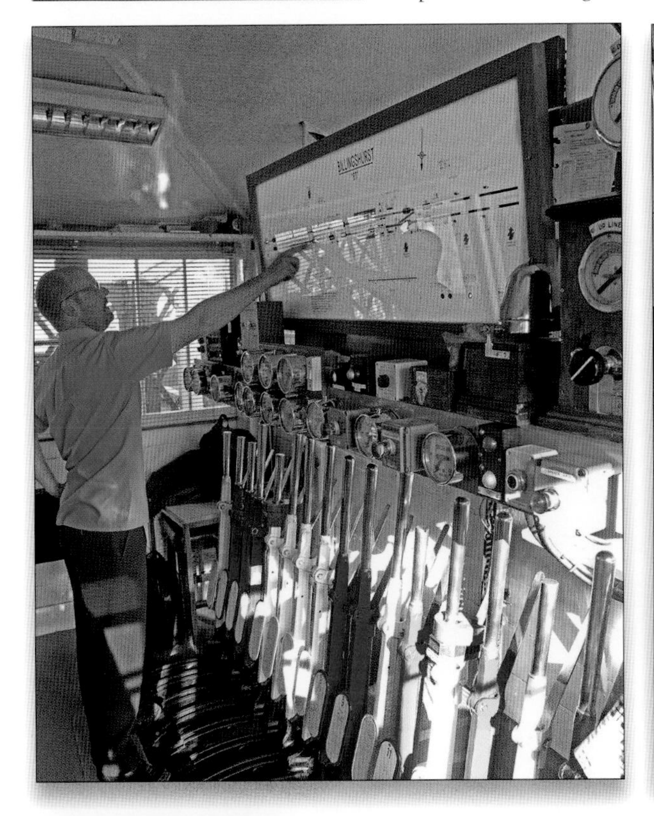

BLANKNEY

Above & right:- Significant strides were made in 2014 in resignalling the Joint Line from Peterborough to Doncaster. This allowed the use of the line 24 hours per day (as compared to just 9 hours per day for the Spalding to Sleaford section of the route). In expanding the availability of the route it was hoped to divert significant tonnages of freight away from the busy East Coast Main Line, but at the time of writing in 2019, this had not happened to any great extent. The signal box at Blankney (adjacent to Metheringham station) was built in 1928, replacing an earlier all-wooden construction built in 1882. It contained a 30-lever frame and a mechanical gate wheel as our interior view shows. Both M. Rhodes

BLOTOFT

Left:- Blotoft signal box opened in 1882 but because of subsidence into the fen was extensively rebuilt in 2003 with the addition of two 'A' frames at either end and steel steps and balcony. It retained its 16-lever frame until closure. M. Rhodes

BRIERFIELD STATION

Above:- In 1983, when this view of Class 104 'power twin' M50500 and M50444 was taken, Brierfield Station had a 12-lever frame in the 1876 Lancashire & Yorkshire Railway box. This was replaced in 1986 by a small IFS panel. Upon closure, control of the station and crossing was handed to Preston power signal box. P. Shannon

GAINSBOROUGH LEA ROAD

Above:- When Gainsborough Lea Road signal box finally closed in 2014, it had been out of use for five years because of fire damage. Here, back in 1996, Class 56 No. 56116 arrives at Gainsborough with 6D90, an empty oil train from Immingham, for loading with crude oil at the Gainsborough inland oil terminal. Built in 1877, the box had an 1895-vintage 35-lever frame; "Lea Road" was added to the name in 1924. M. Rhodes

GOSBERTON CROSSING

Right- For just two years from 2012 to 2014, this unlikely looking crossing keeper's hut contained an NX panel signalling the main line between Mill Green and Blotoft signal boxes. Back in 2010, when the line was still signalled by semaphores controlled by the old Gosberton box (just visible behind the trees in the left background), Class 66 No. 66730 passes with a light engine movement from March to Doncaster. M. Rhodes

HAMWORTHY

Above & right:- Local Operations Manager, Mark Jamieson (a generous contributor to this book) discusses the token machine for the Hamworthy Docks branch with Trevor Maxted (another major contributor to the book). The box was opened in 1893 with a 56-lever frame. It replaced an older box originally called Poole Junction, but renamed Hamworthy Junction in 1872. The new box's name was also shortened to just "Hamworthy" in 1972. The frame was extended to 59 levers in 1901, all of which are visible in our internal view of the box. Both M. Rhodes

HENSALL STATION

Left & below:- In April 2014, Class 66 No. 66595 passes Hensall signal box with an empty MGR from Drax Power Station to Immingham Docks. The box at Hensall dated back to 1875 and contained an 8-lever frame, which had been greatly reduced in size back in 1972 when resignalling took place ready for the new Drax Power Station (opened in 1974). The IFS panel installed as a consequence of this work can be seen in the internal view between the lever frame and the box diagram. Both M. Rhodes

HENWICK HALL

Above:- Henwick Hall was a small but very neat North Eastern Railway SB. Close inspection of the brickwork suggests the access been changed; an exit leading straight onto the running lines would not be considered safe today! Henwick Hall was reduced to a gate box in March 1970 when TCB working was introduced between Shaftholme Junction and Brayton Junction SBs; still the route of the ECML. It wasn't until 1983 that the so-called Selby Diversion was opened leaving Henwick Hall on a branch line. It was photographed on 11 June 1988, by which time the lever frame had been replaced by a small panel. In January 2014 the level crossing was converted to MCB-OD (obstacle detection) supervised by Selby SB. D. Allen

HUNCOAT STATION

Above:- The large L&Y signal box at Huncoat owed its existence to the extensive colliery and power station sidings nearby. These all closed in the late 1970s, leaving the 1902 L&Y box with just 8 levers, retained to control the crossing at Huncoat station. M. Rhodes

HUYTON

Left:- The 36-lever, 1899-vintage LNWR signal box at Huyton controlled the junction of the lines from Liverpool to Manchester and Wigan. It was replaced by the Liverpool workstation in the new Manchester ROC at Ashburys. J. Illingworth

LITTLEWORTH

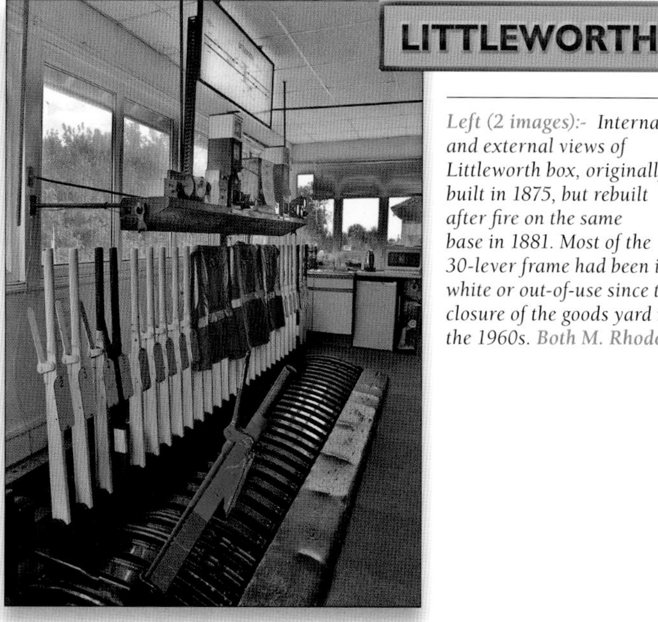

Left (2 images):- Internal and external views of Littleworth box, originally built in 1875, but rebuilt after fire on the same base in 1881. Most of the 30-lever frame had been is white or out-of-use since the closure of the goods yard in the 1960s. Both M. Rhodes

MILL GREEN

Left & above:- *Signalman Eddie Monover accepts a train from Spalding at Mill Green. The box opened in 1882 with a 12-lever frame. This was expanded to 21 levers in 1931, again mostly unused by 2012 when these two images were taken.* *Both M. Rhodes*

PARK ROAD CROSSING

Right:- *As mentioned in the introduction to the events of 2014, the line from Spalding to Sleaford was probably the most expensive route in the UK to operate due to its 10 manual-gated crossings. This, coupled to the sparse traffic, must have cost Network Rail a fortune! Typical of the many small cabins at these crossings is Park Road, north of Spalding, with external levers for locking the gates and cosy accommodation for the crossing keeper, who on the day of my visit was Craig Forde.* *M. Rhodes*

POOLE

Above & right:- *During my visit to Poole signal box in March 2014, signalman Mark Cooper was on duty. The box, originally named Poole West, opened in 1897 with a 27-lever frame which was enlarged to the final size of 51 levers in 1940. The box was renamed Poole 'B' in 1949 and simply "Poole" in 1977.* *Both M. Rhodes*

PULBOROUGH

Right & below:- Pulborough signal box opened in 1878, replacing an older structure which possibly dated as far back as 1864. It contained a 30-lever mechanical frame and in the internal view, Trevor Maxted (resident signaller at Guildford) discusses the workings of the box with John Spears, resident in the box. Both M. Rhodes

ST. JAMES DEEPING

Left & below:- The signalman at St. James Deeping, Richard Dale, had worked in the publishing industry before taking on a resident's role at St. James Deeping signal box. The box dated back to 1876 and had a 32-lever frame, mostly out of use since the 1960s. Both M. Rhodes

SCOPWICK

Below & right:- Signaller Mrs. Hitchins opens the gates at Scopwick during my visit in 2011. Her husband worked as a relief signalman at Lincoln. The 1937 brick-built box replaced an older wooden structure dating from 1882. Originally called Scopwick & Timberland it had 25 levers as well as the gate wheel. Both M. Rhodes

SLEAFORD NORTH

Right, below & below right:- Three images of Sleaford North. The image below is taken from the Sleaford avoiding line (disused at the time) and shows Ray Hilliard opening the gates after a Peterborough to Doncaster train has passed, having joined the main line on the set of points in the foreground at the extreme left of the image. The internal view of the 1882 18-lever frame shows signalman Dafydd Whyles (resident at Gainsborough Trent Junction) chatting with one of the resident signalmen at Sleaford North, Ray Hilliard. Finally, in May 2014, the box is still standing but the area is now controlled from Lincoln signalling centre. Class 66 No. 66732 passes on the newly-refurbished avoiding line with a Middleton Towers to Doncaster sand train, one of hopefully many workings which will use the rehabilitated Joint Line. All M. Rhodes

SLEAFORD SOUTH

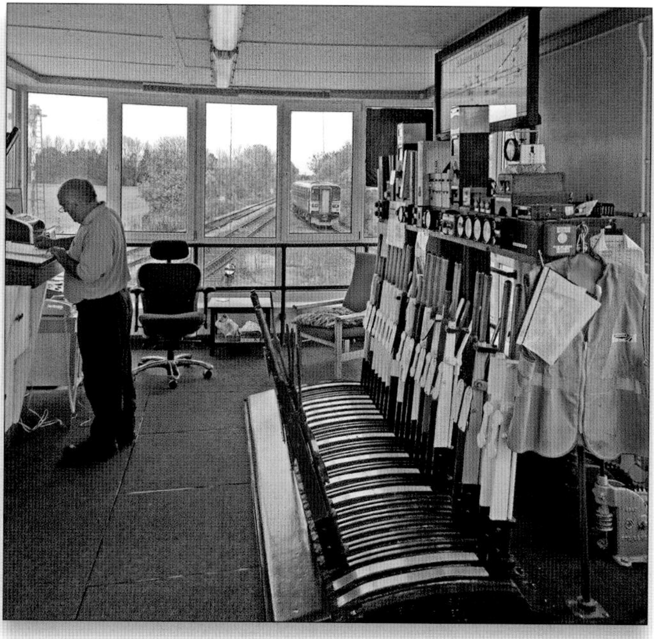

Above & above right:- The brick-built box at Sleaford South competed with Blea Moor as one of the most isolated on the Network, reached either by a walk along the avoiding line from the Boston Road bridge or a 600 yard path from a farmers field. Built in 1957 it was an austerity design with concrete roof and replaced an older wooden structure which had dated back to 1882. The internal view shows the 25-lever frame and signalman filling in the TRB as a single Class 153 unit heads south with the last train of the day over the line to Spalding, which was only open until 1630 at the time of this image. Both M. Rhodes

SMITHY BRIDGE

Right:- Smithy Bridge East SB – renamed Smithy Bridge in 1934 after closure of the West SB – was a hybrid in more ways than one. The base dated from 1874 but the top was replaced in 1903, as was the lever frame. To cope with the traffic, new loops were provided for both directions. In 1973, it became a fringe to Preston PSB as part of Stage C of the East Lancashire Resignalling. Due to financial constraints, the East Lancashire work was the only non-WCML work sanctioned for Preston PSB. In August 2011, as part of the Rochdale Resignalling Stage 1, Smithy Bridge SB was reduced to a gate box. Then in January 2014 it was decommissioned when the level crossing was converted to MCB-OD, supervised from Rochdale West SB. D. Allen

SPALDING

Above & right:- The sheer size of the signal cabin at Spalding suggests a more significant role for the box in the past. In the external view Class 156 No. 156470 leaves with a Doncaster to Peterborough working. Where once there were four routes diverging south from Spalding, now just the one survives. The original 80-lever frame was reduced to 40 levers in 1982 after the closure of the Joint Line to March and then in 1984, all levers were removed and a small IFS panel installed as seen in the 2012 view of signalman Jeff Nichols at work. Both M. Rhodes

SUDFORTH LANE

Left & below:- In the shadow of Kellingley Colliery, Sudforth Lane was a great spot to watch coal trains to and from the power stations at Drax and Eggborough. Opened in 1961, colour lights were introduced to the area in 1968 and this coincided with the installation of an IFS panel, shown in the interior view of the box taken during a visit in August 1998. The external view shows Class 56 No. 56099 passing with 6K86, a Selby Drift mine to Drax Power Station MGR service. Both M. Rhodes

WAREHAM

Below & below right:- Class 444 No. 444025, making up a Waterloo to Weymouth express, slows at Wareham on 4 March 2014. The box here was built in 1928 and had a 30-lever frame. Both M. Rhodes

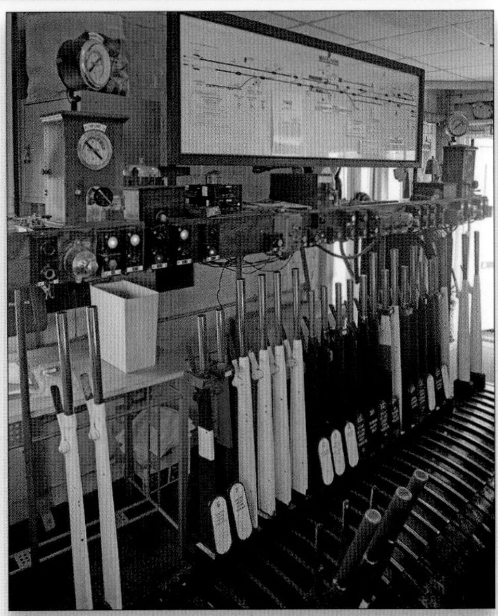

Below & right:- Signalman "Paul" fills in the TRB at Wool box after Class 444 No. 444030 has passed the 1889-vintage signal box there with its 19-lever frame. Both M. Rhodes

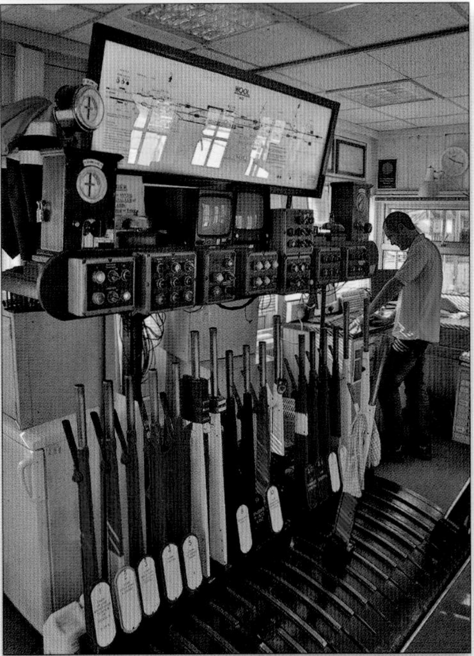

2015

Of all the years from 2000, the changes in 2015 attracted the most attention with the wonderful semaphore signals at Barnetby and Wrawby Junction being demolished as part of the Scunthorpe to Cleethorpes resignalling. Originally the project had been called the North Lincolnshire Resignalling Scheme but cost and timetable over-runs led to the whole scheme being scaled back to just include the main line from Scunthorpe to Cleethorpes and one box on the Immingham branch at Ulceby. One further ground frame was also decommissioned on the Barton-on-Humber branch, at Barton Road. The engineering possession over Christmas and New Year 2015/16 saw the boxes at Appleby (Lincs), Barnetby East, Barton Road, Brocklesby Junction, Elsham, Marsh Junction, New Barnetby, Pasture Street, Roxton Sidings, Stallingborough, Ulceby Junction and Wrawby Junction decommissioned. The crowds during the last two days of Wrawby Junction were something to behold (see below).

A major resignalling between Lewes and St.Leonards, including the Eastbourne branch also took place with control of the area taken over by the Three Bridges ROC. The boxes at Berwick, Bexhill, Eastbourne, Hampden Park, Havensmouth, Pevensey & Westham and Polegate Crossing all closed as a result of this. The East Midlands ROC at Derby took over the remains of the manual signalling on the Nottingham to Grantham line with closure of Bingham and Bottesford West Junction boxes. Crossing boxes in the Doncaster area at Balne and Moss closed with the power signal box at Doncaster taking control, whilst the crossing at Llaneli West was taken over by Port Talbot panel box. The new Manchester ROC at Ashburys assumed control of the Romiley Junction box and a new Gresty Lane signalling centre took over from the old heritage box at Gresty Lane in Crewe.

As part of the strategic plan to concentrate all UK signalling in just twelve ROCs or regional operating centres, the former power boxes at Slough and Wolverhapmpton closed. Their duties were taken over by Didcot ROC and Saltley ROC respectively. Two other important members of the "UK100 club" closed in 2015; Stafford No. 4 and Stafford No. 5. With 105 and 150 levers respectively, they joined Wrawby Junction (with 135 levers) amongst the high profile closures of the 2015 Network Rail programme.

2015		
Appleby (Lincs)	MS&LR - IFS panel - 1885	30/12
Balne	BR (NER) - IFS panel - 1957	25/4
Barnetby East	GCR - 72 levers - 1914	30/12
Berwick	LBSCR - 17 levers - 1879	16/2
Bexhill	LBSCR - 19 levers - 1876	16/2
Bingham	GNR - 40 levers - 1875	30/11
Bottesford West Junction	GNR - 38 levers - 1876	30/11
Brocklesby Junction	GCR - NX panel - 1914	30/12
Eastbourne	LBSCR - NX panel - 1882	16/2
Elsham	MS&LR - IFS panel - 1885	30/12
Gresty Lane	LNWR - IFS panel - 1899	7/12
Hampden Park	LBSCR - 24 levers - 1888	16/2
Havensmouth	RT - IFS panel - 1999	16/2
Llanelli West	GWR - IFS panel - 1877	9/3
Manchester North	RT - NX panel - 1998	7/4
Marsh Junction	GCR - 44 levers - 1908	24/12
Moss	NER - IFS panel - 1873	18/4
Pasture Street	BR (ER) - NX panel - 1962	24/12
Pevensey & Westham	LBSCR - 14 levers - 1876	16/2
Polegate Crossing	LBSCR - 20 levers - 1883	16/2
Romiley Junction	MR - OCS panel - 1899	2/8
Roxton Sidings	MS&LR - 18 levers - 1883	24/12
Slough	BR (WR) - NX panel - 1963	7/4
Stafford No. 4	BR (LMR) - 105 levers - 1960	1/9
Stafford No. 5	BR (LMR) - 150 levers - 1952	1/9
Stallingborough	NR - NX panel - 2007	24/12
Ulceby Junction	GCR - 30 levers - 1910	30/12
Wolverhampton PSB	BR (LMR) - NX panel - 1965	5/5
Wrawby Junction	GCR - 137 levers - 1916	30/12
Closure of 14 mechanical boxes and 15 panel boxes		
Loss of 728 levers		

APPLEBY (LINCS)

Left & above:- The Manchester, Sheffield & Lincolnshire Railway signal box at Appleby (Lincs) opened in 1885 and for most of its life had a 23-lever frame. This was replaced by an IFS panel in 2003 as shown in the internal view. At this stage the crossing barriers were automated and semaphore signals replaced with colour lights. On 11 November 2015, Class 20 Nos. 20308 & 20309 pass by with an RHTT train from Grimsby to Bridlington. Both M. Rhodes

BARNETBY EAST

BARTON ROAD CROSSING

Below:- The small external lever frame at Barton Road level crossing was as far along the Barton-on-Humber branch line as the 2015 North Lincolnshire resignalling reached. The crossing is now controlled from the York ROC. M. Rhodes

Above top & above:- Tony Bradley gives a big smile for the camera in Barnetby East signal box on 23 December 2015, the day before closure. Tony started on the railway 19 years earlier at Kirton Lime Sidings but within a year moved to Marsh Junction, nearer his home in Grimsby, where he worked from 1988 to 2000. He then moved to Ulceby as a Grade 3 General Purpose Relief (GPR) before taking a job in 2012 at Barnetby East as the "Signallers Continuous Assessment Programme Relief" - covering for signalmen and women around North Lincolnshire when they had to attend refresher courses. By the time this picture was taken, Tony was in Barnetby box as the Roxton Grade 5 General Purpose Relief signalman. The box at Barnetby East opened in 1914 and had a 72-lever frame. As the exterior view taken in June 2011 shows, it had been leaning to one side for some years prior to closure. Class 60 No. 60074 passes with an Immingham Docks to Santon iron ore working on 2 June 2011. Both M. Rhodes

BERWICK

Right & below:- The resignalling of the line from Lewes to Bopeep Junction led to the closure of eight boxes including the 1879, 17-lever framed box at Berwick. Both S. Company

BEXHILL

Above & right:- These two views of Bexhill box show the reduced 19-lever frame (originally 21 levers) and the box looking in a somewhat dilapidated state in March 2013. Both S. Company

BINGHAM

Right, below & below right:- *Bingham signal box dates back to 1875 and was significantly extended in 1922. The external close-up of the box shows a curious arrangement in that when it was refurbished in 2006, the upper portion of the westerly end of the box was demolished, leaving a small brick hut at the western end of the box. The smaller box had 40 levers at the time of closure. The general view of the box shows Class 66 No. 66011 passing with the lunchtime Rectory Junction to Immingham empty oil train on 24 February 2012.* *All M. Rhodes*

BOTTESFORD WEST JUNCTION

Above & right:- *Bottesford West Junction opened in 1876 and controlled the junction with the freight-only route to Newark until the early 1980s when this closed. The frame contained 38 levers, rather than the 37 suggested by the interior view, as there was an extra lever at the east end of the frame.* *Both M. Rhodes*

BROCKLESBY JUNCTION

Below (2 images):- Brocklesby box was opened in 1914 in conjunction with the massive GCR development at Immingham Docks. Originally it had a 96-lever frame but by 1998 this had completely gone, replaced by an NX panel perched in the corner of the massive space formerly occupied by all the levers. In June 2013, Sarah Bradley (the daughter of Tony seen in the Barnetby East photograph) is on duty as Class 66 No. 66956 passes with an Immingham Docks to Ratcliffe Power Station coal train. Both M. Rhodes

EASTBOURNE

Right & below:- The imposing structure of Eastbourne signal box had contained 108 levers when it opened in 1882. The frame was reduced to 72 levers in 1935 and then completely replaced by an NX panel in 1991. The panel controlled a much reduced station layout as our internal view illustrates. Both S. Company

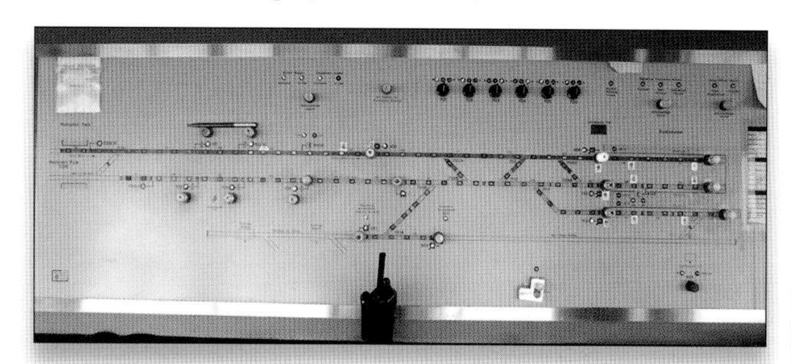

ELSHAM

Right, below & below right- The semaphore signals at Elsham were decommissioned in 2003. The view of Class 60 No. 60015 was taken in 1996 before their demise and shows the locomotive hauling an empty iron ore train from Santon back to Immingham Docks. Contrast this with the 2015 view, with Class 60 No. 60026, now owned by Colas, passing with the empty Preston Docks to Immingham bitumen train. The box steps have been slightly remodelled but the box remains essentially the same. Internally the signalman is seen opertaing the small NX panel as a loaded coal train heads west. All M. Rhodes

GRESTY LANE

Right & below:- Gresty Lane was opened in 1899 but its mechanical frame was removed as long ago as 1978 and replaced with an IFS panel. The panel is seen in operation during a visit in 1990. Both M. Rhodes

HAMPDEN PARK

Below & right:- It seems incongruous to have a signal box with the same name as one of Scotland's premier sporting venues, yet sitting on the south coast. Hampden Park box was originally called Willingdon and opened in 1888. It was renamed Hampden Park in 1930 and contained 24 levers. Both S. Company

LLANELLI WEST

Right:- Llanelli West was originally Llanelli No. 2. It continued to be called Llanelli West until it was decommissioned in February 2015 when both level crossings it controlled were converted to MCB-OD supervised from Port Talbot PSB. Looking at only recent changes, in February 1969 the SB was reduced to a gate box when the AB section was extended from Llanelli East to Llanelli Old Castle Crossing. Then, it survived Stage 5 of the West Wales MAS (Multiple Aspect Signalling) when all semaphores were replaced and TCB working was introduced, controlled from Port Talbot PSB. At this point both Llanelli East and Llanelli West SBs were operating as gate boxes. Then in February 1983, Llanelli East SB was closed and the crossing worked by means of CCTV from Llanelli West. D. Allen

MARSH JUNCTION

Below (2 images):- Just before closure of the box at Marsh Junction a new access road was built overlooking the box, but sadly the bridge was fenced off with palisade fencing. On my visit on 11 November 2015 I was fortunate in that the council parks and maintenance department were on site mowing the grass and I was afforded this view of Class 153 No. 153360 passing with a Barton-on-Humber to Cleethorpes train. In the background, the branch line to the former Great Coates Yard and Immingham Light Railway can be seen. Sadly the RHTT train due that morning never turned up! The box was opened in 1908 and had a 44-lever frame, photographed on 10 October 2012. The box was particularly difficult to access because of extensive 10ft high spiked fencing all around the area. Both M. Rhodes

MOSS

Below:- Dating from just after the line was opened in 1872, Moss SB was typical of those opened by the NER at the time. It was a product of the Southern Division which extended from Shaftholme Junction – just 3 miles to the south – to Darlington. In March 1970, Moss SB was reduced to a gate box with TCB working controlled by Brayton Junction and Shaftholme Junction SBs. In May 1973, Selby West SB replaced Brayton Junction. In turn, Doncaster PSB replaced Shafholme Junction SB in October 1980. In 1983, Stage 2 of the ECML (Selby) Diversion, left York PSB fringing with Doncaster PSB. Then, in September 1989, York IECC replaced York PSB. Moss finally closed in April 2015, when the level crossing was converted to MCB-OD monitored by Doncaster PSB. D. Allen

PASTURE STREET

Above & right:- *The area around Grimsby Town station was particularly intensively signalled with four signal boxes within less than half a mile at Garden Street Junction, Wellowgate, Friargate & Littlefield Crossing. Add to that a 100-lever mechanical box at Cleethorpes and a further seven including Pasture Street between there and Grimsby and it gives an idea of the impact the new cabin at Pasture Street has had since it opened in 1962. The 45-lever frame was replaced by an NX panel in 1985 when the boxes to Cleethorpes closed. Then in 1993 the Grimsby area was added onto the panel, which is seen here in May 2015 manned by signalman Ben Ranshaw. The external view shows Class 185 No. 185136 with a Cleethorpes to Manchester Airport service on the same date.* *Both M. Rhodes*

PEVENSEY & WESTHAM

Above & above right:- *The tiny signal box at Pevensey & Westham was opened in 1876 and contained 14 levers. It closed as part of the Lewes to Bopeep Junction resignalling.* *Both S. Company*

POLEGATE CROSSING

Below & right:- Polegate Crossing was originally called Polegate West Crossing but was renamed shortly after opening in 1883. The 20-lever frame was unusual in that, as our internal view shows, the booking desk with the train register book was plonked straight onto the frame in front of several white levers! Both M. Rhodes

ROMILEY JUNCTION

Below & right:- Romiley Junction signal box was of Midland Railway design and opened in 1899. The frame was replaced by an OCS panel in 1980. Resident signalman Dilip Tailor is seen here on duty during a visit by Anthony McIntyre, the Local Operations Manager. An example of how the railway often really is a "family" is the fact that Dilip had worked with Anthony's father at the start of his career. Both M. Rhodes

ROXTON SIDINGS

Below & right:- The isolated rural crossing at Roxton kept its wheel-operated crossing gates right to the very end in 2015. Opened in 1883 by the MS&LR, it had an 18-lever frame which during my visit was used to store the vacuum cleaner and dining table! Both M. Rhodes

STAFFORD NO. 4

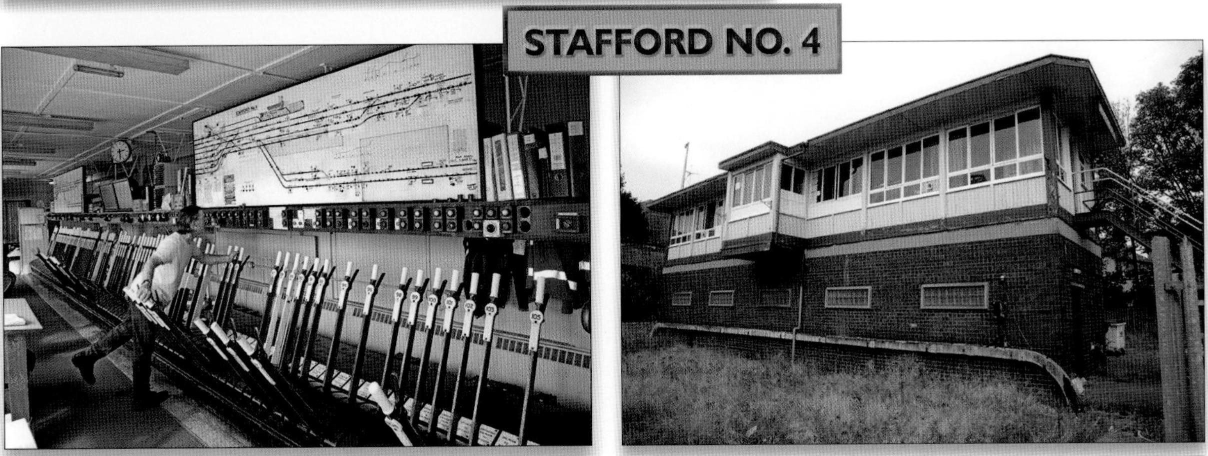

Above & above right- Amazingly, Stafford, one of the busiest spots on the WCML, retained two of the UK's largest mechanical signal boxes until 2015. Stafford No. 4 was opened in 1960 as part of the WCML electrification and contained 105 levers. The box was frantically busy and double-manned. The internal view shows signalman Thomas Larvin, a blur of activity as he has come to help on afternoon turn, having worked the early shift at No. 5 box. Thomas had been on the railway 26 years at this stage, starting at Foley Crossing, moving to Bradwell Sidings and ending up in Stafford. Both M. Rhodes

STAFFORD NO. 5

Above & left- Opened in 1952, Stafford No. 5 was much larger than No. 4 box, with 150 levers, but many of these (69 to be exact) were white. It was therefore single-manned with a meal relief provided. The frame was the second largest in the UK at the time of closure, after the 180-lever frame at Severn Bridge Junction. The external view shows a Plymouth to Manchester train heading north past the box. Both M. Rhodes

STALLINGBOROUGH

Left- Only opened in 2007, when it replaced the mechanical box at Stallingborough, the imposing Network Rail gabled building with its NX panel only lasted seven years in service. M. Rhodes

ULCEBY JUNCTION

Left & above- There's been a points failure and the signalman is on the phone to control. Behind him a Class 66 is stranded on an empty coal train from Scunthorpe CHP to Immingham. The cabin was built in 1910 and had a 60-lever frame, reduced in 1988 to 30 levers with an additional IFS panel. The external view shows the box in 2006 with a Barton-on-Humber to Cleethorpes service in the hands of Class 153 No. 153358. Both M. Rhodes

WRAWBY

Below, right & below right:- In 2015 the third largest signal box on the network was at Wrawby Junction. Opened in 1916 it contained 137 levers, unusually numbered from 1 to 132 with letters A–E at the west end of the frame. In the interior view John Stocks, the LOM, chats with the signalman. Externally, the box was an imposing structure as the view of Class 153 No. 153313 with a Grimsby to Lincoln passenger train shows. The most spectacular view however was of the forest of semaphore signals at Wrawby Junction (and also Barnetby East). Taken on 23 December 2015, Class 66 No. 66186 turns north-west at Wrawby Junction, signalled by Simon Long, with its Immingham to Drax biomass service. To the right of the locomotive is Barnetby East signal box and out of view to the right are dozens of photographers with poles who had to be moved on by the local police, but not before many got excellent pictures of the last of the semaphores at Wrawby Junction. All M. Rhodes

2016

The North Kent resignalling saw closure of five signal boxes but only two of these were heritage structures, at Gillingham and Plumpton gate box. Elsewhere, the headline closure was of the two GWR signal boxes at Banbury, with attempts to save the box at Banbury North eventually proving futile as it was demolished in 2017. Three signal boxes, already mostly out of use due to closure of Thoresby Colliery and Longannet Power Station respectively were finally closed. These were at Thoresby Colliery and Clipstone Junction and then in Longannet Power Station itself. The final major scheme of this year's activity was the completion of resignalling between Nottingham and Newark with closures at Fiskerton Station, Fiskerton Junction, Lowdham, Newark Castle, Rolleston gates and Staythorpe Crossing. This left Swinderby signal box as an isolated remnant of mechanical signalling between the East Midlands ROC and the Lincoln signalling centre.

One anachronistic survivor which finally succumbed in 2016 was the crossing box at Oddingley. The box brought to an end over a century of manual signalling in Worcestershire and was closed as part of the much larger £100 million remodelling of the Bromsgrove area in preparation for electrification. The box, originally constructed in 1908, sat on the 100 mph, 120 train per day main line from Bristol to Birmingham. The mechanical frame was removed in 1969 for control to be handled by the 1875-invented, Annett's Key method. In this system two keys, one for each gate, were kept in an interlocking on the box shelf and only if the line was clear could the gates be opened. The box was secured for preservation by the Chasewater Light Railway at Brownhills in Staffordshire.

2016		
Banbury North	GWR - 95 levers - 1899	30/07
Banbury South	GWR - 67 levers - 1908	30/07
Clipstone Junction	GCR - 26 levers - 1918	18/08
Fiskerton Junction	LMS - 30 levers - 1929	22/10
Fiskerton Station	MR - 15 levers - 1902	21/10
Gillingham (Kent)	SECR - 44 levers - 1913	29/03
Leamington Spa	BR (LMR) - Westcad VDUs - 1985	30/07
Longannet	BR (ScR) - 30 levers - 1969	27/06
Lowdham	MR - 16 levers - 1896	01/10
Newark Castle	MR - 16 levers - 1912	05/11
Oddingley Crossing	MR - Annett's Key - 1908	25/10
Plumpton GB	LBSCR - 21 levers - 1891	08/02
Rainham	BR (SR) - NX panel - 1959	29/03
Rochester	BR (SR) - NX panel - 1959	29/03
St. Fagans GB	BR (WR) - IFS panel - 1969	24/12
Saltley PSB	BR (LMR) - NX panels - 1969	05/11
Sittingbourne	BR (SR) - NX panel - 1959	29/03
Staythorpe Crossing	BR (LMR) - 35 levers - 1950	05/11
Swindon PSB	BR (WR) - NX panel - 1968	22/02
Thoresby Colliery	LNER - 30 levers - 1926	18/08
Closure of 12 mechanical boxes and 8 panel/other boxes. Loss of 425 levers		

BANBURY NORTH

Above & left:- Filling in the gap between the Thames Valley ROC at Didcot and the West Midlands ROC in Saltley took place in 2016, with the closure of the two Banbury boxes and Leamington Spa. Banbury North was opened in 1899 with an 86-lever frame which was expanded to 95 levers in 1956. The box was easily viewed from the bridge to the north of Banbury station, but sadly attempts to preserve it for posterity failed. M. Rhodes & J. Illingworth

BANBURY SOUTH

Below & right:- The box at Banbury South was opened in 1908 and originally had a 66-lever frame. This was enlarged to 87 levers in 1944 but then in 1991 it was shortened back to 67 levers to make way for an NX panel to control the Aynho Junction area. The interior view shows the frame and the NX panel in the distance, whilst the external view shows a Marylebone to Birmingham Snow Hill service made up of Class 168 No. 168218 on 22 August 2012. M. Rhodes & J. Illingworth

CLIPSTONE JUNCTION

Right, below & below right:- Clipstone Junction, originally called Clipstone West Junction, was opened in 1918 and at the time of my box visit in May 2013 had a 26-lever frame reduced from the original 44 levers. This was in order to make way for two NX panels. The first of these was installed in 1986 to cover the route down to Mansfield Concentration Sidings and the collieries at Rufford, Bilsthorpe and Mansfield beyond that. The second came in 1997 and covered the area formerly signalled by Welbeck Colliery Junction signal box. The interior view shows signalman Adrian Stretton on duty, aged 66 and wedded to the railway.

Chatting during my visit he reminisced about how busy the box had been, such that in 1971 there were 120 trains on one shift, mainly because of controlling the northerly entrance and exits from the extensive Mansfield Coal Concentration Sidings. By way of context, the view of Class 20 Nos. 20053 & 20094 on a 7T62, Toton to Clipstone trip freight, taken in 1990, shows the exit from Mansfield Concentration Sidings "down" yard on the left of the picture, with the box hidden behind the train. All M. Rhodes

FISKERTON JUNCTION

Right & below:- Two views of Fiskerton Junction signal box taken in May 2013. The box had controlled the western curve onto the Mansfield line and opened in 1929 with a 30-lever frame. Up until 1983 the signal box was often switched out which meant the associated manual crossing gates had to be operated by the crossing keeper, using a ground frame. To enable this there was a lever in the signal box to disengage control of the gates and thus allow the ground frame to take over. Since the early 1980s however, the box had been open continuously, allowing the ground frame to close and the gates to be operated by the large wheel shown in the internal view. Both M. Rhodes

FISKERTON STATION

Above & above right:- :- The signalman at Fiskerton Station during my visit in 2013 was an avid model railway builder, concentrating on Canadian Railways! Here he puts a lever back in the frame, which was installed in 1902 when the box was opened. At the time it was a 16-lever frame, later reduced to 15 levers. The box at Fiskerton Station was effectively a crossing box manned by a crossing keeper as its block instruments were removed as long ago as 1934. The external view shows Class 60 No. 60011 passing the box (which is leaning significantly by this date), with 6E54, an empty oil train from Kingsbury to Lindsey Oil Refinery in Immingham. Both M. Rhodes

GILLINGHAM

Right:- Way back in 2001 this view of Gillingham signal box clearly shows the Network Rail building in the background that was to become the Gillingham ROC. The box here dated back to 1913 and had a 44-lever frame. I. Stewart

LONGANNET

Left & above:- Built in 1969, in conjunction with the new power station at Longannet, the signal box here had a 30-lever frame which controlled movements within the power station. The internal view, taken during a visit in 1991, shows the unusual signal box diagram of the power station loop. During the same visit, Class 37 No. 37693 is seen leaving the loops at the power station, having unloaded 7G01, an MGR from Westfield Disposal Point and now working on, empty to Millerhill. Both M. Rhodes

LOWDHAM

Above & above right:- Dating from 1896, the signal box at Lowdham escaped too much "modernisation" and retained its sliding sash windows until closure. As the external view shows, there were new metal steps (just visible on the right of our view). Internally it contained a 16-lever frame and it is hoped that both box and frame may be preserved with plans to display them adjacent to the former station offices at Lowdham. Both M. Rhodes

NEWARK CASTLE

Left:- The frame at Newark Castle signal box is unusually located at the back of the box (as compared to all the other boxes along the Nottingham to Newark line - and indeed most Midland Railway signal boxes - where the frame is at the front). It was opened in 1912, replacing an older 1877-vintage structure and as shown in our view had a 16-lever frame which controlled the busy level crossing on the old "Great North Road" and a crossover to allow trains to terminate at Newark. M. Rhodes

ODDINGLEY CROSSING

Right:- The sparsely-used crossing at Oddingley was converted to a full barrier crossing with obstacle detection as part of the Bromsgrove remodelling and resignalling project. The box, which opened in 1908, had a lever frame but this was removed in 1969, leaving just the two Annett keys in the box. M. Rhodes

PLUMPTON

Above:- By the time this image was taken, the frame at Plumpton gate box, between Haywards Heath and Lewes, had just 3 working levers from a total of 21 in-situ. The rest of the frame had been replaced by an IFS panel in 1985. I. Stewart

ROLLESTON

Right:- Class 60 No. 60054 passes the manual gated crossing at Rolleston on 24 May 2013 with 6E54, the empty tanks from Kingsbury to Lindsey Oil Refinery. The distant signal in the view was controlled by Fiskerton Station signal box and the facilities were very basic with just a small green portable building for the crossing keeper, seen behind the trees on the extreme left of this view. The crossing had been protected by its own signals worked from the original Rolleston Junction signal box, but this closed in 1966. M. Rhodes

STAYTHORPE CROSSING

Right & above:- The significant structural problems at Staythorpe are evident in the external view of the box taken in 2013, as indeed are the somewhat garish new uPVC windows. The box opened in 1950, linked to the new rail connections for Staythorpe Power Station and had a 35-lever frame. Staythorpe 'A' Power Station closed in 1984 and the 'B' station in 1994; this is reflected by over a dozen white levers in the frame. Both M. Rhodes

THORESBY COLLIERY

Right & below:- By 2016, Thoresby Colliery signal box had been out of use for most of the previous two years since the closure of the colliery. Opened in 1926, it contained a 30-lever frame and controlled the erstwhile main line to High Marnham as well as the junction to Thoresby Colliery and a small exchange yard. Seen on 18 April 2011, Class 66 No. 66709 arrives with an empty coal train from Worksop which will reverse up the colliery branch to the right of the locomotive and then return to run round in the yard at Thoresby before heading to Cottam Power Station. Both M. Rhodes

2017

2017 was a relatively quiet year in terms of the number of signal boxes to close; the one major scheme to be undertaken during the year was between Preston and Blackpool. Resignalling along this 17-mile stretch of line was needed in preparation for electrification. The opportunity was also taken to remodel several locations along the route. The platforms at Blackpool North station were straightened and the layout at Kirkham simplified. The branch to Fleetwood was also disconnected from the main line at Poulton. In all, five mechanical signal boxes closed as a result of this modernisation scheme.

Further north, the boxes at Elgin, Forres and Nairn were closed as part of the "Inverness–Aberdeen in two hours" project. More double track as well as straightening of the route through Forres was coupled with transfer of control of this stretch of line to the Inverness signalling centre. In central Scotland, the reach of the Edinburgh ROC was extended as far as Larbert North. Again this was part of the plan to resignal as far as Dunblane and electrify the commuter routes between Edinburgh, Glasgow and Dunblane. One final closure was the final decommissioning of Mostyn signal box. The cabin here was often "switched out" and unmanned and finally closed forever in January 2017.

2017		
Blackpool North No. 2	L&Y - 72 levers - 1896	11/11
Carleton Crossing	LMS - 12 levers - 1924	11/11
Carmuirs East	NBR - 28 levers - 1882	31/12
Elgin	BR (ScR) - 26 levers - 1951	7/10
Forres	HR - 24 levers - 1896	7/10
Grangemouth Juntion	RT - NX panel - 1997	31/12
Greenhill Junction	BR (ScR) - NX panel - 1990	31/12
Kirkham	L&Y - 49 levers - 1903	11/11
Larbert North	CR - 59 levers - 1892	31/12
Mostyn	LNWR - 40 levers - 1902	8/1
Nairn	RT - Westcad VDUs - 2000	7/10
Poulton	L&Y - 72 levers - 1896	11/11
Salwick	L&Y - 33 levers - 1889	11/11
Closure of 10 mechanical boxes and 3 panel boxes		
Loss of 415 levers		

BLACKPOOL NORTH NO. 2

Below & right:- With resignalling and electrification to Blackpool completed by the end of 2017, the wonderful Lancashire & Yorkshire Railway signal box at Blackpool North station became surplus to requirements. Built in 1896, the box was fitted with a 120-lever frame which was later reduced to 72 levers (Nos.15-86). Signalman Stuart Marsh was on duty during my official visit in 2012. Both M. Rhodes

CARLETON CROSSING

Right, Below & below right:- Signalman Mark Bradley lowers the gates at Carleton Crossing in February 2017. After 22 years in the box his future was looking uncertain with the Blackpool electrification and resignalling to take place later that year. Opened in 1924, the box had a 12-lever frame of the same age. *All M. Rhodes*

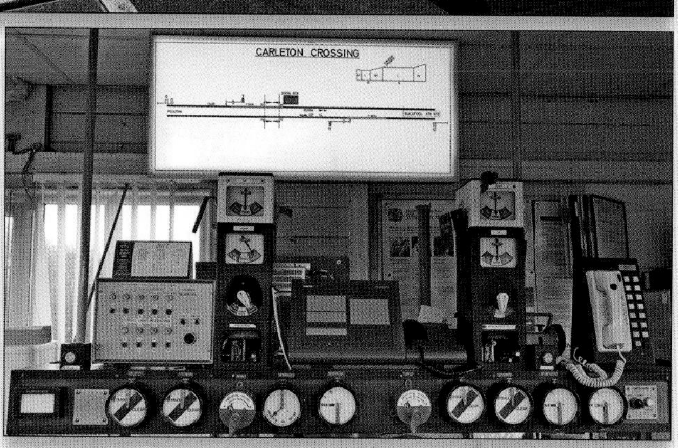

CARMUIRS EAST

Right:- The points are set for this Class 107 DMU to head north to Stirling with a stopping service from Edinburgh Waverley on 31 March 1989. The box here opened in 1882 and had a 28-lever frame. The box closed as part of the electrification of this route. *M. Rhodes*

ELGIN

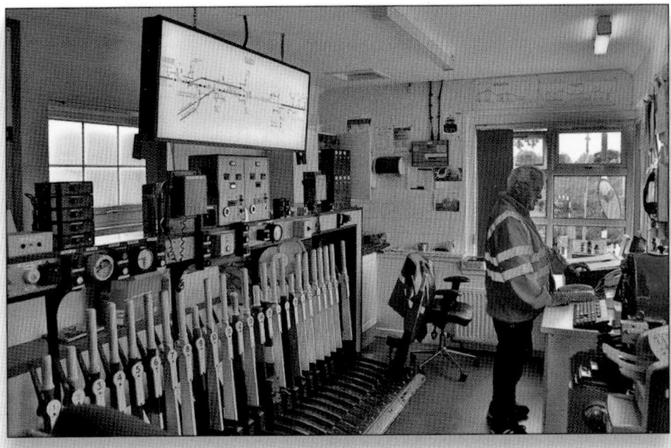

Above, left & below left:- *The signalman a Elgin hands the token for the single line section to Nairn to the driver of an Aberdeen to Inverness service in the hands of Class 158 No. 158712. The signal box here, still named Elgin West, dated from 1951 and had a new frame fitted in 1973. As the signalman logs the passing of the Inverness service in his TRB, he recounts how he had started life as a butcher and enjoyed working for Asda, but left when they were taken over by Walmart to pursue a new career on the railway. The relatively new 1973-built frame contained 26-levers.* All M. Rhodes

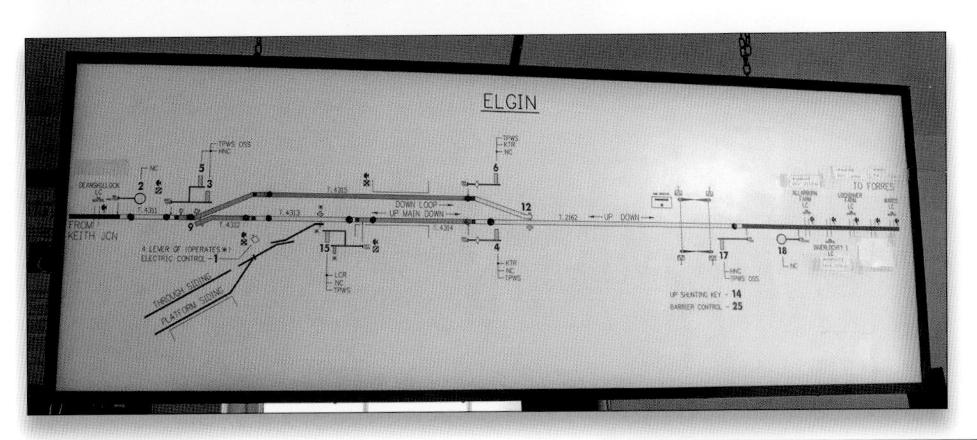

FORRES

Left & above:- *A satellite view of Forres, shows how the current main line bends south to the station and how the ample spare land to the north of the current station could speed the approach and departure from a new Forres station. Hence the days of the box at Forres were numbered. In a scene almost identical to that at Elgin above, signalman Graham Rhind offers the token for the single line to Nairn to the driver of Class 158 No. 158705 as it heads to Inverness. At the time of my visit in 2014, the goods yard was already being cleared for the new line and 300 metal sleepers had been delivered. The whole project offered a 6–7 minute saving on the Inverness to Aberdeen timings. The box dated back to 1896 but contained a much more modern 24-lever frame which dated from 1967.* Both M. Rhodes

MOSTYN

Right:- The Grade II listed signal box at Mostyn already looked in a sorry state in 2012 when this image was taken. Built in 1902, the box had a 40-lever frame which was disconnected from the surrounding tracks and signals in January 2017, after several years when the box was almost permanently "switched out". The box was listed in 1994 because "it was a rare and well preserved early 20th century signal box" - the 2012 image sheds some doubt on the "well preserved" description. M. Rhodes

KIRKHAM

Above, above right & right:- In February 2017, the signalman at Kirkham contemplates his future, having just passed out to work the box six weeks earlier. Opened in 1903 by the Lancashire & Yorkshire Railway, the box was originally called Kirkham North Junction and had a 105-lever frame. This was reduced in the 1960s to 76 levers. More recently there had been further rationalisation with more of the frame removed, leaving just 49 levers above the box floor. A Class 142 'Pacer' DMU approaches the box in 1990. All M. Rhodes

LARBERT NORTH

Above & right:- Track rationalisation has led to rampant bush and buddleia growth at Larbert North, as the external view illustrates. Class 60 No. 60096 passes the box with the Inverness to Oxwellmains empty cement working on 11 May 2017. The box was opened in 1892 and contained a 59-lever frame, here watched over by a signalman who had previously worked in five other boxes in the last 20 years, always told it would be just a one year appointment! Both M. Rhodes

NAIRN

Left & Below:- With the two Nairn mechanical boxes closing in 2000, the new Nairn "signal box" was situated within the station offices. It is a strange concoction of old and new with a modern, 2000-installed workstation, sitting alongside the 1891-vintage block token instruments. Gone are the days when token exchange from Nairn West to Nairn East was conducted by bicycle, but the TRB desk in the station offices retains the historical flavour of the new box with inscriptions on the inside from George Mainnes and Jim Davidson from 1969!. Both M. Rhodes

POULTON

Above & left:- The box was originally called Poulton No. 3 as our external view from summer 1983 shows. Class 37 No. 37228 passes with a Blackpool to Sheffield summer Saturday service. Opened in 1896, the box had a reduced frame of 72 levers at the time of my visit in February 2017. The box diagram is interesting in that it clearly shows the Fleetwood branch, which was still in situ and connected to the main line at the time of my visit. During the summer of 2017 the connection was severed as part of preparatory work for electrification. Both M. Rhodes

SALWICK

Above & left:- At the time of my visit in 2017, Salwick signal box was looking very run down, a sign of its imminent closure. Opened in 1889 it was originally installed with a 30-lever frame. This was extended in 1942 with the addition of levers A to E. Since then it has been reduced to 33 levers and as can be seen in our internal view, most of these have long been redundant as a result of the freight sidings to the Westinghouse Factory closing. Both M. Rhodes

2018

The pace of signal box closures certainly picked up in 2018 with major schemes along the North Wales coast, around Liverpool, along the Humber and finally along the last mechanically signalled Trans-Pennine route.

In North Wales, initial plans had envisaged the resignalling of the whole route to Holyhead, but as with many other projects, cost over-runs and a shortage of contractors to undertake resignalling work led to a scaled-down scheme stretching from Llandudno Junction to Chester, which was completed over Easter. This resulted in the closure of six signal boxes, most notably the splendid LNWR box at Rhyl.

Over on the east of the country, the line from Howden and Goole to Ferriby was due to be resignalled over Easter 2018 but the report was that the new installations along the line would not "talk" to the ROC in York. The reasons for this are not clear but it seems some of the lineside equipment might not have been ready for the switch over to York ROC at that time. Whatever the case, during an engineering possession on 1 September 2018 the points along the line were successfully operated by the ROC in York and definite plans to resignal the entire line were set in stone for the week commencing 26 November 2018. There were slight residual niggles, in that the crossing at Oxmardyke was not wide enough for two HGVs to pass each other. The solution planned for this conundrum was to close the road over the crossing here until such time as it could be widened. A second anachronism of the resignalling of the Hull line is the retention of Crabley Creek signal box as a manual crossing box. The farm to the south of the line has a guarantee of a manned crossing over the access road dating back over a century and granted by parliamentary decree. Even though the owner of the farm was offered an overbridge at Network Rail's expense, he was unwilling to surrender the land needed to create such access. As a result the crossing and box at Crabley Creek survive, operated as a manual crossing box, but no longer a block post.

The gradual takeover of control of the Liverpool area by the Ashburys ROC started with the closure of Halton Junction in May, followed by the 1960s era NX panel at Edge Hill in June. Perhaps the most significant closure occurred in July when the large miniature lever frame controlling Liverpool Lime Street closed. Finally, over Christmas the two large mechanical boxes at Speke Junction and Allerton Junction closed.

Across the Penines, the boxes at Healey Mills, Huddersfield, Halifax, Hebden Bridge, Mill Lane Junction and Milner Royd Junction were all closed during 2018 as well as the cabin at Ashton Moss North Junction. This final closure was partly undertaken in preparation for electrification of the line to Staylybridge, but also because the box was listing to one side and structurally in need of demolition.

2018		
Abergele	LNWR - 60 levers - 1902	24/3
Allerton Junction	BR (LMR) - 70 levers - 1960	31/12
Ashton Moss North Junction	L&Y - 56 levers - 1911	14/4
Broomfleet	NER - 25 levers - 1904	26/11
Brough East	NER - 52 levers - 1904	26/11
Cave Crossing	NER - 16 levers - 1904	26/11
Edge Hill	BR (LMR) - NX panel - 1961	2/6
Gilberdyke	NER - 55 levers - 1903	26/11
Halifax	L&Y - IFS panel - 1884	20/10
Halton Junction	LNWR - 25 levers - 1897	6/5
Healey Mills	BR (ER) - NX panel - 1963	23/1
Hebden Bridge	L&Y - 38 levers - 1891	20/10
Holywell Junction	LNWR - 54 levers - 1902	24/3
Huddersfield	BR (NER) - NX panel - 1958	23/1
Liverpool Lime Street	LMS - 95 levers - 1948	12/7
Melton Lane	NER - 26 levers - 1921	
Mill Lane Junction	L&Y - IFS panel - 1884	20/10
Milner Royd Junction	L&Y - 20 levers - 1874	20/10
Prestatyn	LNWR - 45 levers - 1897	24/3
Rhyl	LNWR - 90 levers - 1900	24/3
Rockcliffe Hall	RT - IFS panel - 1995	24/3
Runcorn	LMS - 45 levers - 1940	6/5
Saltmarshe	NER - NX panel - 1905	26/11
Speke Junction	LNWR - 86 levers - 1907	24/12
Talacre	LNWR - 24 levers - 1903	24/3
Welton	NER - 6 levers - 1904	26/11
Closure of 19 mechanical boxes and 7 panel boxes		
Loss of 888 levers		

ABERGELE

Below & right:- Built in 1902, Abergele signal box had a 60-lever mechanical frame. Class 175 No. 175106 is seen passing the box in 2013 with a Manchester to Llandudno service. Both M. Rhodes

ALLERTON JUNCTION

Above & right:- Relief signalman John Illingworth stands guard over the 70-lever frame at Allerton Junction in summer 2016. The box here, built in 1960, controlled not only the main line, but also the access to Allerton depot. Both M. Rhodes

ASHTON MOSS NORTH JUNCTION

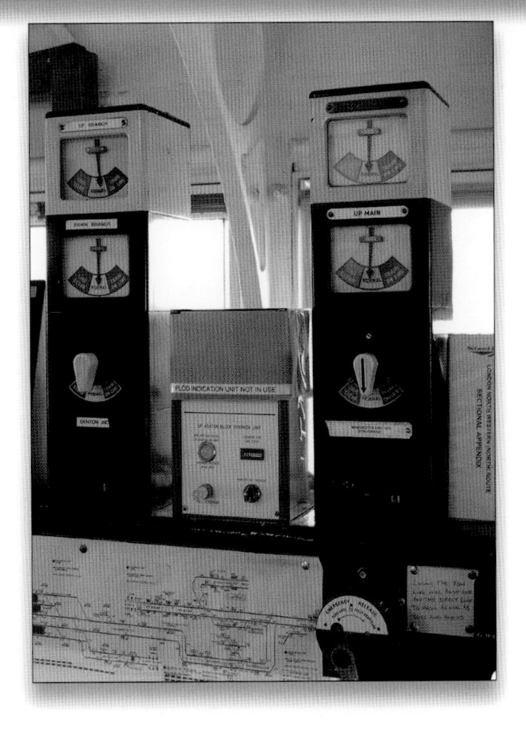

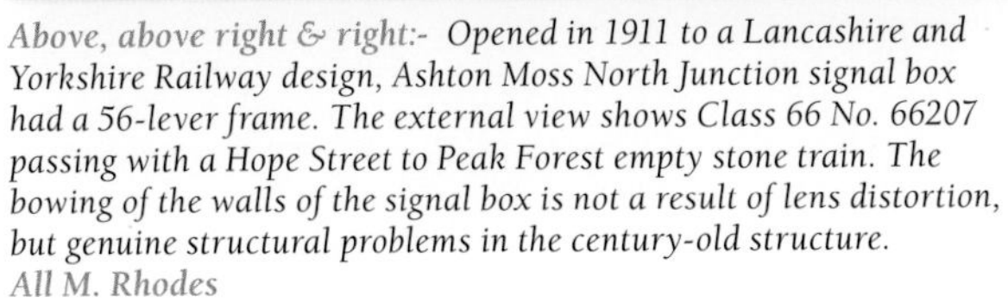

Above, above right & right:- Opened in 1911 to a Lancashire and Yorkshire Railway design, Ashton Moss North Junction signal box had a 56-lever frame. The external view shows Class 66 No. 66207 passing with a Hope Street to Peak Forest empty stone train. The bowing of the walls of the signal box is not a result of lens distortion, but genuine structural problems in the century-old structure. All M. Rhodes

BROOMFLEET

Above & above right:- Resident signalman Richard Charnock is seen in action in Broomfleet signal box. Opened in 1904, the box had a 60-lever frame but this was significantly reduced in size as the internal view shows, with just 11 levers left at the west end, 13 to the east and then a gap to a final lever controlling the interlocking for the level crossing. The external view shows a bit of the "lean" of the box as Class 66 No. 66051 passes on 1 October 2012 with 6H25, a Hull Docks to Drax Power Station coal train. Both M. Rhodes

BROUGH EAST

Above & above right:- The external image of Brough East shows Class 180 No. 180101 passing with a King's Cross to Hull service in July 2012. It also emphasises the labour intensive nature of the manually-signalled Selby to Hull line. The crossing box at Welton is seen to the right of the line in the distance, whilst the semaphores at Melton Lane can be seen further away. The box was opened in 1904 and had a 52-lever frame from which just 11 levers were still in use in 2018. Both M. Rhodes

CAVE CROSSING

Above & right:- Built in 1904, the signal box at Cave Crossing was originally fitted with a 16-lever frame, but by 2018 this had several gaps in it and just seven operational levers as the interior view shows. Both M. Rhodes

GILBERDYKE

Left & above:- Resident signalman in Gilberdyke box, and well known model maker, James Wells, offers a train to Saltmarshe on the Goole line. The signal box here was originally called Staddlethorpe West but shortly after opening in 1903 was renamed Gilberdyke. It had a 55-lever frame. Class 66 No. 66057 is seen passing the junction on 17 April 2015 with an empty biomass train from Milford West sidings to Hull Docks, where it will be loaded with biomass for Drax Power Station. Both M. Rhodes

HALIFAX

Above:- Formerly known as Halifax East, the signal box at Halifax opened in 1884. The mechanical frame was replaced by an IFS panel in 1970. M. Rhodes

HEBDEN BRIDGE

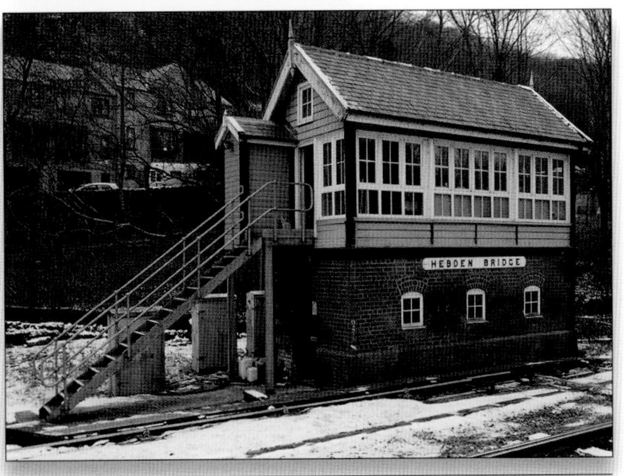

Above:- In 2007 Hebden Bridge signal box was restored to as close to original condition as possible and featured on a 2012 list of recommendations from Historic England for Grade 2 listing. Opened in 1891 it contained a 38-lever frame. M. Rhodes

HALTON JUNCTION

Right:- The LNWR SB at Halton Junction dates from when the branch line from Frodsham Junction opened in 1897; it had a 25-lever frame. The essential charm of the original structure was affected by the bricked-up locking room windows and the addition of a relay room in 1960. The latter was required for the second stage of the resignalling between Crewe and Liverpool when running signals were replaced by colour lights and the method of working on the main line converted to TCB. This view, taken on 30 July 1990, shows Class 37 No. 37015 returning light engine from Ellesmere Port to Garston. D. Allen

HOLYWELL JUNCTION

Right:- Two Virgin Voyager diesel multiple units speed past Holywell Junction in May 2012. The signal box here opened in 1902 and was equipped with a 54-lever mechanical frame. It was relatively sympathetically refurbished with double glazed windows in 2004. M. Rhodes

LIVERPOOL LIME STREET

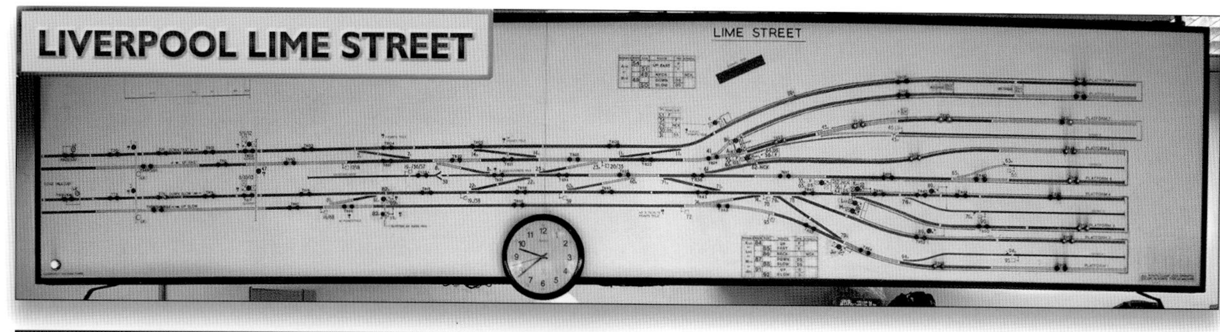

Top, above and right:- In 2018, the UK's largest surviving electro-mechanical miniature lever frame was at Liverpool Lime Street, where a 95-lever frame controlled the terminus at Lime Street. On the day of my visit in 2014, signalman John Piercy was on duty refreshing his knowledge of the box from resident signalman Tony Prince. With a career starting in 1980 at Huyton and moving via Allerton and Sandhills to Lime Street by 1991, where he spent eight years, he was able to recount much about signalling on Merseyside. Having become a MOM in 1991 and then returned to signalling in 1999 covering Huyton, Fiddlers Ferry and then Rainhill, John was back on his old patch at Lime Street. The box was opened in 1948, built to a similar "wartime" design as the box at Hull Paragon, albeit on the LMS. All M. Rhodes

MELTON LANE

Left & above:- The signal box at Melton Lane opened in 1921 with a 34-lever frame. This was later reduced to 26 levers and in 1980 a small IFS panel was installed to control the Ferriby area. Tree clearance which took place during 2015 in preparation for resignalling and electrification allowed this view of Class 47 No. 47812 with a Doncaster Decoy Yard to Hull Docks freight; it has been many years since the signal box at Melton Lane had been visible from Brickyard Lane. Both M. Rhodes

MILL LANE JUNCTION

Right:- Mill Lane Junction box opened in 1884 and became much more significant in 1973 following the demolition of the old Bradford Exchange station and construction of the much smaller station in use today. At this time the mechanical frame was removed and an IFS panel installed controlling not just the junction area, but the whole station as well. M. Rhodes

MILNER ROYD JUNCTION

Left:- Milner Royd Junction signal box lies on the former L&Y main line to the east of Sowerby Bridge and controls the Junction with the line towards Halifax. In 2018 it was the oldest operational L&Y signal box, dating from 1874. Of the 20 levers, six were spare and four missing. There were no longer any semaphores. A lone survivor, the "up" distant, lingered on until 2009 when nearby Greenland SB was closed, and the AB working replaced by TCB. During the 1980s, BR seriously considered singling the section between Milner Royd Junction and Halifax but fortunately this was met with much local opposition. Indeed in 1997, because of delays between Milner Royd Junction and Hebden Bridge station where it wasn't possible to run trains at less than eight-minute intervals, Railtrack installed colour light signals on both tracks to the east of Mytholmroyd. D. Allen

PRESTATYN

Left & above:- Class 175 No. 175114 leaves Prestatyn station with a Manchester to Llandudno service. By way of contrast on another rainy day, but 50 years earlier, a DMU pauses at Prestatyn with a Chester-bound service. The infrastructure that has disappeared is shocking; the four-track main line, the semaphore signals and the water troughs seen towards the horizon, to name but three items. The signal box here was built in 1897 and had a 30-lever frame but this was enlarged to 45 levers in 1931. M. Rhodes & M. Rhodes Collection

RHYL

Left & below:- Whilst the signal box at Rhyl still has LMS name boards stating "Rhyl No. 1", the box has been called simply Rhyl since the closure of Rhyl No. 2 in 1990. The box opened in 1900 and on the day of my visit, signalman Mark Pendlebury can be seen hard at work in front of the 90-lever mechanical frame. Sadly, this splendid structure closed in 2018. Both M. Rhodes

RUNCORN

Above & right:- Built in 1940, just as the Battle of Britain was under way, Runcorn signal box has a robust concrete roof to protect against bombing. The box contained a 45-lever frame, which is seen in 2016 with relief signalman John Illingworth reviewing some files between trains. Both M. Rhodes

SALTMARSHE

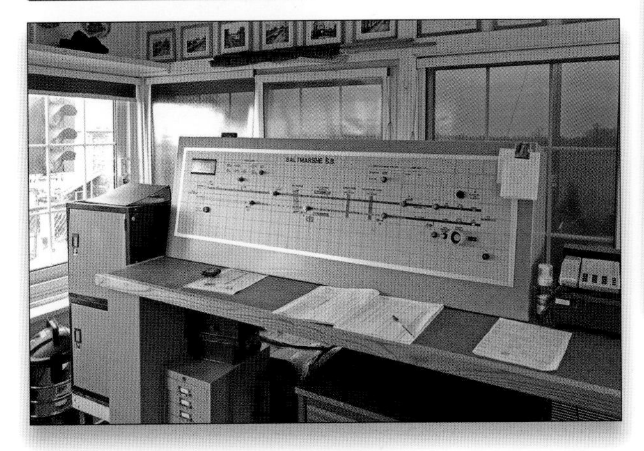

Left & above:- Built in 1905, Saltmarshe signal box had a 19-lever frame until 2006, when this was replaced by the small NX panel illustrated in our internal view. A Class 66 is seen passing the box in March 2012 with a coal train from Hull Docks to Drax Power Station. Both M. Rhodes

SPEKE JUNCTION

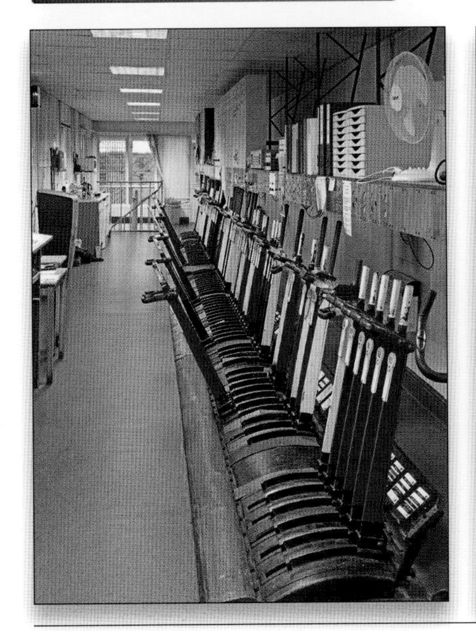

Above & above right:- The box at Speke Junction controlled the main line, the entrance to the former Speke Yard and further on to Garston Freightliner Terminal. The old yard, which had contained over 30 sidings, became the site of the compound to oversee the resignalling of the area in 2018. The box at Speke Junction was opened in 1907 and contained levers numbered to 93, within what was (because of adjustments) an 86-lever frame; levers 8–93 were still in situ. Our external view shows GB Railfreight Class 66 No. 66712 arriving to run round in the remaining loops at Speke Junction with a Dagenham to Garston Car Terminal train on 11 August 2016. Both M. Rhodes

TALACRE

Right:- Class 175 No. 175108 passes Talacre signal box with a Holyhead to Birmingham International service on 9 May 2012. The box here opened in 1903 and contained a 24-lever mechanical frame which came second hand from nearby Gronant signal box, situated between here and Prestatyn. M. Rhodes

WELTON

Above:- Welton crossing box was opened in 1904 and contained a 6-lever frame. Class 66 No. 66539 is seen passing the box on 16 September 2013 with 4D52, an empty coal train from York Holgate Yard to Hull Docks. The close proximity of signal boxes along this line lead to an unusual situation, in that the signal above the locomotive holds the Welton home signal, but also the distant signal for Melton Lane box to the east. A similar arrangement is found looking the other way with the Brough East distant (currently at danger in this view) below the Welton "up" home signal. M. Rhodes

Britain's Surviving Signal boxes

Introduction

In this, second section of the directory, it is aimed to illustrate all of the surviving heritage or mechanical signal boxes that were still operational at the beginning of 2019. As I am sure the reader will appreciate, modernisation of the network continues apace, and some of the boxes illustrated in this section may well have closed during the finalising of this book. Where possible this will be indicated in the captions to the relevant images.

By way of background to this section, it is helpful to understand the plans laid out by Network Rail for the "Control Period" from 2009 to 2014. Planning by Network Rail is made in five-year blocks which are called control periods and these fit in with the financial year running from 1st April to 31st March. As I write this we are approaching the end of the 2014 to 2019 control period, called CP6. Back at the start of 2010, Network Rail finalised a plan for CP5, between 2010 and 2014, to move control of the entire network to fourteen ROCs or Regional Operating Centres. As part of this plan a detailed list of signal box closures was drawn up with dates for the closure of every signal box in mainland Britain. Two key pillars of this programme were the construction and fitting-out of the ROCs placed in Edinburgh, Glasgow, York, Manchester (Ashburys), Derby, Birmingham (Saltley), Rugby, Cardiff, Didcot, Romford, Basingstoke, Three Bridges, Gillingham & Ashford and the introduction of a new low-cost resignalling system. It should be noted that the ROCs planned for Saltley and Ashford have subsequently been allocated for merger; Saltley into Rugby and Ashford probably to Gillingham.

Low-cost resignalling with easy-to-install equipment was the second key element of this nationwide plan. Low-cost resignalling systems were trialled by Signalling Solutions on the Norwich to Ely route and Invensys on the Crewe to Shrewsbury line. Significant delays occurred on both projects as well as cost over-runs. Most notable were the teething problems with the new "Obstacle Detection" level crossings, first trialled at Filey in 2010. Concerns of Network Rail managers about the safety of the proposed radar detection equipment (used very effectively in Germany and Austria) led to expensive and time-consuming "retro-engineering work". This added a low-level radar detector (LIDAR) to the standard obstacle detection used overseas. Concern had been expressed that the standard detection only reached to a level of 18 inches above the ground and to what might happen if a toddler was crawling across the crossing, or maybe a dog?! Unforeseen problems occurred very early with the equipment at Shippea Hill, where in the autumn of 2012, mud from the hundreds of sugar beet lorries using the crossing here, obscured the lens on the LIDAR. This caused it to register the crossing as occupied and therefore prevent the signaller in Cambridge power box from closing the gates and allowing a train to pass. Mobile operations managers had to be sent out to wipe the lens clean before the railway could start running again. Further work was then undertaken to provide a shield for the detection lens and eventually a new design of LIDAR with a retractable cover was introduced. This remains closed until just before the crossing is scanned and most of the detection problems seem to have been solved with this new crossing design. The new idea wasn't, however, in time to avoid total chaos in December 2012 when it snowed in East Anglia and all the LIDAR along the Norwich to Ely line registered the crossings as occupied! Mobile Operations Managers were again called upon to man the old mechanical boxes and open and close the crossings manually.

This saga, a very minor one when considering the entire Network Rail CP5 plans, illustrates just how much chaos unplanned and ill-thought-out alterations can cause. It also illustrates why Sir Peter Hendy was asked to produce a report for the Secretary of State about the "re-planning of Network Rail's Investment Programme". A mixture of situations similar to that of obstacle detection crossings, linked to shortages of sufficient engineering expertise and manpower had led to major over-runs on all Network Rail infrastructure projects. Signalling and the new ROCs are hardly even mentioned in Sir Peter's report. Instead he highlights that there may be delays to major CP6 projects like the electrification schemes to Cardiff, Bristol and Oxford or Manchester to Leeds and York. There is also concern that the electrification from Bedford to Corby may not be completed in CP6. As we now know, electrification of the South Wales mainline will not make it to either Bristol or Oxford during CP6, whilst the other two schemes are not even going to be anywhere near finished.

Even in the early years of CP6, many signalling projects have been quietly altered as cost over-runs and engineering delays set in. One example is the North Lincolnshire Resignalling Scheme which headlined the complete resignalling of North Lincolnshire. Some nine months before the scheme was due to be introduced (over Christmas and New Year of 2015/2016), it was quietly renamed the Scunthorpe to Cleethorpes resignalling scheme. As costs escalated and time began to run out, it was decided to leave the signal boxes on the Grimsby light railway, the Barton-on-Humber Branch and the Brigg line for another day. That is not to say that the relentless modernisation and removal of mechanical signalling isn't carrying on, but with a debt in 2017 of £51 billion and strict new borrowing controls imposed on Network Rail, things have slowed down when compared to the original grand plan published in 2010.

This background is by way of explanation because, in the absence of any new definitive closure schedule, I have chosen to include the original tables, published by Network Rail, recognising they have many dates that have proven to be incorrect and many more which will eventually be shown to be over optimistic. I have tried to draw attention to these in each section, but the tables should give some idea of the order in which each area is to be resignalled, even if the dates may slip as Network Rail's debt grows and priority has to be given to more headline schemes like main line electrification or major station redevelopments. One additional aid which I have attempted to include for each signal box is the postcode and an indication as to how easy it is to observe from a public place. It is hoped this will allow readers to find and observe many of the surviving mechanical signal boxes around the country.

Scotland

The centrally-planned strategy for Scottish resignalling is perhaps the most inaccurate of all the regional plans. Two key Scottish government infrastructure projects have turned the resignalling timetable on its head. The first of these concerns improvements to the Inverness to Aberdeen route, which envisage a train every hour between the two cities with a journey time of just two hours. The first phase of this project, due for completion in 2019, sees resignalling between Inverness and Elgin - necessitated by the relocation of the line through Forres which effectively maroons the old mechanical signal box there. Thus, whilst the box at Forres was allocated a renewal in 2024, it is expected to close more than five years earlier.

A second major Scottish government rail scheme is electrification to Dunblane. Preparatory work began on the route as early as 2012/13 with removal of the semaphore signals at Stirling (albeit with retention of the two mechanical signal boxes controlling colour light signals). The aim was to have electrification of the routes from Glasgow and Edinburgh to Stirling and Dunblane, as well as the Alloa branch, completed by December 2018. The implications for heritage signal boxes along the route were closure in 2018 for Larbert North, Stirling Middle, Stirling North and Dunblane, rather than the originally planned 2025. Interestingly other events in the region led to the closure of Longannet signal box in 2016 as the power station closed; this much earlier than the projected 2025.

Signal Boxes Scheduled to Close per Network Rail 2010 Masterplan

Glasgow ROC	
2011	Paisley SC, Carmuirs West Junction
2013	Cathcart
2015	Yoker IECC
2016	Motherwell SC
2023	Annan, Dumfries, Holywood, Hurlford, Kirkconnel, Mauchline, New Cumnock, Thornhill SC, Barrhead, Kilmarnock, Lugton
2025	Fort William
2040	Banavie
Edinburgh ROC	
2012	Polmont
2013	Millerhill
2017	Cowlairs, Greenhill Junction
2018	Carmuirs East Junction, Grangemouth Junction
2021	Auchterarder, Barnhill, Blackford, Dunkeld, Errol, Hilton Junction, Longforgan, Perth, Pitlochry, Stanley Junction, Aviemore, Blair Atholl, Dalwhinnie, Kingussie
2024	Aberdeen, Arbroath, Carmont, Carnoustie, Craigo, Inverkeilor, Laurencekirk, Montrose North, Newtonhill, Stonehaven, Dyce, Elgin, Forres, Huntly, Insch, Inverurie, Keith Junction, Kennethmont, Nairn
2025	Larbert North, Stirling Middle, Stirling North, Cupar, Leuchars, Tay Bridge South, Dunblane, Greenloaning, Dundee SC, Fouldubs Junction, Longannet
2035	Clachnaharry, Inverness SC

Aberdeen–Dundee

ARBROATH

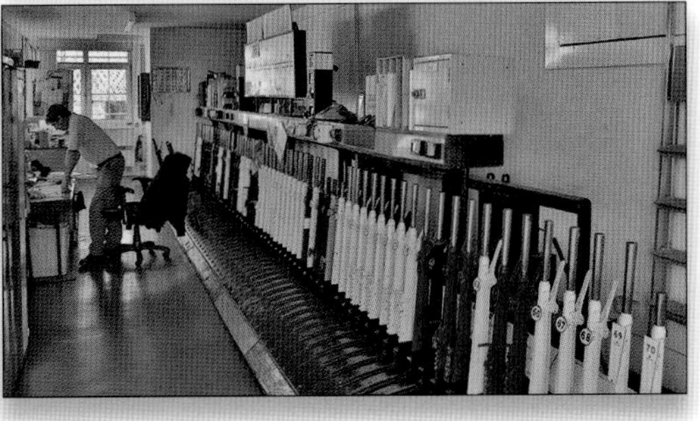

Above, above right and right:- The distinctive signal box at Arbroath North is seen in summer 1991 as Class 158 No. 158706 passes with an Aberdeen to Glasgow "express". The narrow base with a large overhang is a design often employed where there is insufficient space for a box base, as was the case when the box here was opened in 1911. At that time there were extensive goods sidings hemming the box in. Internally the box retains its 72-lever frame with just 70 levers still in situ as our view from 2014 illustrates. All M. Rhodes

Location: *DD11 1RT*

Visibility: *Whilst visible from the north end of the station platform at Arbroath, the box is best observed from the public footbridge linking Hume Street and Spink Street.*

CARMONT

Above & right:- The concrete pebble-dash on the walls of the signal box at Carmont somewhat spoils the appearance of the 1876 Caledonian Railway structure. During my visit in 2014, signalman Terry Bagnall was on duty, extolling the peace and tranquillity of the location after relocating from London. The box has an 18-lever frame and is located at a level crossing making observation of the box very easy. Both M. Rhodes

Location: *AB39 3YJ*

Visibility: *The signal box controls a level crossing not at Carmont, but at Newmill and easy to observe. The roads in the area are unnamed but the box is a five minute drive to the north of the A90, south of Stonehaven.*

CARNOUSTIE

Above & above right:- Carnoustie signal box stands to the west of the passenger station at Carnoustie and is seen as Class 170 No. 170422 passes with an Aberdeen to Glasgow service. The 1898-vintage cabin contains a 20-lever frame which is thought to have been salvaged from Slateford Junction signal box and reduced in size to fit in Carnoustie. Both M. Rhodes

Location: *DD7 6AR*

Visibility: *Excellent from station crossing and footbridge.*

CRAIGO

Above:- The signal box at Craigo is often "switched out" with trains signalled directly between Laurencekirk and Montrose. Built in 1877, it has a 21-lever frame. M. Rhodes

Location: *DD10 9LB*

Visibility: *The image shown is taken with permission from 26 Mill Place in Craigo; only a partial view of the box is possible from a public place.*

INVERKEILOR

Above right and right:- The external view of Inverkeilor signal box shows the new metal roof and the large extension to the rear of the original signal box, added at the start of the 21st century to accommodate an internal toilet and a kitchen area. An Aberdeen to Edinburgh train formed by Class 170 No. 170429 is seen passing on 7 August 2014. Internally there is a 22-lever frame. Both M. Rhodes

Location: *DD11 5RY*

Visibility: *The signal box is visible from the road overbridge to the north on Station Road, Inverkeilor.*

LAURENCEKIRK

Above & right:- The 1910 Caledonian Railway box at Laurencekirk has a 40-lever frame. Most levers are still in use in our 2014 view thanks to the survival of the goods yard here, albeit hanging by a thread. In the external view a CrossCountry Voyager passes with one of the UK's longest distance services from Aberdeen to Plymouth. *Both M. Rhodes*

Location: *AB30 1AJ*

Visibility: *The signal box is a significant distance north-east of the station and visibility is very poor from public places.*

MONTROSE NORTH

Above (4 images):- The signal box at Montrose North took over the work of both Montrose South box and Usan in 2010, necessitating a new box diagram which is illustrated here. The box itself dates from 1881 and is fitted with a much more modern 1953-built 51-lever frame. The semaphores to the south of Montrose were replaced by colour light signals in 2010, but the semaphores at the north of the station remain, although since the view of Class 66 No. 66622 with an empty Craiginches to Oxwellmains cement working taken back in 2006, the signal posts have been replaced with somewhat utilitarian, short steel examples as our second external view illustrates. *All M. Rhodes*

Location: *DD10 8JN*

Visibility: *The signal box is visible in the distance from the station footbridge at Montrose station. A closer view is possible from the A92, heading north from the station.*

NEWTONHILL

Above & above right:- The Caledonian Railway signal box at Newtonhill dates from 1876 and contains a 30-lever frame. Both M. Rhodes

Location: *AB39 3TZ*

Visibility: *A clear broadside view of the box is available from Old Mill Road in Newtonhill.*

STONEHAVEN

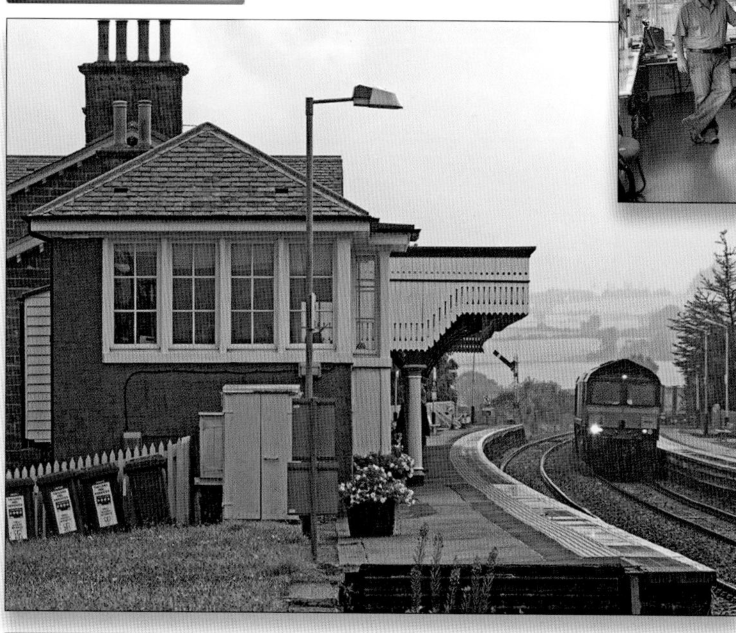

Left, above & below:- Signalman Phil Barlow surveys the 40-lever frame at Stonehaven signal box in 2014. Phil had 13 years on the railway in 2014 after a 13-year stint in the prison service and hoped the boxes along the Aberdeen to Dundee route would last him through until retirement. Stonehaven box was opened in 1901 and is seen in our external view in the pouring rain as Class 66 No. 66301 passes with a Grangemouth to Aberdeen intermodal service. All M. Rhodes

Location: *AB39 2NE*

Visibility: *The box is situated on the north end of the "up" platform at Stonehaven station and easily visible.*

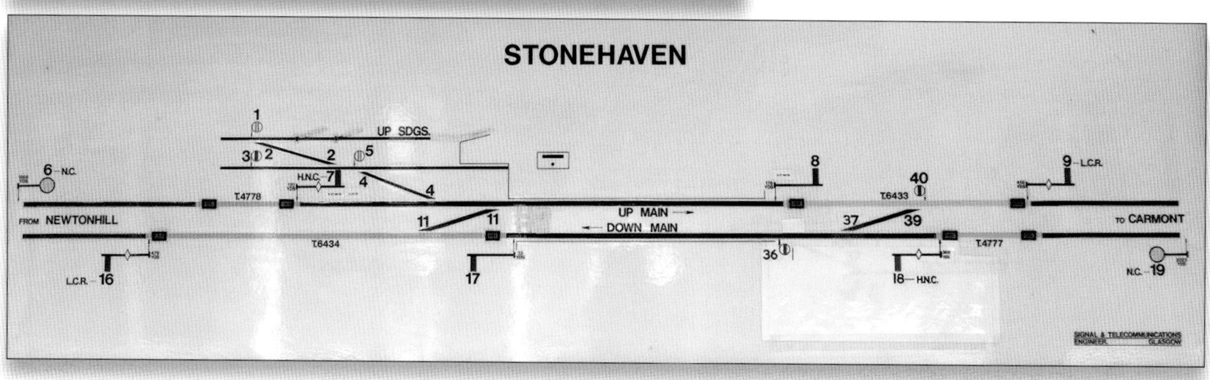

Aberdeen–Inverness

DYCE

Top & above:- Back in July 1988, Class 47 No. 47644 arrives at Dyce with an Aberdeen to Inverness express. At this time, the Great North of Scotland box, dating from 1880, had a 26-lever frame which had been reduced with the closure of the Fraserborough and Peterhead branches from its full extent of 46 levers. By the time of my visit in 2014, the frame had been replaced by a 2007-vintage NX panel, installed as part of the changes instituted to open the Raithes Farm freight depot. Both M. Rhodes

Location: *AB21 7BA*

Visibility: *Easily observed from Dyce station as it sits at the south end of the "up" platform.*

HUNTLY

Top & above:- There had been three signal boxes at Huntly; the current Huntly signal box was formerly Huntly South. The 1890-construction had simply been a gate box until it received its frame in 1970. At this stage, a 25-lever frame was installed controlling the station and the goods yard, which remained busy with timber traffic into the 1990s. Extensively refurbished, the box has lost much of it's original Great North of Scotland Railway architecture. Both M. Rhodes

Location: *AB54 8AX*

Visibility: *Really poor from public places – visible in the distance from Huntly station.*

INSCH

Above & above right:- Flower boxes aside, Insch is a pretty featureless signal box. Opened in 1886, it has a 20-lever frame and was extensively modernised and expanded to include an inside toilet in 2000. Both M. Rhodes

Location: *AB52 6XP*

Visibility: *Sits on the western end of the north side platform and is easily visible from both the station and the B9002 overbridge.*

INVERURIE

Above, above right & right:- An imposing structure, set back to the north of the main line, west of Inverurie station, the signal box at Inverurie was originally called Inverurie New Station. Opened in 1902, it had a 96-lever frame but this was reduced to 30 levers in 1970 as an aftermath of the Beeching closures in the area. To the right, Class 37 No. 37015 passes as track rationalisation is taking place in the late 1980s. Ironically, 30 years later the tracks are being reinstated. All M. Rhodes

Location: *AB51 0GZ*

Visibility: *The box is visible in the distance from the end of the platform at Inverurie station; one can get closer in the PC World car park but views are not good.*

KEITH JUNCTION

Top & above:- Originally called Keith South, back in 1884 when it was first built, the box was rebuilt in 1905 and named Keith Junction. It contains a 40-lever frame as illustrated, and on the day of my visit was manned by signalman Peter Dobson, an "emigree" from Northumberland. Both M. Rhodes

Location: *AB55 5GB*

Visibility: *The only place to clearly see the signal box is from the eastern end of the station platform at Keith, although it can also be seen in the distance from the B9116 overbridge to the east of the station.*

KENNETHMONT

Top & above:- The goods yard at Kennethmont used to handle both coal and Ardmore whiskey until the end of Speedlink services. Even her majesty the Queen has overnighted in the sidings here. Sadly, those days are long gone and the 1888 signal box at Kennethmont has been extensively refurbished. Opened in 1888, the original 20-lever frame remains largely unchanged inside the box. Both M. Rhodes

Location: *AB54 4NH*

Visibility: *The box can be seen in the distance from Station Road crossing to the east.*

Inverness–Stanley Junction

AVIEMORE

Right & below right:- The internal view of Aviemore signal box reflects the many changes that have taken place at this location. The NX panel dating back to 1979 (on the left of the view) controls the interlockings at Carrbridge, Kincraig, Moy, Slochd & Tomatin. The frame, which is almost all visible, has just 30 levers. When it opened back in 1892, it had 85 levers but soon reduced to 46 in 1898 when the new box at Aviemore South was enlarged. This state of affairs continued until 1971 when rationalisation as a result of Beeching led to just 30 levers being retained. The external view shows signalman Duncan McCrae, a veteran of 30 years, watching as Class 66 No. 66432 passes with an Inverness to Mossend intermodal service on 5 August 2014. The semaphore on the right of the image relates to the Aviemore to Boat of Garten line of the Strathspey Railway. Both M. Rhodes

Location: *PH22 1RH*

Visibility: *The box is visible from the northern end of the platform at Aviemore station but directly visible from the car park of the Strathspey Railway*

BLAIR ATHOLL

Above & left:- The signal box at Blair Atholl is a curious mix of Absolute Block and Scottish Tokenless Block. Our internal view shows signaller, Margaret, using the Scottish Tokenless Block machine to Pitlochry. The box was opened in 1890 and had an 18-lever frame, reduced to 17 in 1978 when an IFS panel was added for control of the "down" line to Dalwhinnie. Both M. Rhodes

Location: *PH18 5SJ*

Visibility: *Easily viewed from the Ford Road crossing, which the box controls.*

DALWHINNIE

Below, below left & below right:- Dalwhinnie is the UK's highest signal box at 351m above sea level and also the coldest inhabited place in the UK with a mean annual temperature of 6.6°C. The box here was built in 1909 and has a 20-lever frame installed in 1966. In 1978 an IFS panel was added to control the line to Aviemore. On the day of my visit I was fortunate to have signalman Geoff Drucquer on duty who is a keen photographer and he kindly provided the snowy shot to give an idea of winter at Dalwhinnie. M. Rhodes (2) & G. Drucquer

Location: *PH19 1AD*

Visibility: *The signal box can be well seen from the short Station Cottages Road, to the north of Dalwhinnie station.*

DUNKELD

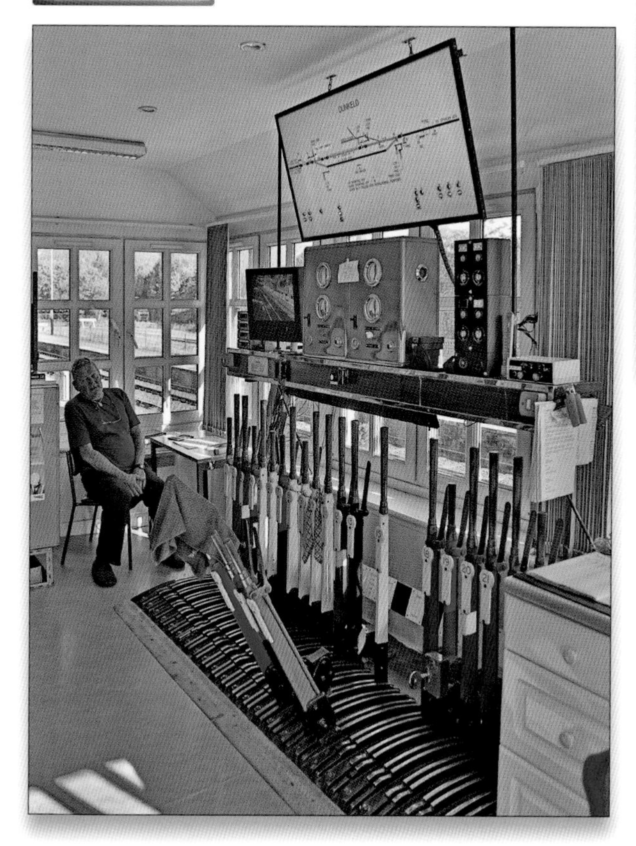

Left & above:- Signalman Fred Meiklen sits in the box at Dunkeld in August 2014. He joined the railway at the age of 49, responding to an advertisement in the newspaper for a signalman's job arising when the line through Dunkeld went over to 24 hour operation, 15 years earlier. The signal box at Dunkeld was built in 1919 and has a 23-lever frame, reduced from 35 levers. Gardening is an avid pastime for at least two of the signallers resident here! Both M. Rhodes

Location: *PH8 0DS*

Visibility: *Visible from the south end of Dunkeld station platform but also better views from the car park in the old station goods yard.*

KINGUSSIE

Above & right:- The signal box stands at the north east end of the "down" platform and was built in 1924. The external view shows an Edinburgh to Inverness express in the hands of Class 158 No. 158718. The frame was originally 17 levers and was increased to 18 in 1928, but as our internal view from 2014 shows, it is back down to 17 with a vacant slot in the frame at the far end. Both M. Rhodes

Location: *PH21 1EW*

Visibility: *Views of the box are excellent from the station, station footbridge and the crossing.*

PITLOCHRY

Left & above:- The signal box at Pitlochry was opened in 1911 with the same 24-lever frame that it uses today. Both M. Rhodes
Location: *PH16 5AN*
Visibility: *This is limited from the station, but a good view is afforded 400 yards west along Station Road.*

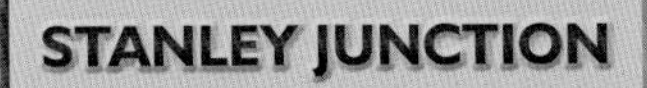

Left, above & below:- Signalman Eddie Low watches carefully as I photograph the frame at Stanley Junction. Once an important junction for the line to Aberdeen via Forfar, most of the 45-lever frame has been out of use since the route to Aberdeen closed to through traffic in the late 1960s. The signal box here was opened in 1965 at the time of modernisation in the Perth area with a new power signal box at Perth itself and the new hump marshalling yard north of Perth. The external view shows the new order; Class 170 No. 170417 passes with an Edinburgh to Inverness express. All M. Rhodes
Location: *PH1 4QS*
Visibility: *This is poor although the box can be seen from the car park at the end of Station Road in Stanley.*

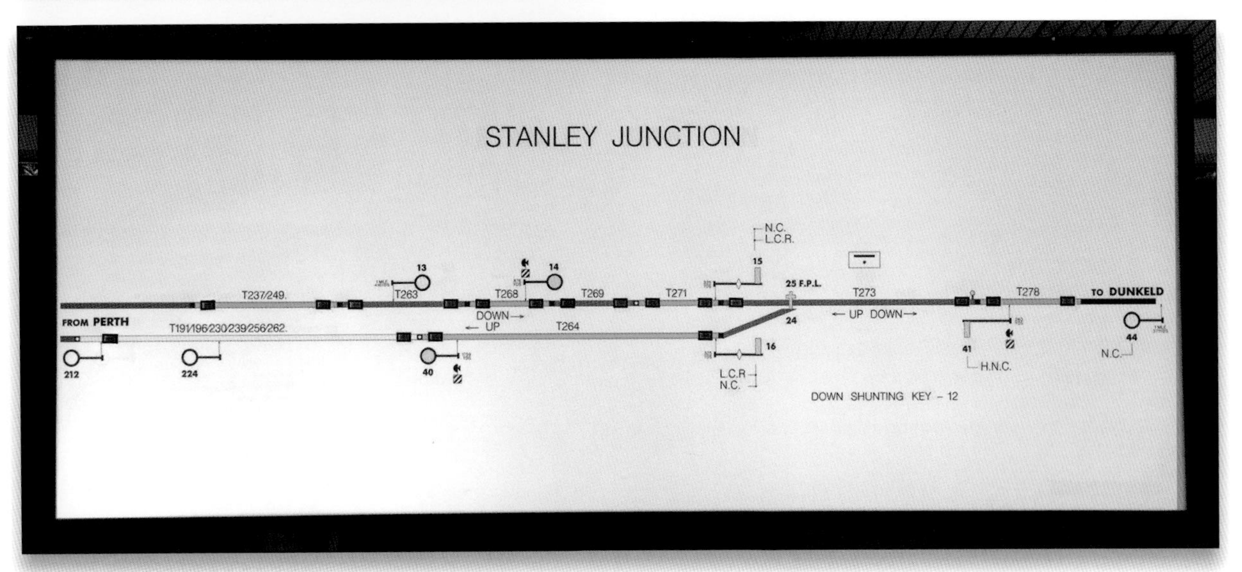

Dundee–Falkirk & Ladybank

AUCHTERADER

Right:- The 1895 Caledonian Railway signal box at Auchterader is relatively well preserved, albeit with the addition of metal box steps and a corrugated iron extenson for an inside toilet. The box contains 16 levers. M. Rhodes

Location: *PH3 1PS*

Visibility: *This is very poor and the only place one can glimpse the box is from the car park of Alan Dougan.*

BARNHILL

Left:- Hidden away in suburban Perth this box is almost impossible to find! It opened in 1874 and has a 20-lever frame. M. Rhodes

Location: *PH2 7HS*

Visibility: *Turn off the A85 into Island View, east of Perth and keep going beyond the end of the cul-de-sac, where one can glimpse the box.*

BLACKFORD

Right:- The signal box at Blackford is a relatively recent construction, built by the LMS in 1933 and with a 25-lever frame. M. Rhodes

Location: *PH4 1PZ*

Visibility: *The box can be well observed from the B8081 local road, which is the access into Blackford from the A9 and crosses the railway adjacent to the signal box.*

CUPAR

Left & above:- It is not clearly known when the signal box at Cupar opened although it seems likely it was around 1888 when the other boxes along the line were built. The box has a 32-lever frame and the box itself has a rearward extension to accommodate a toilet. *M. Rhodes & J. Illingworth*
Location: *KY15 5BZ*
Visibility: *The box is visible in the distance from the east end of Cupar station*

Right:- Located to the north of Dunblane station, the signal box at Dunblane was originally called Oban Junction, Dunblane. It was renamed simply Dunblane in 1955 and at this stage had a 55-lever frame installed. *M. Rhodes*
Location: *FK15 9AF*
Visibility: *A view of the box is possible from Caledonian Place in Dunblane.*

ERROL

Right & far right:- The 1877-constructed signal box at Errol has a 20-lever frame, installed in 1911. *Both M. Rhodes*
Location: *PH2 7SN*
Visibility: *The signal box lies adjacent to the level crossing on Station Road, which is just over a mile north of the village of Errol.*

FOULDUBS JUNCTION

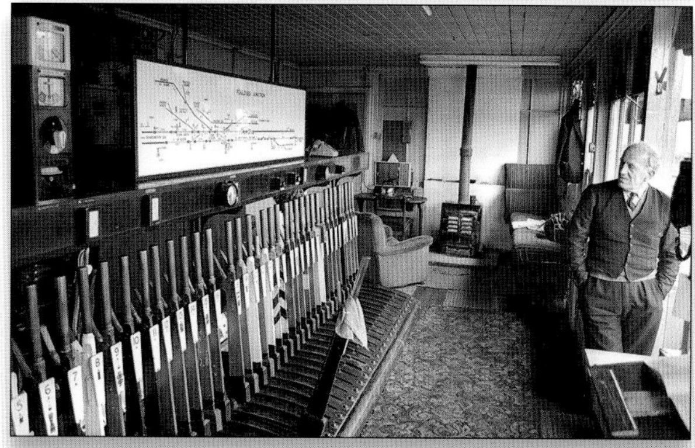

Top & above:- *The signal box at Fouldubs Junction dates back to 1908 when it opened with 77 levers. The frame was enlarged to 80 levers in 1951 and controlled the access to Grangemouth locomotive depot as well as the freight sidings here. The frame, as shown in our internal view, taken in 1986, was then reduced to 40 levers in 1972. The box now controls access along the branch to the Port of Grangemouth as well as the entrance to the intermodal depot on the site of the old locomotive shed.* *Both M. Rhodes*
Location: *FK3 8TR*
Visibility: *The box is visible from the A905 overbridge just to the west of Fouldubs Junction.*

GREENLOANING

Above:- *Class 66 No. 66092 approaches the disused loops at Greenloaning on 7 August 2014 with an Aberdeen Waterloo goods depot to Mossend freight service. The 1891-constructed box, with its 32 levers, is often switched out, although it may become more frequently manned in future if plans to improve services between Glasgow, Edinburgh and Perth come to fruition.* *M. Rhodes*
Location: *FK15 0LX*
Visibility: *The box is visible in the distance from the A822 overbridge at the old Greenloaning station, to the west of the signal box.*

HILTON JUNCTION

Left & above:- *Signalman Stephen Shaw overlooks the cramped cabin at Hilton Junction with its unusual layout of frame set at 90 degrees to the box diagram. Having started work at Carmuirs West, then moved to the portable building at Polmont when that box closed, he enjoyed the rural quiet at Hilton Junction. The box was built in 1873 and contains a 20-lever frame.* *Both M. Rhodes*
Location: *PH2 8PY*
Visibility: *The box is very hard to see from a public place – the access road through Hilton Farm is the only way to the box and is not a public right of way.*

LEUCHARS

Above & right:- When opened in 1920 the box at Leuchars possessed 54 levers, but the frame has subsequently been reduced to 38 levers. The box now stands well back from the main line as a result of track rationalisation, as our external view showing Class 170 No. 170431 on its way from Aberdeen to Edinburgh demonstrates. M. Rhodes & J. Illingworth

Location: *KY16 0AA*

Visibility: *The box is visible in the distance from the station footbridge.*

LONGFORGAN

Above & above right:- The signalman at Longforgan had been resident here for 17 years when this view of the frame was taken in 2017, having started on the railway at Barnhill signal box, just down the line in Perth. The 1929 signal box has a 20-lever frame. The highlight of my visit in 2017 was witnessing the devastation behind the box caused by newly introduced beavers who had gnawed down several large trees along Huntly Burn! Both M. Rhodes

Location: *DD2 5HT*

Visibility: *The box can be well seen from the level crossing on an un-named road, a mile south of Longforgan village.*

PERTH

Above:- Not strictly heritage nor mechanical, the panel box at Perth has recently been refurbished with new cladding and a new roof. Opened in 1962, it replaced eight mechanical signal boxes and a total of 455 levers. Class 67 No. 67021 is seen passing with the Euston to Inverness sleeper on 5 August 2014. M. Rhodes
Location: *PH2 0DU*
Visibility: *The box can be well seen looking south from St. Leonard's Bridge.*

STIRLING NORTH

Right- Stirling North was opened in 1900 and had a 102-lever frame which was enlarged to 108 levers in 1950. Subsequent Beeching closures and rationalisation saw the frame reduced to 48 levers in 1972 and this is how it remains today. M. Rhodes
Location: *FK8 - Burghmuir Road*
Visibility: *The box is best viewed from the overbridge north of Stirling station called Forth Place.*

STIRLING MIDDLE

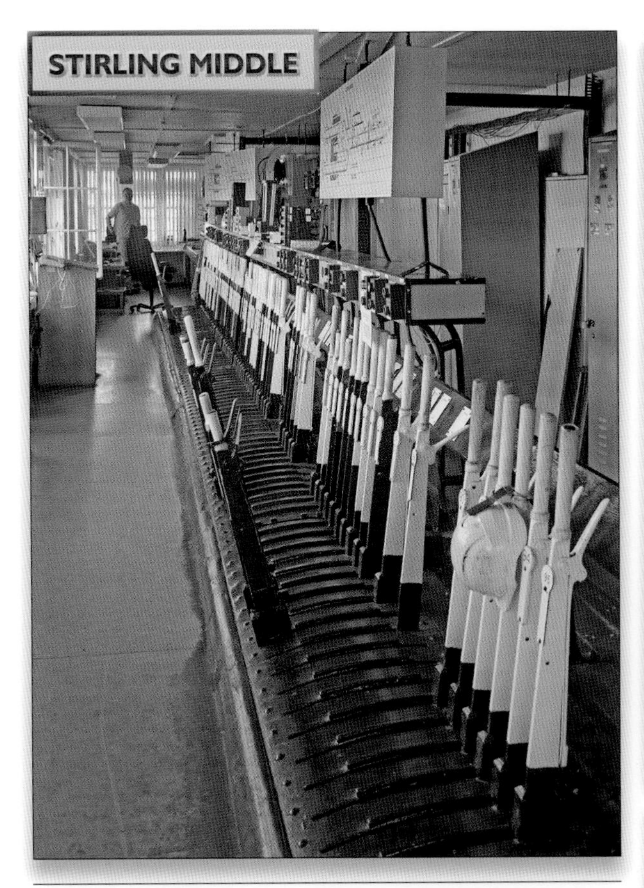

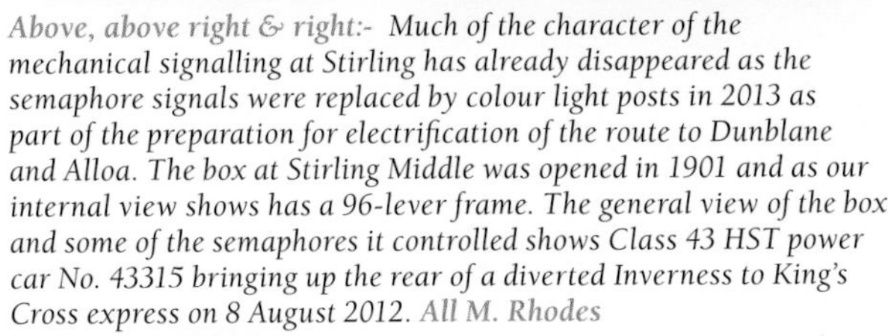

Above, above right & right:- Much of the character of the mechanical signalling at Stirling has already disappeared as the semaphore signals were replaced by colour light posts in 2013 as part of the preparation for electrification of the route to Dunblane and Alloa. The box at Stirling Middle was opened in 1901 and as our internal view shows has a 96-lever frame. The general view of the box and some of the semaphores it controlled shows Class 43 HST power car No. 43315 bringing up the rear of a diverted Inverness to King's Cross express on 8 August 2012. All M. Rhodes

Location: *FK8 1QZ*

Visibility: *The box is 400 yards south of the station and visible from the platform.*

TAY BRIDGE SOUTH

Above & above right:- The signal box at Tay Bridge South is unusual in that it has no timber upper deck like those present on most boxes. Because of the salt spray from the neighbouring Tay estuary, it is built completely in brick. The external view shows Class 170 No. 170461 with an Aberdeen to Edinburgh express, whilst the internal view was taken back in 1990, when visiting Dundee to learn laparoscopic surgery! The 27-lever frame has remained largely unchanged through the life of the box although the white levers are the result of closure of the Newport-on-Tay branch under Beeching. Both M. Rhodes

Location: *DD6 8LU*

Visibility: *The box can be well observed from Bridgehead Place in Wormit.*

West Highland Line

FORT WILLIAM JUNCTION

Right:- The West Highland Line was resignalled in 1987, with the whole route controlled from the Banavie signalling centre. The whole route, that is, except the station tracks at Fort William, which are controlled by Fort William Junction signal box. Built in 1894 and formerly called Mallaig Junction, it was fitted with an NX panel in 1975 for the station tracks, in addition to the reconditioned 30-lever mechanical frame dating from 1973. Here, in December 2016, Black Five No. 45407 passes the box on a very gloomy day, which only serves to highlight the signalman at work in the box. Bob Avery

Location: *PH33 6SU*

Visibility: *In the distance from The Earl of Inverness Road overbridge.*

Glasgow–Carlisle

ANNAN

Below:- Class 156 No. 156496 departs from Annan passing the signal box with a Carlisle to Glasgow service. The box opened in 1876 and contains a 20-lever frame. M. Rhodes

Location: *DG12 6AS*

Visibility: *The box can be seen from the west end of the station platforms.*

BARRHEAD

Above right:- Afflicted with a steel outside toilet, the box at Barrhead was opened in 1894 and contains a 25-lever frame which was installed as recently as 1973. M. Rhodes

Location: *G78 1AA*

Visibility: *The box is visible from the north end of Barrhead station platforms.*

DUMFRIES

Right:- The box at Dumfries station opened in 1957, replacing Dumfries No. 1 & No. 2 boxes. When opened it contained a 28-lever frame as well as an OCS and IFS panel. When colour light signals were introduced in 1997, the lever frame was decommissioned. Here in 2012, Class 156 No. 156449 passes with a Glasgow to Carlisle stopping service. The large brick structure behind the main box contained what were called "extended welfare facilities" which basically meant a toilet and a cooker! M. Rhodes

Location: *DG1 1LU*

Visibility: *The box is visible from the northern end of the station platforms at Dumfries.*

KIRKCONNEL

Above:- The box and signals at Kirkconnel are seen from the north in 2012. The cabin opened in 1911 and has a 42-lever frame. M. Rhodes
Location: *DG4 6LX*
Visibility: *The box can be viewed from either the station footbridge or the farm track overbridge to the west of the station.*

HOLYWOOD

Above:- The box at Holywood opened in 1920 and contains a 23-lever frame of the same date. It is one of the more difficult boxes to locate in the UK, situated on a country lane nearly a mile off the A76. M. Rhodes
Location: *DG2 0RL*
Visibility: *Easily viewed from the road crossing on the unnamed road that heads east from the A76 in Holywood.*

HURLFORD

Above:- The signal box at Hurlford has been almost constantly "switched out" for the last 11 years. Built in 1926 and originally called Hurlford South, it had a 67-lever frame. It was renamed simply Hurlford in 1934 at which stage the frame was reduced to 56 levers. Further rationalisation in 1976 reduced the frame to 20 levers. The box's main claim to fame is that it was the first post on the railway for Jimmy Knapp, the erstwhile head of the NUR and RMT. D. Allen
Location: *KA1 5AU*
Visibility: *The box can be seen from waste ground at the end of Station Drive in Hurlford.*

MAUCHLINE

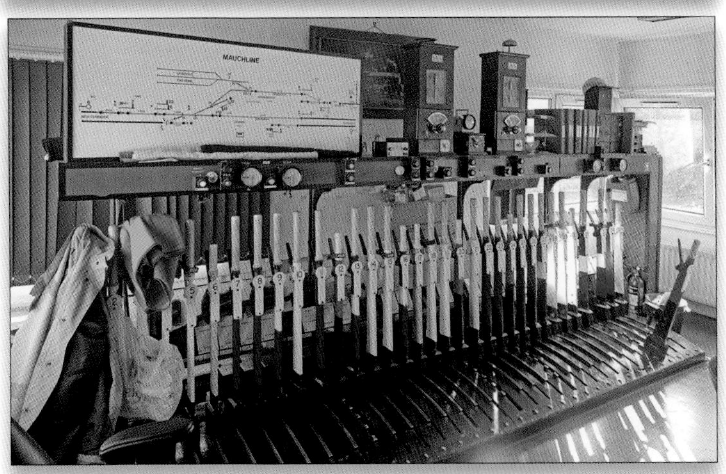

Right & above right:- Class 66 No. 66109 is seen passing Mauchline signal box with 6E99, a Greenburn coal disposal point to West Burton coal train. The train was banked by Class 66 No. 66161. Opened in 1877 and originally called Mauchline North, the box was renamed simply Mauchline in 1970. It contains a 35-lever frame, slightly smaller than its largest extent which was 41 levers. Both M. Rhodes
Location: *KA5 5EW*
Visibility: *Partial views of the box can be obtained from Station Road in Mauchline.*

LUGTON

Left:- *Class 26 No. 26040 is shunting the sidings at Lugton having arrived with the 6T19 trip freight from Mossend conveying feriliser, on 25 June 1991. I had ridden with the freight and was able to catch this shot of the box at Lugton. Originally called Lugton Junction, the box opened in 1929 and had a 55-lever frame which was reduced to 35 levers in 1973.* *M. Rhodes*
Location: *KA3 4DX*
Visibility: *The box can be seen in the distance from the crossing to the south-west, but close views are difficult.*

THORNHILL

Right:- *The concrete "bomb resistant" design at Thornhill is evident in this view of the 1943-vintage box taken in 2012. Class 156 No. 156449 passes with a Carlisle to Glasgow train. The box has a 30-lever frame.* *M. Rhodes*
Location: *DG3 5DX*
Visibility: *The box is difficult to observe from a public place.*

NEW CUMNOCK

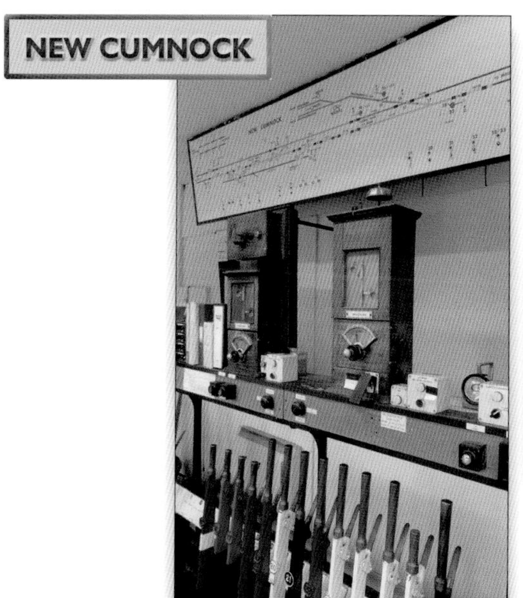

Left & above:- *The largely wooden structure at New Cumnock opened in 1909 and has a 40-lever frame. With expansion in the Scottish coal industry in the early part of this century, an OCS panel was added to control Greenburn Junction and the access to the opencast coal loading site there.* *B. Avery & M. Rhodes*
Location: *KA18 4DF*
Visibility: *The signal box is on New Cumnock station and well visible.*

Stranraer Line

BARRHILL

Far left & left:- *The tiny cabin at Barrhill was installed on the platform in 1935, having been reclaimed from Portpatrick. It originally contained 18 levers, but as the internal view from 2017 shows, these have been reduced to 17. The block token instruments for the single line sections either side of the station are in the station office rather than the signal box, which is so small there is quite literally no room to swing a cat!* *Both M. Rhodes*
Location: *KA26 0QF*
Visibility: *Excellent from the station platform.*

DUNRAGIT

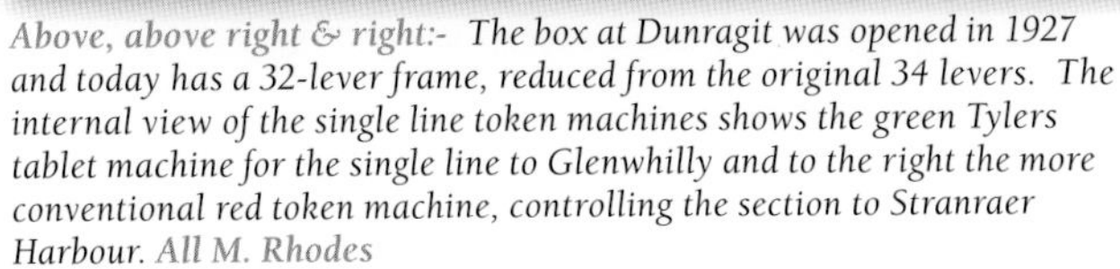

Above, above right & right:- The box at Dunragit was opened in 1927 and today has a 32-lever frame, reduced from the original 34 levers. The internal view of the single line token machines shows the green Tylers tablet machine for the single line to Glenwhilly and to the right the more conventional red token machine, controlling the section to Stranraer Harbour. All M. Rhodes

Location: *DG9 8PW*

Visibility: *The box can be well observed from the road crossing in Dunragit.*

GIRVAN

Above & right:- The signalman at Girvan looks askance at the photographer as he takes a "line block" in early 2017. The box here opened in 1893 and contains a 30-lever frame. There is also an adjacent ground frame that controls access to the former goods yard. The box has had several name changes, starting out as Girvan Station in 1893, changing to Girvan No. 3 in 1906, then Girvan No. 2 in 1935 and finally simply Girvan in 1973. Both M. Rhodes

Location: *KA29 9EN*

Visibility: *The box is at the south end of the station platform at Girvan.*

GLENWHILLY

Above (3 images):- *Glenwhilly is perhaps one of the most isolated signal boxes in the UK. Signalman John Harvey is seen taking the tablet for the single line to Dunragit from the driver of Class 156 No. 156495 and exchanging it for the tablet allowing access to the section to Barrhill. The box opened in 1905 and has a 20-lever frame. It is unusual in that the coal stove has been retained in spite of refurbishment because "electricity is not 100% reliable out here". John Harvey recalls his boss was once stranded in the box for three days following heavy snowfall.*
All M. Rhodes

Location: *DG8 0LX*
Visibility: *The box is easily visible from the old station yard at Glenwhilly.*

KILKERRAN

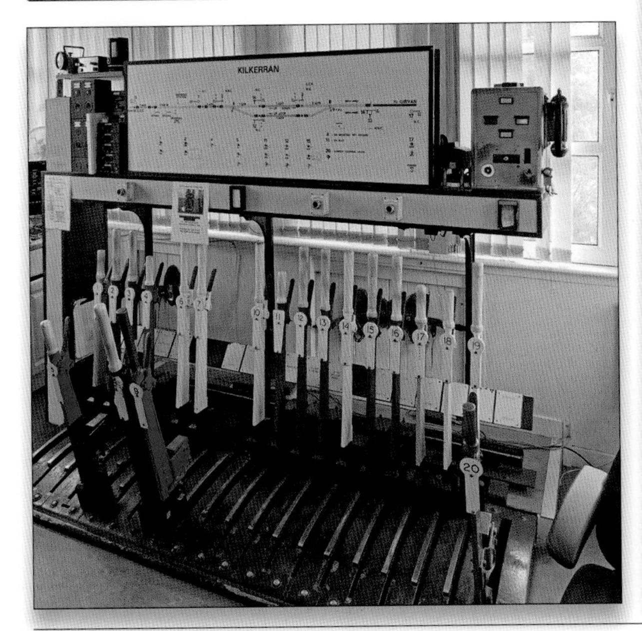

Above & above right:- The box in Kilkerran opened in 1895 and had a 21-lever frame which was reduced to 20 levers in 1973. Both M. Rhodes
Location: *KA19 7SE*
Visibility: *The box can be well seen from the farm crossing, which it controls on a lane off the B741.*

STRANRAER

Above:- Opened in 1897, the signal box at Stranraer Harbour boasts a 56-lever frame which is sadly mostly out of use as the track layout at Stranraer Harbour has been greatly simplified. The box is largely switched out and has been since 2011. Questions about the integrity of the pier at Stranraer Harbour and the move of the Irish Ferry north to Cairnryan raise serious questions about the future of both station and signal box here. M. Rhodes
Location: *DG9 8EL*
Visibility: *The box can be well seen from the station platform.*

North West England

The Regional Operating Centre to control most of the area covered in this section is at Ashburys in Manchester. Opened in July 2014, the ROC will eventually control the network from Carlisle to Crewe and then from the Welsh border as far east as Todmorden. The first piece of track to be controlled from the new centre was between Huyton and Roby, near Liverpool and in 2015 several routes in north Manchester were "migrated" to the ROC. Once fully operational it will have a staff of 400 including controllers from Network Rail as well as from the TransPennine and Northern passenger franchises.

Looking at the original Network Rail table for signal box closures it is evident that there has been some slippage in the North West. The big change for 2017 was the resignalling of the Preston to Blackpool line in preparation for its electrification. This led to the closure of signal boxes at Blackpool North, Carleton Crossing, Poulton, Kirkham and Salwick. This had been scheduled for 2015, as indeed had been the closure of Liverpool Lime Street. The 2016 plans for the Allerton and Speke Junction area were also deferred - until 2018, two years later than planned, whilst changes further ahead are hard to predict.

One bright spot in the North West is the possibility that mechanical signalling will survive around Peak Forest for another decade, making one of the most popular spots to watch freight trains safe from modernisation for the time being.

Signal Boxes Scheduled to Close per Network Rail 2010 Masterplan

Manchester ROC	
2013	Atherton Goods Yard, Blackrod Junction, Crow Nest Junction, Walkden
	to Preston PSB - Bare Lane, Hest Bank, Huncoat, Brierfield LCF
	to Chester PSB - Hooton
	to Castleton - Smithy Bridge
2014	to Manchester East - Romiley
	to Burscough Bridge - Four Lane Ends XGB
2015	Liverpool Lime Street, Blackpool North No. 2, Carleton Crossing, Kirkham North Junction, Poulton, Salwick
2016	Warrington PSB, Allerton Junction, Speke Junction, Ditton, Halton Junction, Runcorn
2017	Bamber Bridge LCF, Daisyfield Station, Horrocksford Junction, Preston PSB, Towneley XGB, Midge Hall, Rufford (NW), Baguley Fold, Denton Junction, Diggle Junction, Dinting Station
2018	Burnside Higher XGB, Carlisle PSB, Parbold, Rainford Junction, Wigan Wallgate, Chapel Lane LC
2019	Ashton Moss North Junction, Manchester North PSB, Astley, Bromley Cross LC, Eccles, Manchester Piccadilly, Burscough Bridge, Chester PSB, Deansgate Junction, Greenbank, Mobberley, Northenden Junction, Plumley West, Edge Hill, Huyton, St Helens Station, Castleton East Junction, Vitriol Works
2021	Arnside, Askam, Barrow in Furness, Bootle, Bransty, Carnforth Station, Dalton Junction, Drigg, Foxfield, Grange over Sands, Kirksanton XGB, Limestone Hall XGB, Maryport, Millom, Park South Junction, Sellafield, Silecroft, Skelly Crag XGB, St Bees, Ulverston, Wigton, Workington Main No. 2, Workington Main No. 3, Salcoats LC
2022	Arpley Junction, Fidlers Ferry, Monks Siding, Chinley, Earles Sidings, Edale, Grindleford, New Mills Central, New Mills South Junction
2024	Ellesmere Port, Frodsham Junction, Helsby Junction, Mickle Trafford, Norton (NW)
2025	Dee Marsh Junction, Buxton, Chapel-en-le-Frith, Furness Vale, Great Rocks Junction, Peak Forest South, Hazel Grove, Norbury Hollow
2027	Appleby North, Blea Moor, Culgaith, Garsdale, Hellifield, Howe & Co's siding, Kirkby Stephen, Kirkby Thore, Low House Crossing, Settle Junction
2028	Edgeley Junction No. 1, Edgeley Junction No. 2, Heaton Norris Junction, Stockport No. 1, Stockport No. 2, Manchester South SC
2033	Merseyrail IECC, Glazebrook East Junction, Hunts Cross, Warrington Central

Cumbrian Coast

ARNSIDE

Above:- The signalman is silhouetted in the box window at Arnside on 29 May 2012 as Class 185 No. 185137 passes with a Barrow to Windermere service - a most unusual service that runs into Lancaster and reverses. The Furness Railway signal box at Arnside dates back to 1897 and contains a 35-lever frame. M. Rhodes
Location: *LA5 0HF*
Visibility: *The box can be seen from both the end of the station platform and also Station Road in Arnside.*

BARROW

ASKAM

Top & above:- The signalman at Askam prepares to lower the barriers as the morning nuclear flask train from Crewe approaches. The box was opened in 1890 and of Furness Railway design. It contains a 22-lever frame, albeit with several levers removed and their slots covered with draught excluding carpet, as our internal image shows. Class 57s Nos. 57009 and 57007 double-head 6C53, a Crewe to Sellafield flask train past the box in May 2012. Both M. Rhodes
Location: *LA16 7AL*
Visibility: *As our image shows, the signal box is on the southern end of the platform at Askam station.*

Above left & left:- In October 2015, Class 37 No. 37423 departs from Barrow with a train to Carlisle, whilst two further local services fill the other two platforms at Barrow station. The signal box, as can be seen from the external view, lies to the north of the station and indeed was formerly called Barrow North. Opened in 1907, the box contains a 67-lever frame which was reduced to 55 levers as the internal image taken in 2017 shows. Both M. Rhodes
Location: *LA14 5QZ*
Visibility: *The box is visible from a short distance away on the north end of the island platform at Barrow station.*

BOOTLE

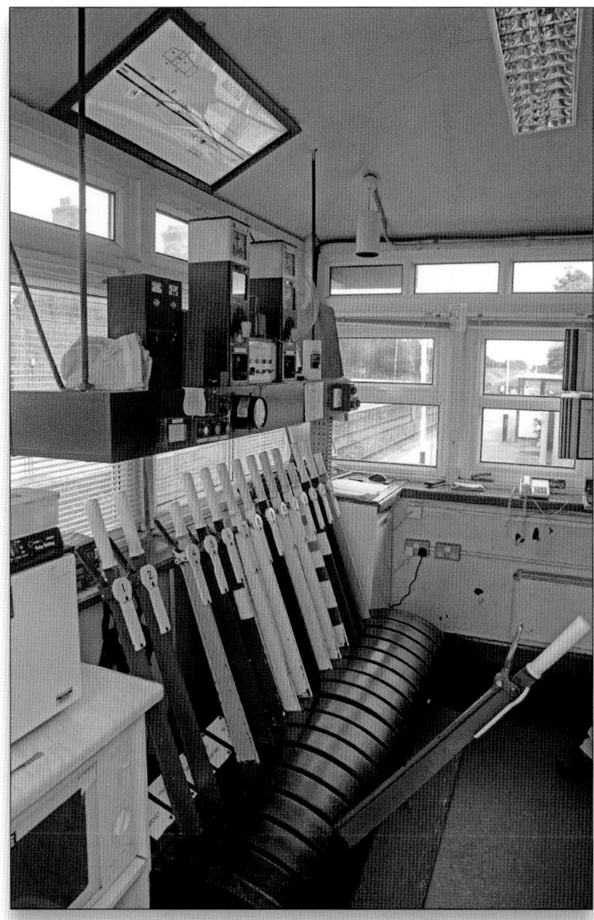

Top & above:- A Carlisle to Preston service passes over the crossing at Bootle on 6 August 2012 in the hands of Class 156 No. 156444. The box here, which lies at the north end of the "down" platform, opened in 1871 in preparation for the line doubling of 1873, which makes it one of the oldest surviving signal boxes in the country. The 15-lever frame was installed as late as 1977 and came from the signal box at Netherton. Both M. Rhodes

Location: *LA19 5UY*

Visibility: *Well seen from the crossing and the station.*

BRANSTY

Top, above & below:- The Ugg boots of the lady signaller in charge at Bransty in March 2017 protrude beneath the booking desk at Bransty signal box. The cabin opened in 1899 and was formerly known as Bransty No. 2. It has a 60-lever frame but the majority of the levers are white and out of use since the colliery at Whitehaven closed in the late 1980s. All M. Rhodes

Location: *CA28 6AX*

Visibility: *Partial views are possible from the end of the platform at Whitehaven station.*

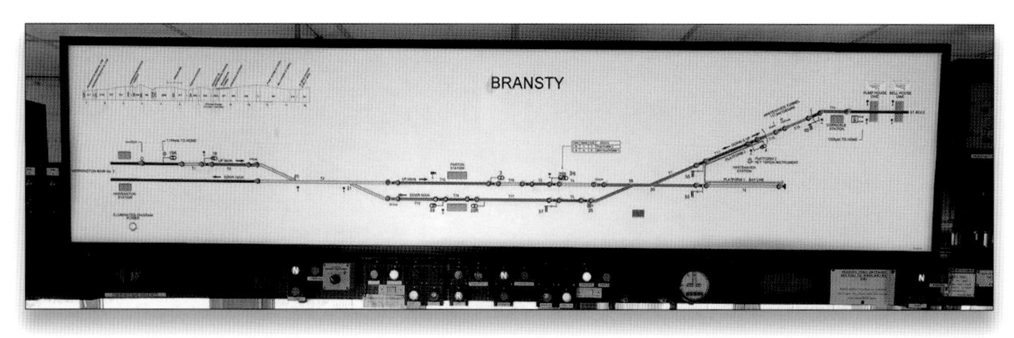

CARNFORTH STATION JUNCTION

Top & above:- Renowned railway photographer Steve McGahon stands to attention in his place of work for the last 34 years. Steve started work as a trainee in Appleby box in 1978 and transferred to Culgaith as a resident, but decided to move to Carnforth in 1983 when the closure notices for the Settle and Carlisle line were posted! He has since enjoyed a long and illustrious career as the resident signalman at Carnforth. The box here is formally known as Carnforth Station Junction and opened in 1903. The frame originally contained 64 levers but has been reduced to 59 slots. Just 56 levers remain as our internal image shows. Both M. Rhodes

Location: *LA5 9TR*

Visibility: *The box can be seen in the distance from the end of the Barrow line platforms at Carnforth station.*

DALTON JUNCTION

Right top, middle and above right:- The close-up external view of Dalton Junction (taken in 2017) is interesting as the metal grilles over the windows, visible in the 2015 view of Class 37s Nos. 37059 & 37609 on a Sellafield to Heysham flask train, have been removed. The box opened in 1902 and has a 20-lever frame. The box is switched out on Saturdays and Sundays which means that any nuclear flask traffic must travel round via Barrow station rather than using the short cut to Park South Junction. All M. Rhodes

Location: *LA15 8LH*

Visibility: *The box is best seen from the Abbey Road overbridge in Dalton, Cumbria. Close up views are difficult.*

DRIGG

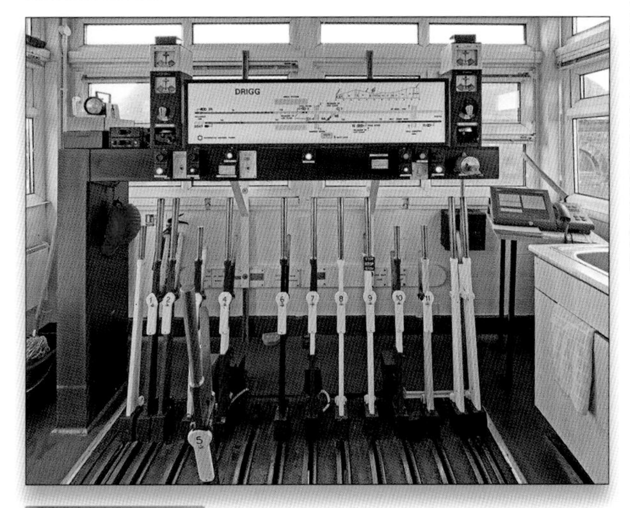

Left and above- *The signal box at Drigg is one of the oldest in the country, built by the Furness Railway in 1871. The frame currently in use was installed in 1882 and has 14 levers. Passing the box in 1989 is Class 47 No. 47292 with 7A40, the daily Speedlink service from Workington to Willesden Yard. Prominent in its load is nuclear traffic from Sellafield to the south coast nuclear power stations and steel rails from British Steel at Workington.* *Both M.Rhodes*
Location: *CA19 1XH*
Visibility: *From the level crossing on Shore Road, which the box controls.*

FOXFIELD

Above & right- *As can be seen from our external view, the signal box at Foxfield is on the station platform and was originally incorporated into the station buildings. Since the closure of the Coniston branch these have all been demolished, leaving the signal box standing alone. Opened in 1879 the box has a 52-lever frame which never contained more than 51 levers and by 2012, when our internal view was taken, had just 10 operational levers.* *Both M. Rhodes*
Location: *LA20 6BX*
Visibility: *On the station platform.*

GRANGE-OVER-SANDS

Right- *Class 25 No. 25191 passes the box at Grange-over-Sands on 19 July 1984 with the 1821 Barrow to Liverpool Lime Street. The box is the most modern along the Cumbrian Coast line, opened in 1956 and contains 25 levers.* *M. Rhodes*
Location: *LA11 6PH*
Visibility: *The box is best seen from the beach-side promenade which runs along the coast and can be accessed off Lindale Road.*

KIRKSANTON CROSSING

Above:- The permanent way team are working on Kirksanton ground frame, which is situated south of Silecroft. M. Rhodes
Location: *LA18 5LL*
Visibility: *Visible from the crossing at this postcode.*

LIMESTONE HALL CROSSING

Above:- Situated between Kirksanton and Silecroft, this second ground frame is still in operation. M. Rhodes
Location: *LA18 5LN*
Visibility: *Visible from the crossing at this postcode.*

MARYPORT

Top & above:- Opened in 1933, Maryport currently has a 50-lever frame, reduced from 70 levers in the early 1970s. The box itself was constructed in 1933 but was extensively modernised and refurbished in the early part of the century. Both M. Rhodes
Location: *CA15 6NH*
Visibility: *The box is visible from the end of the station platform.*

MILLOM

Above:- Hard to believe that in the 1960s, there was a large ironworks at Millom. Class 156 No. 156451 passes the box at Millom which was built in 1891. It contains a 30-lever frame and had to be rebuilt in 1913 after a derailed train ran into it. M. Rhodes
Location: *LA18 4HX*
Visibility: *The box is best viewed from George's Road overbridge.*

PARK SOUTH

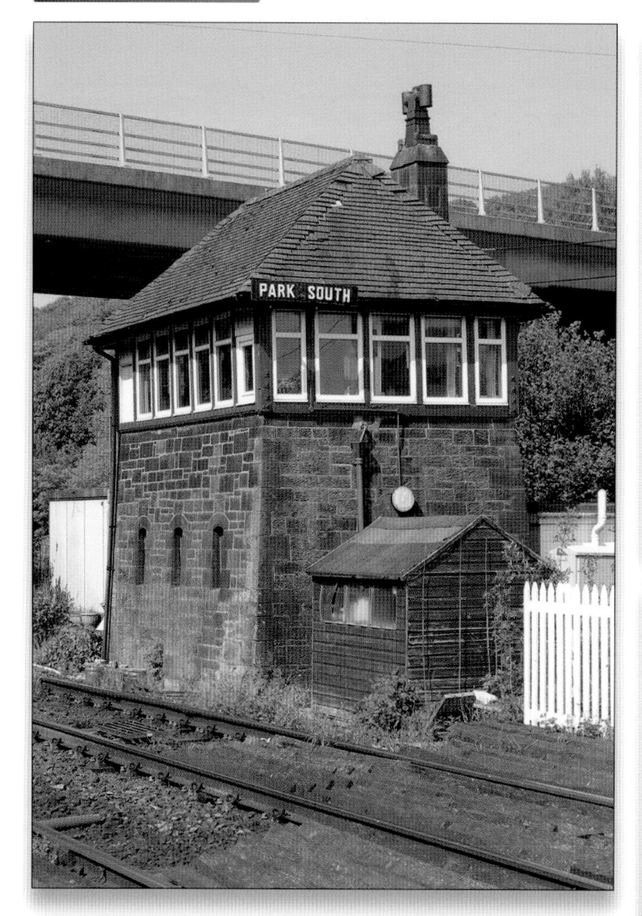

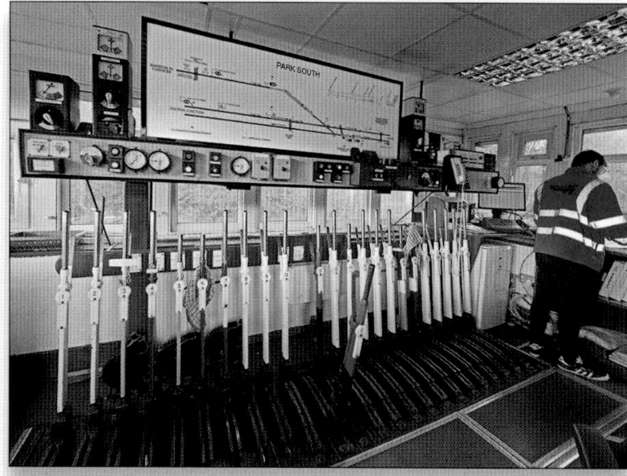

Top & above:- The signal box at Park South controls the junction between the Barrow avoiding line and the single track to the north end of Barrow station. Opened in 1883, it has a 24-lever frame. This was salvaged from Coniston in 1962 when the box there closed. Both M. Rhodes

Location: *LA14 4QH*

Visibility: *The box is visible to the north of the level crossing on St. Helen's, which the box controls.*

SELLAFIELD

Top & above:- A Carlisle to Barrow service arrives at Sellafield and the driver hands over to the signalman the single line token for the stretch of line from St. Bees. The box here opened in 1918 and has a 49-lever frame. Interestingly this was installed in 1918, well before the British Nuclear Fuels facility and associated sidings were built. The sizeable lever frame was a reflection of the fact that Sellafield was the junction for the branch to Beckermet, closed in the 1960s, but given the developments at Seascale most of the levers remain in use. Both M. Rhodes

Location: *CA20 1PF*

Visibility: *The signal box is on the north end of the "down" platform at Sellafield station.*

SILECROFT

Right:- The box at Silecroft was opened in 1923 and currently has a 15-lever frame controlling the crossing gates, crossover and signals. During my visit in 2012 the signal lady on duty got very upset at my taking this picture and threatened to call the police, hence no internal views of the box are included in this book! M. Rhodes

Location: *LA18 5LP*

Visibility: *As shown in our image, the box can be well seen from the station platform.*

ST. BEES

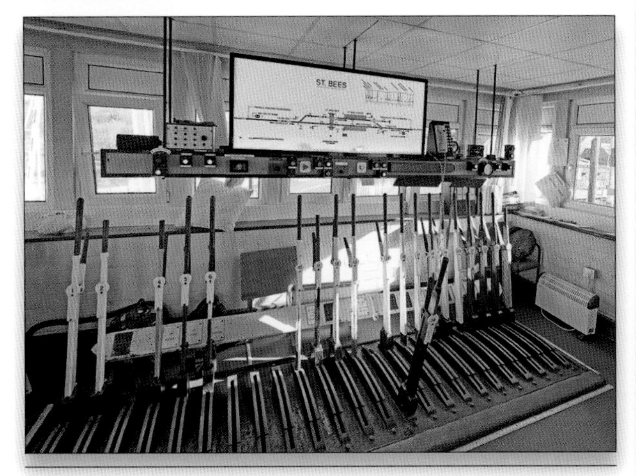

Above:- Nestled under the station footbridge at St. Bees, the signal box is on the "down" platform and controls a crossing and the only passing loop between Whitehaven and Sellafield. It was built in 1891 and has a 24-lever frame. M. Rhodes
Location: *CA27 0DG*
Visibility: *On the station at St. Bees.*

ULVERSTON

Above right & right- The signalman on duty on the day of my visit to Ulverston was Darren Goodsir who had worked for over a quarter of a century on the railway, starting as a signalman at Grange-over-Sands, moving to Arnside and Plumpton Junction, before settling in Ulverston 19 years ago when Plumpton Junction closed. The box at Ulverston was built in 1900 and retains a 22-lever frame which as our image shows had been reduced in the 1970s when the goods yard closed. The external view shows Class 37 No. 37409 passing the box on 2 March 2017, with 2C47, a Preston to Barrow passenger working. Both M. Rhodes
Location: *LA12 0DP*
Visibility: *The box is difficult to see clearly but can be seen in the distance from Ulverston station and also from the A590 overbridge to the west of Ulverston station.*

WIGTON

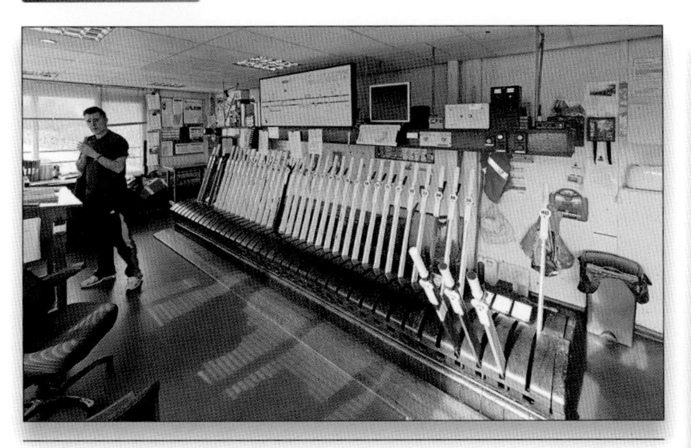

Above & right- The 1957-built BR (LMR) signal box at Wigton has a 40-lever frame. As our internal view shows, 80% of the frame is not used and the box simply acts as a block post between Carlisle and Maryport, the sidings and goods yard which it controlled having long since been ripped up. Both M. Rhodes
Location: *CA7 9BA*
Visibility: *The box can be seen in the distance from the station footbridge at Wigton and the rear of the box can be seen from the A596 bypass to the west of the station.*

WORKINGTON NO. 2

Top, above & right:- *By March 2017 when I visited Workington, the numerous sidings controlled by Workington No. 2 signal box were all rusty and clearly out of use. The 1889-constructed box retained levers up to Number 60, but the frame had two slots removed making it a 58-lever frame.*

Class 47 No.47333 passes Workington in 1981 with 6L64, a Maryport to Fiddlers Ferry Power Station MGR service. In this view, taken from Workington No. 2 signal box, the smaller Workington No.3 box can be seen just above the loaded coal wagons. Emphasising how much the railway infrastructure at Workington has been rationalised, there are six locomotives stabled in the station (08419, 25135, 40014, 40015, 47229 & 47429) as well as the coaching stock for the night mail train to London. All M. Rhodes

Location: *CA14 3YW*
Visibility: *The box can be seen in the distance from the south end of Workington station and also close up from the Morrisons car park on the Derwent Retail Park.*

WORKINGTON NO. 3

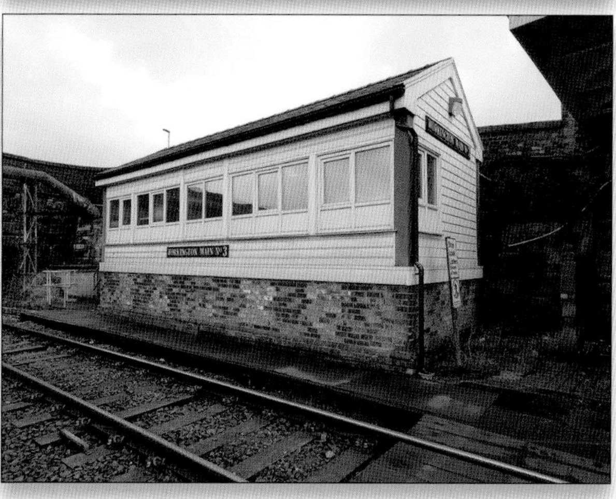

Top & above:- *As can be seen from the internal view, Workington No. 3 signal box has levers numbered 19-43 in use. The frame was originally 55 levers when the box was opened in 1886. Externally the box has been extensively modernised and even boasts a house number style sign on the main door welcoming the visitor to "No. 3".* Both M. Rhodes

Location: *CA14 2XE*
Visibility: *Sits at the north end of the "up" platform at Workington station.*

Settle & Carlisle

APPLEBY NORTH

Top & above:- Back in June 1981, Class 25 No. 25069 passes in front of Appleby signal box shunting the 9T35 trip freight from Carlisle Kingmoor Yard. It is detaching wagons for the Warcop branch, which still handled revenue-earning freight at this time. Built in 1951, the box contains a 25-lever frame. Both M. Rhodes

Location: *CA16 6TT*

Visibility: *The box is visible in the distance from the north end of the station.*

BLEA MOOR

Above (3 images):- Blea Moor signal box is undoubtedly the most isolated in the UK. Indeed, back in the late 1970s, the first freight of the day would deliver water to the box. In 2019, there is still a half-mile walk to the signal box which was built in 1941 and has 30 levers. The middle view shows Class 66 No. 66848 passing with 6J37, a Carlisle to Chirk log train. In the bottom view, Class 66 No 66750 runs round its stone train in the shadow of the signal box. All M. Rhodes

Location: *LA6 3AU*

Visibility: *Apart from seeing the box from a passing train, the only way to see the signal box is to hike from the car park at Ribblehead (postcode above), for one mile past Ribblehead viaduct and up the hill towards Dent.*

CULGAITH

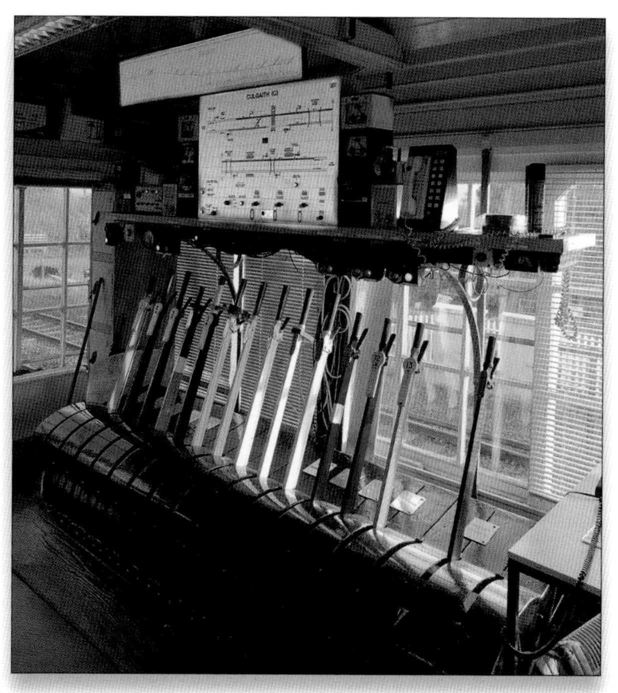

Above & right:- Culgaith box was sympathetically modernised in 2006 and retains its distinctive Midland Railway appearance. Opened in 1908, the box contains a 16-lever frame. Both M. Rhodes

Location: *CA10 1QQ*

Visibility: *Easy to observe from the level crossing on Station Road in Culgaith.*

GARSDALE

Above, far right & right:- The large porch added to Garsdale signal box in 2006 and made to look as close to original as possible, is looking very much in need of redecoration in this 2017 view. The box opened in 1910 and contains a 40-lever frame which in 2019 only contains 33 levers.

Class 40 No. 40031 obscures Garsdale signal box as it passes the "down" starter signal at Garsdale in 1980 with 8M81, the daily Llandeilo Junction to Carlisle Kingmoor mixed freight service. All M. Rhodes

Location: *LA10 5PP*

Visibility: *On the down platform at Garsdale station and easy to see into.*

HELLIFIELD SOUTH JUNCTION

Above & right:- *Signalman Dave Grogan explained that the box at Hellifield had been comprehensively refurbished in 2007, but a decade later the north side of the cabin certainly needs cleaning and repainting. The box was opened in 1911 and has 58 levers in the frame with a 64-lever frame beneath the floor.* Both M. Rhodes

Location: *BD23 4HL*

Visibility: *On the south end of the island platform at Hellifield station.*

HOWES SIDING

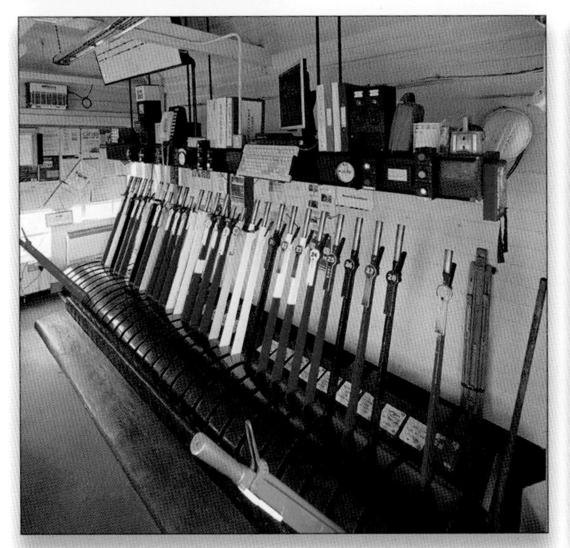

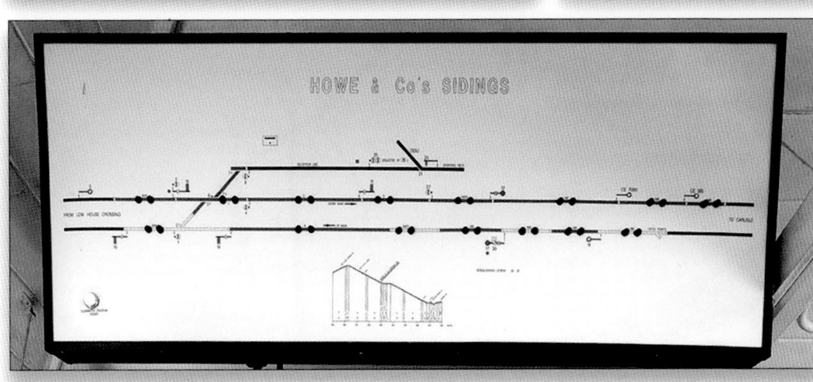

Above left, above & left:- *The box at Howe & Co's Siding has been restored to its original state with timber windows, albeit with double glazing. Opened in 1916 it has a 30-lever frame. Sadly, the sidings after which it is named are long since removed.* All M. Rhodes

Location: *CA4 0AY*

Visibility: *This is almost impossible from a public place. The box lies 400 yards north of the crossing on a minor road at Lonsdale Park.*

KIRKBY STEPHEN

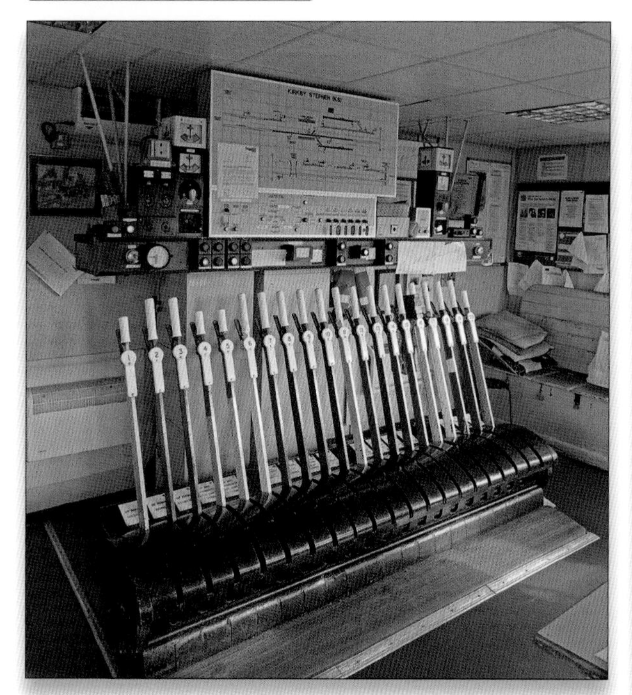

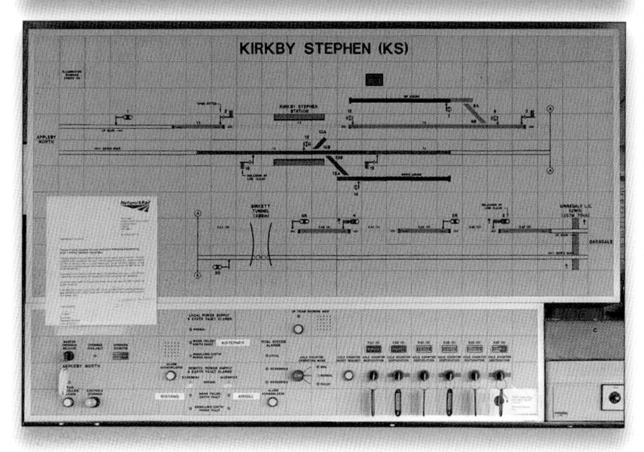

Above (3 images):- Class 66 No. 66708 passes Kirkby Stephen in 2006 with 4M32, a West Burton Power Station to Newbiggin gypsum service. The box at Kirkby Stephen opened in 1974 and as relief signalman (and well known photographer), Jay Hartley explained to me, the 20-lever frame came from Kendal in 1973 with the box super-structure coming from Shap Quarry in the same year. All M. Rhodes

Location: *CA17 4LF*

Visibility: *The box can be seen in the middle distance from the footbridge at Kirkby Stephen station.*

KIRKBY THORE

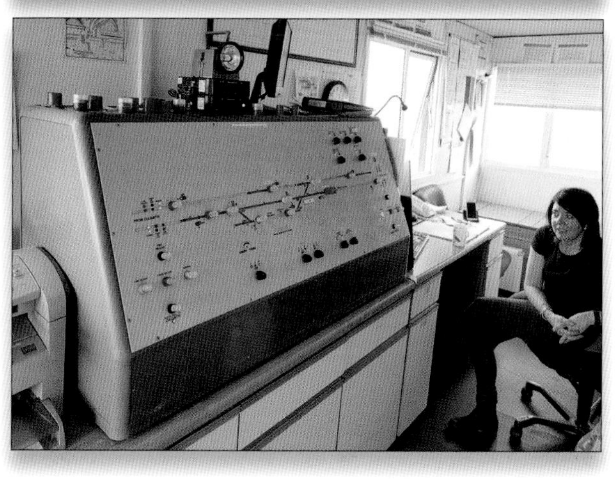

Top & above:- It is fair to say that the signal box at Kirkby Thore is neither heritage nor mechanical! It's basically a double-decker portable building. However in the interests of completely covering the Settle and Carlisle line it is included here. Opened in 1994 and containing a small IFS panel, the box controls the main line as well as the gypsum sidings at Kirkby Thore. Both M. Rhodes

Location: *CA10 1XU*

Visibility: *There is a footpath from the car park at Kirkby Thore (where access is strictly forbidden), which leads along the line and from which the box can be glimpsed.*

LOW HOUSE CROSSING

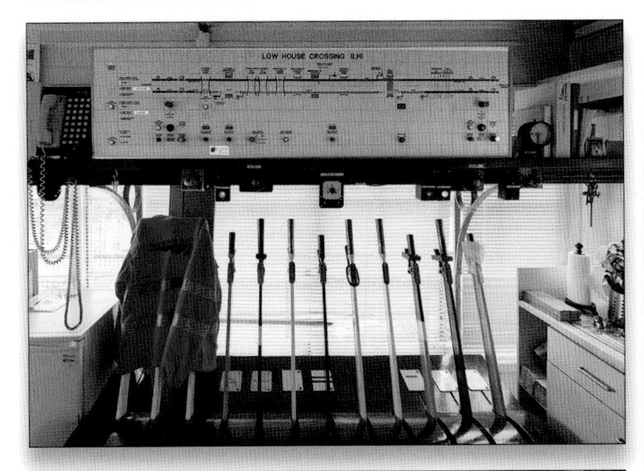

Top & above:- The tiny signal box at Low House Crossing was restored in 2007 to its original state, albeit, again with double glazing. The box was opened in 1900 and contains a 12-lever frame.
Both M. Rhodes
Location: *CA4 9SP*
Visibility: *The box is visible from the level crossing on Station Road.*

SETTLE JUNCTION

Top, above & below:- In March 1982, with the threat of closure looming large over the Settle to Carlisle railway, Class 40 No. 40079 passes Settle Junction. The train is 8M64, A Healey Mills to Carlisle Kingmoor fitted freight. The interior of the box at Settle Junction is seen on 28 February 2017 when the signalman on duty was Mick Guilfoyle. As he pointed out to me, the section to Carnforth, 26 miles long and taking 36 minutes to traverse, is probably the longest Absolute Block section in the UK. The box contains a 31-lever frame, the last lever of which is covered by Mick's high visibility vest.
All M. Rhodes
Location: *BD24 9JY*
Visibility: *The best place to see the box is from the farmer's crossing to the north, from where the black and white image in this section is taken. The box can also be seen from a lay-by on the A65, but is best viewed from the farmer's crossing.*

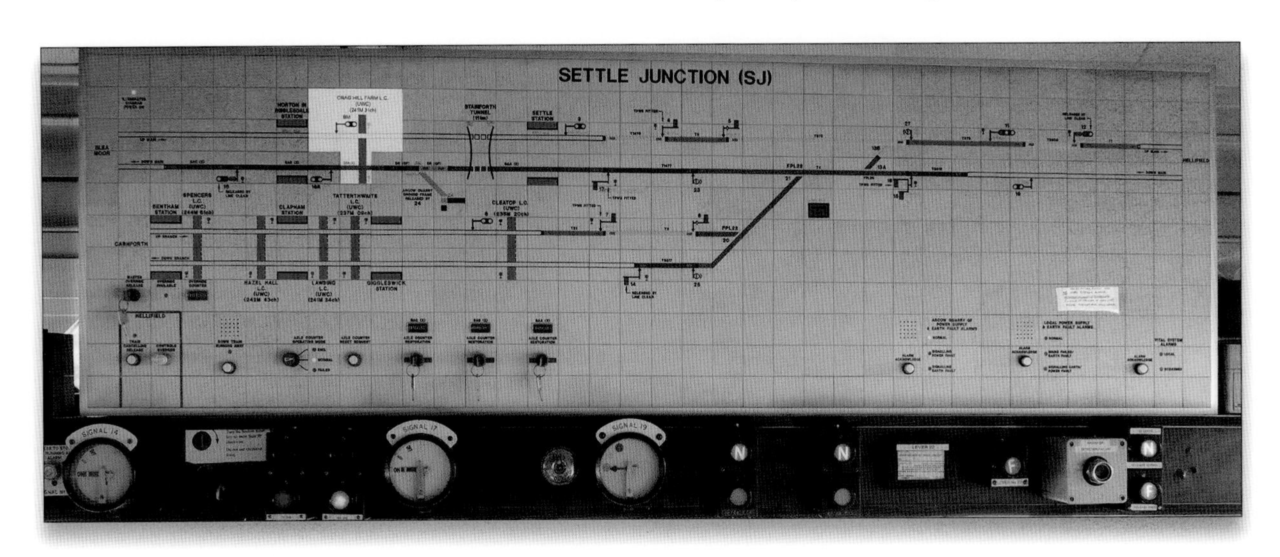

Liverpool Area

CANNING STREET NORTH

Right:- Perhaps this wonderful little signal box should be in the closures section of this book because it has been out of use for many years and was severely damaged by fire in 2008. Yet the shell of the box is still listed as extant, albeit out of use. Opened in 1900 the box had/has an 18-lever frame. Our external view, taken in 1983, shows Class 03 No. 03189 passing the signal box with a load of plate steel to R.Smith's private siding at Shore Road in Birkenhead. It goes without saying that they still made ships in Birkenhead in those days. P. Shannon
Location: *CH41 1FF*
Visibility: *The remnants of the signal box can just be seen from the Rendel Street overbridge.*

DITTON

Left- Again the purist may argue that Ditton is neither heritage nor mechanical - and that would be true. The box is included for completeness of the Liverpool area and because it replaced the two mechanical boxes at Ditton which feature in our closures section. Signalman. John Illingworth, a regular in this book, is at repose in the 2000-built box with its NX panel. Fascinating are the plastic templates which are used for different line blockages, much like the metal collars used in mechanical boxes. M. Rhodes
Location: *WA8 8TN*
Visibility: *The box can be seen in the middle distance from the Hale Road overbridge at this postcode.*

ELLESMERE PORT

Right- Called just Ellesmere Port in 2017, but as this view shows, formerly Ellesmere Port No. 4, the signal box here is unusual as the frame is older than the structure containing it. Built in 1972, the box contains a 1924, 64-lever LNWR-design frame. It is seen here in 1996 with a Merseyrail electric in the platform at the limit of the third rail. Electrification doesn't extend as far as the M53 overbridge from where this view was taken. M. Rhodes
Location: *CH65 4EH*
Visibility: *The box can be seen from the westbound M53 and also in the distance from Ellesmere Port station, but it is difficult to observe at close quarters.*

FIDLERS FERRY

Right & below:- An Interesting fact illustrated by our external view is the unusual spelling of 'Fidlers' in the signal box name, as opposed to the more common 'Fiddlers' used for the adjacent power station. Taken in 1991 the external view shows Class 20 Nos. 20141 & 20013 winding out of the power station with 6T77, an empty MGR to Bickershaw Colliery. This was a wonderful day in the box and the driver of the train even stopped to ask for a copy of the picture I had taken, which I duly sent to him! The box itself was opened in 1967 and contained a 45-lever frame. Both M. Rhodes
Location: *WA5 2UN*
Visibility: *The box can be glimpsed from the end of Marsh Lane at this postcode, but is difficult to see.*

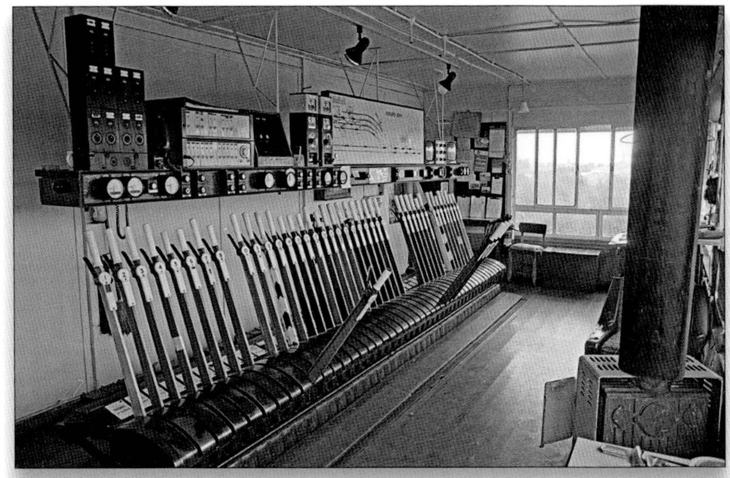

ST. HELENS STATION

Left:- Surrounded by dense foliage and rusting buried sidings, St. Helens Station signal box is hardly recognisable from the busy scenes of the 1980s when freight to and from the local glassworks kept the old yard busy. Opened in 1891 and with a 24-lever frame of the same date, the box had an IFS panel added in 1995 to control the sidings to Ravenhead Oil Terminal. M. Rhodes
Location: *WA10 1DQ*
Visibility: *The box is best viewed from the Corporation Street overbridge to the east of the station.*

Cheshire

ARPLEY JUNCTION

Right, below right & below:- The external view of Arpley Junction signal box was taken in the summer of 1983 and shows just how busy the lines here used to be after the closure of the direct route to Manchester via Latchford. Class 45 No. 45009 arrives at Arpley Yard with a trip freight from Ditton, which has run round at Arpley, whilst Class 37 No. 37246 is seen heading for the Latchford loops with an empty coal train from Garston to Mansfield Coal Concentration Sidings; much coal was exported through Garston Docks to Ireland at this time. The stabling sidings contain locomotives Nos. 25303, 40096, 47229 & 47246. What a contrast to our internal views, taken in 2017 when the day before my visit there had been no movements at all past the box during the 12-hour day shift and on the day of my visit there were just three light engine movements. One operational peculiarity at Arpley is the use of laminated sheets of paper to indicate which arrival siding at Arpley the locomotive or train should use. These are all held up at once by signalman John Illingworth for illustration purposes only. The box was built in 1918 and contains a 54-lever frame. All M. Rhodes

Location: *WA1 1PS*
Visibility: *The box is best seen from the road overbridge on Slutchers Lane. Beware, parking here is strictly monitored beyond the bridge and I have had my car clamped there which cost me £125!*

BASFORD HALL JUNCTION

Below & right:- The survival of mechanical signal boxes around Crewe, controlling the West Coast Main Line and its passing Pendolinos, is a bit of an anachronism in 2019 and nowhere more so than at Basford Hall Junction. Our external view shows Class 86 No. 86253 passing the box with an "up" express, with my minder perched on a lineside chair on the left of the view. The box was opened in 1897 and has levers numbered to 66 as the internal view shows, but rationalisation means the frame has been reduced to just 48 slots. Both M. Rhodes
Location: *CW2 5NJ*
Visibility: *Distant views of the box are possible from Weston Lane to the north and Casey Lane to the south of the box.*

BEESTON CASTLE & TARPORLEY

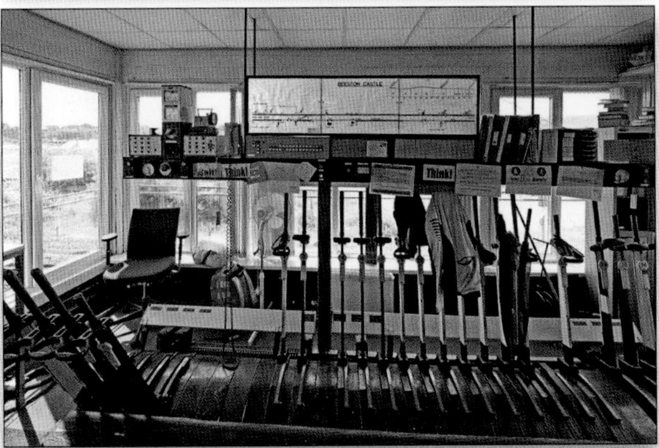

Top & above:- Beeston Castle & Tarporley SB, which stands precisely mid-way between Crewe and Chester, was opened in 1915 to a LNWR design and has a 26-lever frame. It became a fringe to Chester PSB on 6 May 1984 during Stage 5 of the resignalling when Chester No. 2 and No. 4 SBs were decommissioned. Towards Crewe, it continues to supervise one end of the 'AB island' to Steel Works SB. It is located north of the site of the former station and opposite a number of sidings. Sadly the station closed in 1966 and the last of the trackwork associated with the goods facility was taken out of use in 1992. There is a mix of semaphores and colour lights which control the main running lines and trailing crossover. This meagre layout is operated from a 26-lever frame of which 12 are not used and three are missing! Both M. Rhodes

Location: *CW6 9NJ*

Visibility: *A distant view of the box is possible from the Lock Gate Coffeehouse car park at this postcode.*

CREWE COAL YARD

Top & above:- Built in 1939 at the start of WWII, the box at Crewe Coal Yard had the concrete and brick construction typical of the era. The box contains 65 levers. Both M. Rhodes

Location: *CW1 2BD*

Visibility: *Partial views are possible from the car park near the box on Thomas Street.*

CREWE SORTING SIDINGS NORTH

Left & above- Crewe Sorting Sidings North was one of three signal boxes that controlled the yards at Basford Hall. Opened in 1962, it is the only one of the three that survives in 2019. It contained a 1962 era IFS panel, which as our internal view shows was recently replaced by a new panel . In contrast, the box at Sorting Sidings South, opened in 1901 had a 75-lever frame, whilst that at Sorting Sidings Middle was a similar 1962 construction with an IFS panel. Back in July 1991, Class 90 No. 90047 is seen passing the box with 4Z63, a Carlisle to Southampton freightliner service, necessitated because the previous day's Coatbridge to Southampton had been declared a failure at Carlisle Kingmoor Yard. M. Rhodes & I. Stewart

Location: *CW2 6EL*

Visibility: *The box is at the north end of Basford Hall Yard and is not usually visible except on the occasion of a railway open day.*

CREWE STEEL WORKS

Left & above:- *Situated along the line from Crewe to Chester at the point where the overhead catenary ceases and built in 1935 to an LMS design, Crewe Steel Works has a 20-lever frame. Class 47 No. 47799 is seen passing the box in 2002 with 1D67, the 1007 Birmingham to Holyhead express.* *I. Stewart & M. Rhodes*
Location: *CW2 7UD*
Visibility: *The box is difficult to see clearly from a public place.*

FRODSHAM

Left:- *Class 158 No. 158837 races past Frodsham signal box (formerly Frodsham Junction). The box was opened in 1912 but contains an older frame which dates back to 1893. It has 32 levers.* *M. Rhodes*
Location: *WA7 3EH*
Visibility: *Distant views of the box, as our image shows, can be obtained from the Halton Station Road overbridge.*

HELSBY

Above & above right:- *Carefully restored with timber-framed windows with double glazing, Helsby signal box was opened in 1900. The 45-lever frame is easily observed at close quarters as it is on the station platform at Helsby station.* *Both M. Rhodes*
Location: *WA6 0AE*
Visibility: *From station platform.*

LITTON'S MILL CROSSING

Right:- The box at Litton's Mill opened in 1890 with a 16-lever frame which was replaced by an 18-lever frame in 1922. Further change came in 2012, when the box was removed as a block post and simply remained to control the level crossing. This led to the removal of levers 1–12, with just six levers left in the frame to control the 1982-installed crossing gates, which came from Sealand signal box. M. Rhodes

Location: *WA5 1AP*

Visibility: *From Quay Road level crossing, which the box controls.*

MICKLE TRAFFORD

Right:- Formerly controlling the freight-only Chester diversion to Dee Marsh, Mickle Trafford signal box was built in 1969 and contains a 35-lever frame. A local service from Chester to Warrington Bank Quay is seen passing the box in 1990. M. Rhodes

Location: *CH2 4TA*

Visibility: *The box is visible in the distance from the signalman's car park off Station Lane.*

MONKS SIDING

Above & right:- One of the UK's oldest signal boxes is Monks Siding, which opened in 1875 with a 20-lever frame. The external view shows Class 20 Nos.20195 & 20159 with 7T75, a Parkside Colliery to Fiddlers Ferry Power Station MGR service, taken in April 1991. I. Stewart & M. Rhodes

Location: *WA5 1AR*

Visibility: *From the level crossing on Quay Fold, which the box controls.*

NORTON

Right:- Norton was one of three mechanical fringe SBs opened when Warrington PSB was commissioned in 1972. It was built to the standard pattern favoured by the London Midland Region at the time and fitted with a 10-lever mechanical frame. Flat roofed and pre-fabricated, it was built in timber throughout. Class 158 No. 158750 passes with a Manchester to Llandudno service. D. Allen.
Location: *WA7 6EP*
Visibility: *In the distance from the end of Runcorn East station platform.*

PLUMLEY WEST

Left:- Built by the Cheshire Lines Committee in 1908, Plumley West signal box has a 26-lever frame. Here, Class 47 No. 47237 passes with an Appley Bridge to Northenden empty waste train. M. Rhodes
Location: *Moss Lane, WA16*
Visibility: *Difficult to see clearly from a public place.*

SALOP GOODS JUNCTION

Below left & below:- Salop Goods Junction SB dates from 1901, when the LNWR greatly enlarged Crewe station and provided a network of avoiding lines. It needed extending in 1936 to accommodate a conventional 65-lever frame which replaced the power frame installed when the SB was new. Converging from the north are the AB Liverpool Independent Lines to Crewe Coal Yard; the TCB Manchester Independent Lines towards Sandbach South Junction controlled from Manchester South SC and the TCB "up" Chester Independent from Crewe North Junction supervised by Crewe PSB. Approaching from the south is one of the few remaining four-track AB sections in the UK from Crewe Sorting Sidings North as well as the Salop lines controlled by Gresty Lane SCC. Back in the early 1990s Class 47 No. 47079 passes with empty vans from Deanside in Glasgow, having delivered pet food there the previous day. M. Rhodes & D. Allen
Location: *CW2 6EF*
Visibility: *Partially visible from Gresty Lane football ground car park but difficult to see clearly.*

WARRINGTON CENTRAL

Left & below:- Liverpool Relief signalman John Illingworth sits on the frame at Warrington Central signal box discussing the "Monday line blocks" with the resident signalman. If the permanent way staff need to walk the line then there are frequent phone calls in-between the 10 minute peak service frequently to warn when the track is clear and when a line block has to be withdrawn because of an approaching train - a far cry from the days of a single platelayer wandering along a route at a leisurely pace, watching out himself for approaching trains! The box was opened in 1973 and both the box and the 55-lever frame came from Platt Bridge. Both M. Rhodes
Location: *WA2 7TS*
Visibility: *On the end of the station platform.*

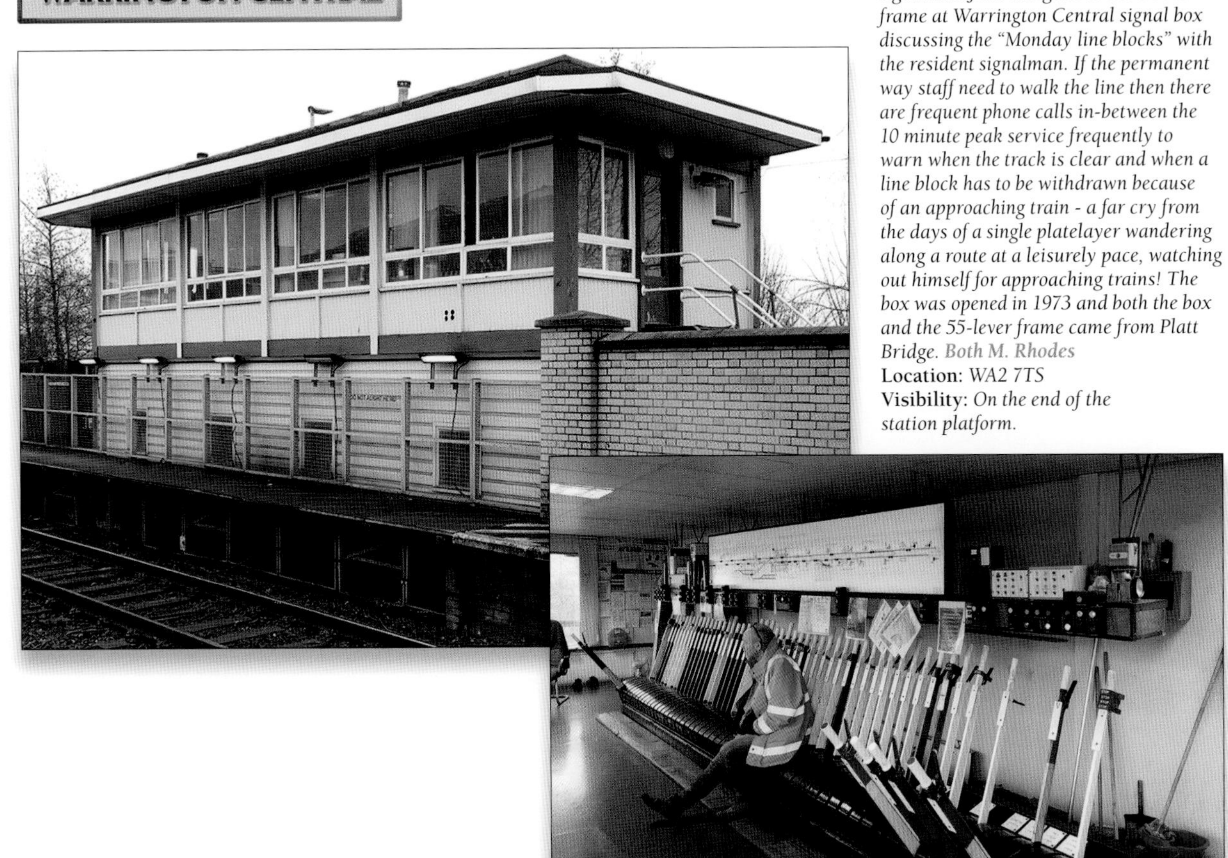

WINSFORD

Above:- Winsford signal box was built in 1897 and functions today with a reduced frame of 41 levers, numbered 12-52. An NX panel was added to the box in 1997 to control the Hartford and Weaver Junction areas. J. Illingworth
Location: *CW7 3BL*
Visibility: *Partially visible from Deakins Road which used to cross the WCML here but is now severed.*

Greater Manchester

ASTLEY

Top & above:- One of the UK's most recently constructed mechanical signal boxes is at Astley on the Manchester to Rainhill and Liverpool line. Built in 1972, it contains a 15-lever frame which remarkably was salvaged from the Fylde in 1954 and kept in storage for nearly two decades before finding a second use at Astley. Signalman Jim Roach watches on as his two guests record the frame for posterity. The pattern of his 13 year history as a signalman is a common one driven as much by closures as career progression, moving from Oldham to Smithy Bridge, to Shaw Street, then working as Rochdale relief before moving to Astley. Both M. Rhodes

Location: *M29 7LS*

Visibility: *From the Rindle Road crossing, which the box controls.*

BAGULEY FOLD JUNCTION

Top & above:- *The first heritage box out from Manchester along the route to Stalybridge is at Baguley Fold. Opened in 1890 by the Lancashire & Yorkshire Railway, it contains an IFS panel as our internal view from 2014 shows. One of the North West's longest serving signallers, now a Local Operations Manager, "Tony Mac" chats to the signalman about the days, pre-1988, when the box had a 21-lever mechanical frame.* Both M. Rhodes

Location: *M40 2HJ*

Visibility: *The box is almost impossible to see from a public place and is west of the Lord Street underpass at this postcode.*

CASTLETON EAST

Top & above:- *Rochdale relief signalman, Ian Garside, chats about the finer points of the box at Castleford East with Garston relief signalman John Illingworth. The box here opened in 1963 and was installed with a 65-lever frame which, as our internal view shows, now has quite a few vacant slots. The last two semaphores and the new colour light signals at Castleford East are used to frame Class 66 No. 66742 which is seen passing on a gloomy January day in 2017 with 4M37, an empty biomass train returning from Drax Power Station to Liverpool Docks.* Both M. Rhodes

Location: *OL11 3AU*

Visibility: *Can be seen in the distance from the Manchester Road overbridge at Castleton station.*

DEANSGATE JUNCTION

Right:- *Built in 1957, Deansgate Junction signal box in Altrincham originally had a 20-lever mechanical frame. In 1991 it was fitted with an NX panel which also controls the Manchester Metrolink line into Trafford Park.* M. Rhodes

Location: *WA15 6SQ*

Visibility: *From the Deansgate Lane level crossing, which the box controls.*

DIGGLE JUNCTION

Above:- Opened by the LNWR in 1885 with a 59-lever frame, the signal box at Diggle Junction was enlarged in 1891 to 81 levers. Even though the "junction" for the line to Staley & Millbrook closed in 1966, it was not until 1980 that the lever frame was rationalised down to 26 levers and a partition placed to keep the box warm more easily. Here in 2017, Class 185 No. 185118 speeds past with a Leeds to Liverpool express with the verdant tree growth disguising any signs of a former major railway junction. M. Rhodes

Location: *OL3 5JT*

Visibility: *Best seen from the Ward Lane overbridge at this postcode but close up views are possible from a public footpath running along the railway to the right of this view.*

ECCLES

Top & above:- Opened in 1933 by the LMS, Eccles signal box originally had a 60-lever frame. This was replaced by an NX panel in 1998 as our internal view shows. Both M. Rhodes

Location: *M30 0AG*

Visibility: *The box is visible from the signalman's parking ramp off the M602/A576 roundabout.*

DINTING STATION

Left:- With the former Woodhead route looking forlorn, the signal box at Dinting Station is seen in 2017. Opened in 1905 with a 40-lever frame, the box was extended in the early 1930s to a 43-lever frame which survives today. M. Rhodes

Location: *SK13 7EB*

Visibility: *On the station platform.*

EDGELEY NO. 1

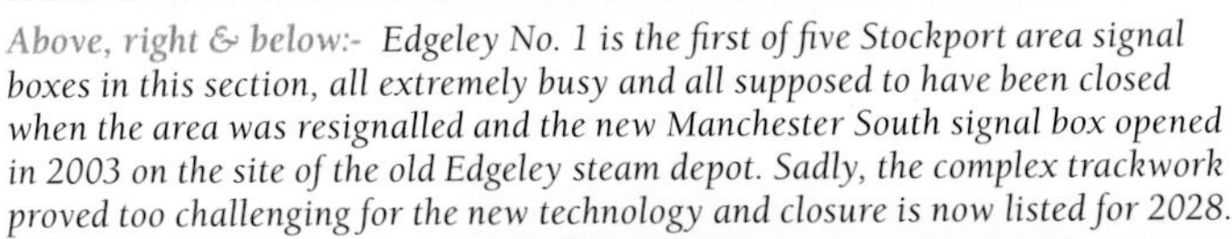

Above, right & below:- *Edgeley No. 1 is the first of five Stockport area signal boxes in this section, all extremely busy and all supposed to have been closed when the area was resignalled and the new Manchester South signal box opened in 2003 on the site of the old Edgeley steam depot. Sadly, the complex trackwork proved too challenging for the new technology and closure is now listed for 2028. No. 1 box was opened in 1884 and originally had a 90-lever frame which is now reduced to 54 levers as signalman Eamon Maher explains to me on my official visit in 2012.* *All M. Rhodes*
Location: *SK3 9QW*
Visibility: *This is poor but the box can be seen in the distance from Booth Street and Stockholm Road overbridges.*

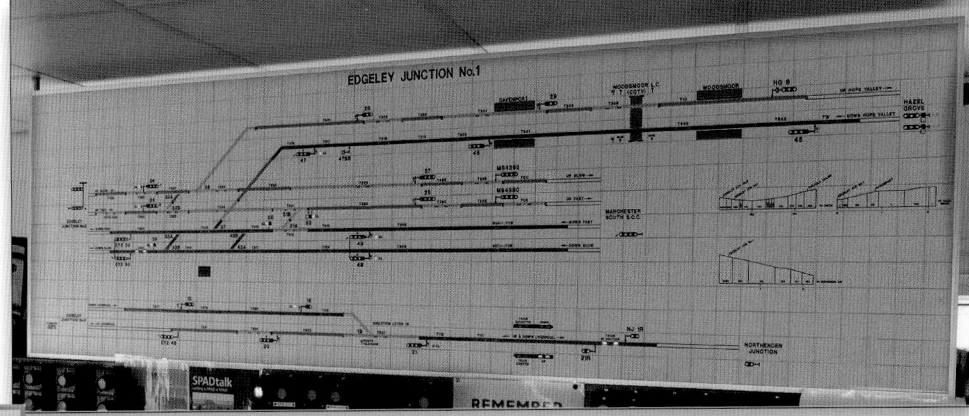

EDGELEY NO. 2

Above & above right:- *Edgeley No. 2 box was also opened in 1884 and has always had a 54-lever frame, most of which is redundant in 2019 as our internal view shows. Back in November 1983, Class 37 No. 37078 double heads Class 40 No. 40079 with 6H33, an empty cement train from Widnes to Earles Sidings. The locos are passing Edgeley No. 2 box whilst No. 1 box can just be seen above the rear of the train. The picture is taken from Booth Street.* *Both M. Rhodes*
Location: *SK3 9DG*
Visibility: *From Booth Street looking south.*

GLAZEBROOK EAST JUNCTION

Top & above:- *The signal box at Glazebrook East Junction was built in 1961 and had 80 levers, most of which were out of use by the time of this view in 2017; this because of the closure of the sidings and branch line to the Manchester Ship Canal.* Both M. Rhodes

Location: *M44 5YE*

Visibility: *A partial view is possible from the Glazebrook Trail which runs from the end of Fir Street.*

HEATON NORRIS

Top & above:- *Situated at the north end of Stockport viaduct, where the line to Guide Bridge diverges from the main line, Heaton Norris box was opened in 1955. Originally it contained 125 levers and still has the 125-lever frame but only levers 31 to 90 are functional. The central bank of levers was selected in order that the box could be single-manned.* Both M. Rhodes

Location: *SK4 2LY*

Visibility: *Partial views are possible from Dunblane Avenue and Stitch Lane.*

NORTHENDEN JUNCTION

Left:- *Northenden Junction signal box was opened in 1881 by the Cheshire Lines Committee and contains 25 levers.* M. Rhodes

Location: *M22 4SS*

Visibility: *Well observed from Longley Lane overbridge.*

STOCKPORT NO. 1

Left & below:- Because of the size of the lever frames and the intensity of the traffic, both Stockport signal boxes are double-manned. Here, signalmen Lee Chadderton and Dave Vincent are seen on duty in 2015. The box was opened in 1884 with a 113-lever frame but in 2019 just levers Nos. 16–113 remain above the frame, making 98 levers in all. The external view shows a Euston to Manchester express passing the box which sits on the south end of the "down" platform at Stockport station. Both M. Rhodes

Location: *SK3 9HZ*

Visibility: *From the station platform*

STOCKPORT NO. 2

Left, above & overleaf top:- Back in 2014, signalman Geoff Andrew is seen with a colleague at Stockport No. 2, just weeks before he retired. The box here was opened in 1890 and originally had a 120-lever frame, now reduced to 90 levers with Nos. 31–120 retained. A second image shows signalmen Andrew Law and Guy Henry at work in 2015; the sheer intensity of the traffic means that both of them are on their feet most of the time. All M. Rhodes

Location: *SK3 9HZ*

Visibility: *The box is to the north of the "up" platform at Stockport station.*

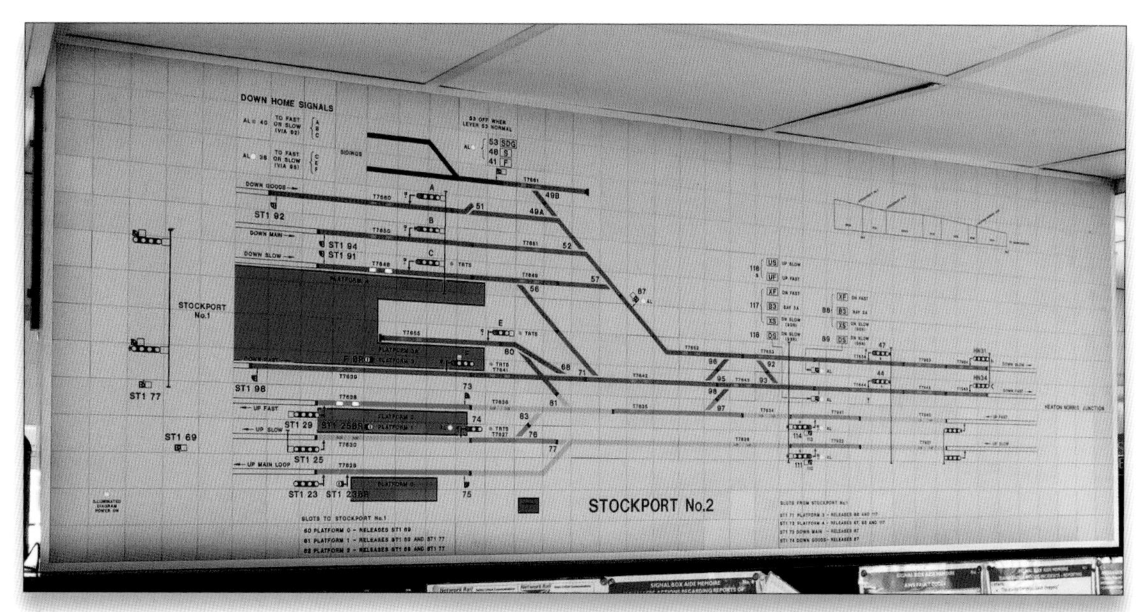

VITRIOL

Right & below:- The signal box at Vitriol Works retains its London Midland name boards, as the external view of Class 66 No. 66547 passing with 4E10, a Fiddlers Ferry to Ferrybridge empty coal train shows. Opened in 1954, the box still has 65 levers although with the closure of all the local sidings, only nine remain in use. Both M. Rhodes

Location: *OL9 0JA*

Visibility: *Partial rear views are possible from the Broadway Business Park*

Peak Forest & Hope Valley

BUXTON

Top & above:- The classic 1894-constructed LNWR box at Buxton is seen just after repainting in 1990. Our internal view shows signalman Richard Stockton filling in the TRB during a visit by LOM Anthony McIntyre in 2014. The box was fitted with a 60-lever frame, but now has just 45 levers with Nos. 4–48 still in use. Both M. Rhodes
Location: *SK17 7AT*
Visibility: *Partial views of the box are possible from Lightwood Road and it can be seen in the distance from the end of the platform at Buxton station.*

CHAPEL-EN-LE-FRITH

Top & above:- Signalman Steven Allen chats to LOM Anthony McIntyre at Chapel-en-le-Frith signal box. The box was rebuilt here in 1957 after the fatal crash of two freight trains, so eloquently remembered in the Ballad of John Axon, who was posthumously awarded the GC for his bravery. The 20-lever frame has just five operational levers in 2019 and the box is only manned for two shifts, there being no night shift here. Both M. Rhodes
Location: *SK23 9UJ*
Visibility: *Well visible from the end of the station platform.*

CHINLEY

Left & above:- Built in 1980 to replace the Midland Railway Chinley North signal box, the cabin at Chinley contains an OCS panel controlling the routes down to Peak Forest as well as the Hope Valley main line. Both M. Rhodes
Location: *SK23 6EH*
Visibility: *Partial views possible from the A624, Hayfield Road.*

EARLES SIDINGS

Top & above:- Class 185 No. 185150 passes the box at Earles Sidings with a Manchester Airport to Cleethorpes express in 2012. The box was built to a Midland Railway design in 1929 and as can be seen has been rebuilt with a flat roof. It contains a 35-lever frame which is almost all in use controlling the sidings for the Hope cement works here. Both M. Rhodes
Location: *S33 6SF*
Visibility: *Distant views are possible from the west on Fulwood Stile Lane (S33 6TF).*

EDALE

Top & above:- The 1893-built box at Edale was refurbished in 2005 with the ubiquitous uPVC windows. It is fitted with a 20-lever frame dating back to the same year. Both M. Rhodes
Location: *S33 7ZP*
Visibility: *It is visible in the distance from the station platform and a closer view is possible from waste ground on the former goods yard at Edale.*

FURNESS VALE

Above & above right:- Class 156 No. 156423 passes Furness Vale signal box with a mid-morning Manchester Piccadilly to Buxton service in autumn 2013. The box here opened in 1887 and the original mechanical frame was extended to its current 20 levers in 1909. Both M. Rhodes
Location: *SK23 7QS*
Visibility: *From the station footbridge.*

GREAT ROCKS JUNCTION

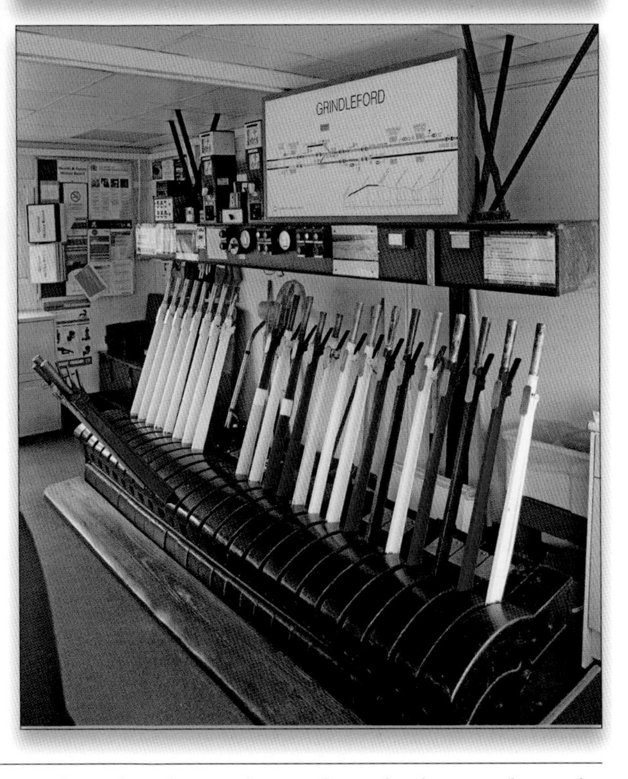

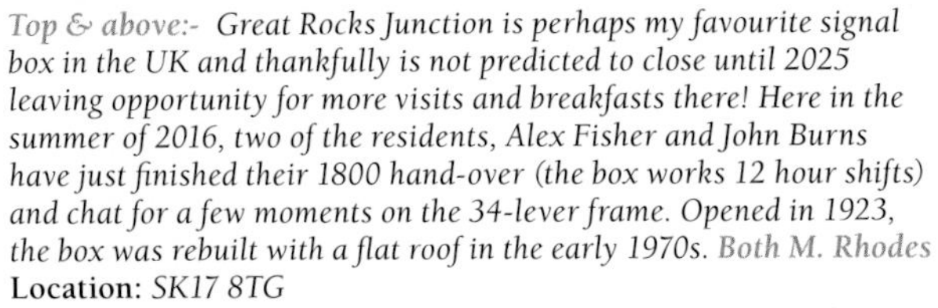

Top & above:- Great Rocks Junction is perhaps my favourite signal box in the UK and thankfully is not predicted to close until 2025 leaving opportunity for more visits and breakfasts there! Here in the summer of 2016, two of the residents, Alex Fisher and John Burns have just finished their 1800 hand-over (the box works 12 hour shifts) and chat for a few moments on the 34-lever frame. Opened in 1923, the box was rebuilt with a flat roof in the early 1970s. Both M. Rhodes

Location: *SK17 8TG*

Visibility: *Good views from the Waterswallows Road overbridge.*

GRINDLEFORD

Top right & above right:- The signal box at Grindleford was built in 1938 with a 25-lever frame and was modernised with new windows and steps in 2005. Both M. Rhodes

Location: *S32 2HY*

Visibility: *Distant views from the end of the station platform with closer views possible from the waste ground of the old goods yard.*

NEW MILLS CENTRAL

Top & above:- *The Midland Railway box at New Mills Central opened in 1938 with a 25-lever frame. It is nestled under the road bridge to the east of the station. Both M. Rhodes*
Location: *SK22 3JB*
Visibility: *Right underneath the Station Road overbridge.*

NORBURY HOLLOW

Above & right:- *Ern Sweetmore stands proudly in front of the 6-lever frame at Norbury Hollow crossing. Built in 1974, the box is surrounded by sunflowers grown by Ern and has an adjacent rock garden dedicated to his beloved Manchester United FC. Both M. Rhodes*
Location: *SK7 6NE*
Visibility: *From the crossing it controls on Norbury Hollow Road.*

NEW MILLS SOUTH

Top & above:- *Built in 1903 by the Midland Railway, the box was fitted with a 55-lever frame in 1960. Both M. Rhodes*
Location: *SK23 7QE*
Visibility: *In the distance from the Marsh Lane overbridge at this postcode.*

PEAK FOREST

Above (3 images):- Local Operations Manager Anthony McIntyre signs the TRB whilst signalman Gary Steer makes us a cup of tea on a gloomy day in October 2013. The box at Peak Forest, originally called Peak Forest South, opened in 1925, but has a much more modern 50-lever frame, fitted in 1974. It must be one of the most photographed boxes in the UK as the bridge to the north, from where our first external view is taken is a popular train watching spot. Class 60 No. 60066 departs with a Peak Forest to Attercliffe stone train on 9 August 2016. Looking from the box towards the bridge, Class 66 No. 66143 arrives with 6P62 from Hope Street on 28 October 2013, as Class 60 No. 60099 runs onto the stabling point. All M. Rhodes

Location: *SK17 8BR*

Visibility: *In the distance from the Batham Gate Road overbridge.*

TOTLEY TUNNEL EAST

Above & right:- Class 66 No. 66622 passes Totley Tunnel East signal box in April 2014 with 6E08, a Hope Earles Sidings to West Burton freight. Opened in 1893, the box has a compact 12-lever frame of the same vintage. Both M. Rhodes

Location: *S17 3QT*

Visibility: *Well seen from the footbridge off Totley Brook Road at this postcode.*

Northern Lancashire

BAMBER BRIDGE

Above:- Class 40 No. 40153 is seen passing "Bamber Bridge station level crossing frame" in December 1982, with 9079, the afternoon unfitted freight from Blackburn to Arpley Yard. The box was built by the Lancashire and Yorkshire Railway in 1906 and fitted with a 12-lever mechanical frame. This was replaced by an IFS panel in 1972. M. Rhodes
Location: *PR5 6EA*
Visibility: *From Station Road crossing, which the box controls.*

BURSCOUGH BRIDGE

Above:- Burscough Bridge Junction SB has for many years not been a junction and no longer controls any points. Opened in 1922, it had a 40-lever frame until 1993 when this was replaced by an IFS panel. At this time, the remaining sidings and crossover at Burscough Bridge were removed. Burscough Bridge SB became a fringe to Merseyrail IECC during Stage 2 of the Merseyrail Northern Lines Resignalling in March 1994. Here a pair of Class 47s pass light engine on their way to the Appley Bridge waste terminal. D. Allen
Location: *L40 0RZ*
Visibility: *Well seen from the A59 overbridge to the east of Burscough Bridge station.*

DAISYFIELD CROSSING

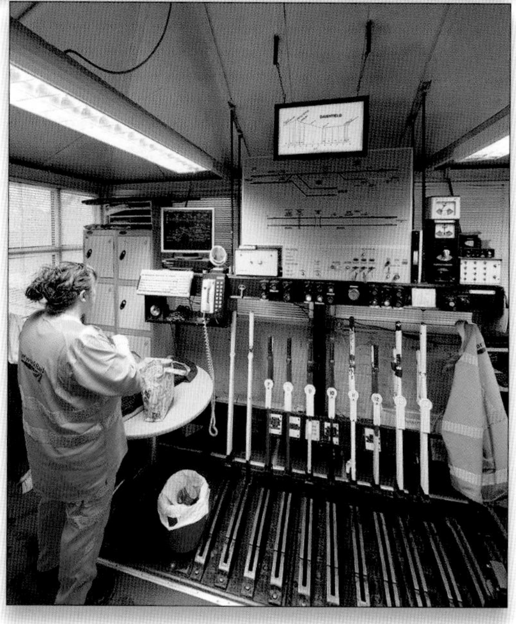

Top & above:- Trainee signaller, Jeanette Davis is listening to signalman Lawrence Cox as he explains the operation of Daisyfield Crossing box. The cabin here was built in 1873 and had a reconditioned lever frame with 16 levers fitted in 1943. Originally called Daisyfield Station, the box became known simply as Daisyfield Crossing in the 1960s after the station here closed. Both M. Rhodes
Location: *BB1 5JT*
Visibility: *From the crossing on Moss Street which the box controls.*

HORROCKSFORD JUNCTION

Top & above:- *Class 66 No. 66117 arrives at Horrocksford Junction on 6 August 2015 with an empty cement train from Hansons in Avonmouth to Clitheroe Cement Works. The train is having to reverse from the "down" line to the "up" line because there is no direct access to the cement works from the "down" line. The box, which is partially visible behind the trees, was built in 1873 and contains an 8-lever frame installed in 1928. Resident signalman Paul McGarvie is seen putting the points back during my visit in February 2017.* Both M. Rhodes

Location: *BB7 2BN*

Visibility: *Close up views are possible from Pimlico Road and a good general view is possible from the Pimlico Road overbridge.*

MIDGE HALL

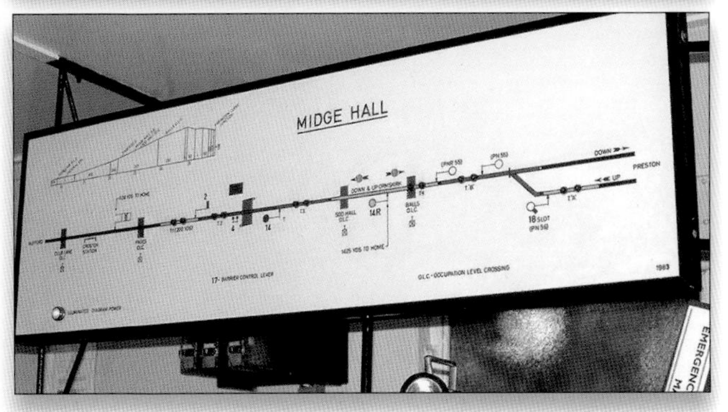

Top & above:- *Class 142 No. 142011 passes Midge Hall, which was one of five new mechanical SBs built as fringes when the London Midland Region resignalled the WCML north of Weaver Junction in 1972/73. It opened with a 20-lever frame, as part of Stage 2 of the Preston resignalling, replacing a life-expired structure located on the opposite side of the tracks at the Liverpool end of the disused station. Midge Hall is today in an unusual position; a signal box situated on a single line without a passing loop.* Both D. Allen

Location: *PR26 6TN*

Visibility: *From the crossing on Midge Hall Lane, which the box controls.*

PARBOLD

Above:- *Back in September 1984, Parbold signal box had just been rebuilt and fitted with a 1983-vintage 20-lever frame. Opened originally in 1877, the rebuild had been precipitated by collapse of the old mechanical frame. Metropolitan-Cammell DMU Nos. 51558 & 51550 pass with a Southport to Leeds train.* M. Rhodes

Location: *WN8 7NU*

Visibility: *From the crossing on Station Road, which the box controls.*

RAINFORD JUNCTION

Right:- The driver of Class 150 No. 150270 hands the single line passenger token to the signalman at Rainford Junction with a Kirkby to Blackburn via Manchester Victoria and Copy Pit Service - a journey made possible by the reopening of the westerly curve at Todmorden. There is another freight token which unlocks the ground frame at Knowsley. The base of the signal box at Rainford Junction dates back to 1874 and there is a 56-lever frame still in situ below the floor. A new top was built on the box in 1933 and in 2019 there are just 10 working levers which were the old Nos.21–30 but are now numbered 1–10. M. Rhodes
Location: WA11 7JX
Visibility: *From the station footbridge.*

WIGAN WALLGATE

Right & below:- Wigan Wallgate is the only survivor of three new Air Raid Precaution (ARP) SBs opened when the LMS resignalled Wigan in 1941. It replaced Wigan Wallgate No. 2, 3, 4 and 5 SBs. The internal view, taken on 16 January 1988, shows the box diagram and part of the 1977-installed 75-lever frame. The box was closed in 2004 to allow the frame to be replaced by an NX panel. Since the resignalling of WCML north of Weaver Junction in 1972/73, it has been a fringe to Warrington PSB. Our external view, on the same date, shows DMU Nos. 54261 & 53978 standing in the "up" siding No. 2 waiting to be attached to the Saturday-only 1827 Wigan Wallgate to Bolton, part of their move home to Newton Heath depot for repair. Both D. Ingham
Location: WN6 7TP
Visibility: *In the distance from the end of the station platform or from a side road off Prescott Street.*

North East England

The York ROC, which is the largest of the new regional operating centres, will eventually control the whole of the North East as well as much of the territory to the East of the main London to Edinburgh main line. Whilst many of the signal box closures in the North East happened roughly as predicted, there has been considerable slippage as compared to the 2010 Network Rail plans. In particular the resignalling of the line from Gilberdyke to Hull, which was scheduled for 2016, did not take place until 2018. A £34.5 million contract was awarded to Ansaldo STS and Linbrooke Servers in February 2016, which precipitated the closure of boxes at Melton Lane, Welton, Brough East, Crabley Creek, Broomfleet, Cave Crossing and Gilberdyke - see also 2018 Chapter in section 1 for details. The review of Network Rail finances undertaken by Sir Peter Hendy in 2015 suggests many schemes listed below may be deferred as higher profile projects like the electrification of Midland Main Line, Great Western Main Line and Manchester to Leeds route have all suffered from cost over-runs.

Signal Boxes Scheduled to Close per Network Rail 2010 Masterplan

2012	Horsforth, Rigton, Heck Ings GC, Cutsyke Junction
2013	Crofton Old Station GC, Joan Croft GC, Godnow Bridge, Medge Hall, Bonsall Lane, North Carr
	To Doncaster PSB - Dormer Green, Balne, Moss, Balne Lowgate, Barcroft, Fenwick, Heyworth, Noblethorpe
	To Lincoln SCC - Bearty Fen, Blankney, Blotoft, Blue Gowts, Brewery Lane, Cheal Road, Church Lane, Flax Mill, Gainsborough Lea Road, Golden High Hedges, Gosberton, Littleworth, Mill Green, Park Road, Rowston, Saxilby, Scopwick, Sleaford North, Sleaford South, Spalding, St. James Deeping, Stow Park, Sykes Lane, Water Drove
	To Ferrybridge SB - Hensall, Sudforth Lane, England Lane, Heck Lane, High Eggborough
	To Selby - Henwick Hall, Thorpe Gates, Barlby, Burn Lane, Sandhill Lane
	To Bowesfield - Urlay Nook
2015	Appleby Lincs, Barnetby East, Brocklesby Junction, Elsham, Wrawby Junction, Beckingham
2016	Castleford, Red Lane GC, Wakefield Kirkgate, Batley, Bradford Mill Lane, Halifax, Healey Mills, Hebden Bridge, Horbury Junction, Huddersfield, Milner Royd Junction, Broomfleet, Brough East, Cave, Crabley Creek, Gilberdyke Junction, F Lane, Oxmardyke, Welton, Marsh Junction, Pasture Street, Roxton Sidings, Stallingborough, New Barnetby, Barnsley, Woolley Coal Siding, Barrow Road Crossing, Barton Road, Bystable Lane, Goxhill, Oxmarsh Crossing, Ulceby Junction, Brigg, Gainsborough Central, Gainsborough Trent Junction, Kirton Lime Sidings, Northorpe, Immingham East Junction, Immingham West Junction, Immingham Reception, Lincoln SCC, Swinderby
2017	Billingham on Tees, Greatham, Norton East, Norton South, Norton station, Norton West, Ryhope Grange
2018	Goole Bridge, Goole, Green Oak Goit GC, Saltmarshe, Selby, Bowesfield, Crag Hall, Grangetown, Longbeck, Low Gates, Middlesbrough, Nunthorpe, Redcar, Tees yard, Whitehouse
2019	Belmont, Cattal, Hammerton Road, Hammerton, Harrogate, Hessay, Knaresborough, Marston Moor, Poppleton, Starbeck, Whixley, Wilstrop, Ferrybridge, Prince of Wales, Ancaster, Rauceby, Sleaford East, Sleaford West, Eastfield, Peterborough PSB, Woodcroft
2020	York IECC 2, Bardon Mill, Blaydon, Brampton Fell, Corby Gates, Denton Village, Haltwhistle, Haydon Bridge, Hexham, Lane Head, Low Row, Milton Village, Prudhoe, Wylam, Doncaster PSB, Norton GB, Bellwater Junction, Heckington, Hubberts Bridge, Sibsey, Skegness, Thorpe Culvert, Wainfleet, West Street Junction, Carlton GB, Claypole GB, Grassthorpe Lane GC, Helpston GB, Finningley GB, Ranskill GB
2021	Butterwell B shunt box, Spittal, Tweedmouth, Hull Paragon, Bedlington North, Bedlington South, Freemans, Hirst Lane, Marcheys House, Newsham, North Seaton, Winning
2022	Gascoigne Wood, Milford, part of York IECC, Keadby Canal, Scunthorpe PSB, Holton le Moor, Langworth, Wickenby
2023	Great Coates No. 1, Pyewipe Road
2025	Beverley, Bridlington, Driffield, Gristhorpe, Hessle Road, Hull River Bridge, Lebberston Road, Seamer, Barton Hill, Common Road, Howsham, Kirkham Abbey, Malton, Strensall, Weaverthorpe
2026	Thrumpton
2027	Ferryhill, Heaton Control Tower, Tyneside IECC, Heighington, Shildon
2029	Alnmouth
2030	Hickleton, Moorthorpe
2044	Seaham
2051	Belasis Lane, Selby Swing Bridge
2056	Morpeth

Newcastle–Carlisle

BARDON MILL

Above:- HST power car No. 43082 leads the way on a diverted Edinburgh to King's Cross service in April 1989. The box at Bardon Mill opened in 1874 but is fitted with a much more modern 20-lever reconditioned mechanical frame, dating from 1966. M. Rhodes
Location: *NE47 7HY*
Visibility: *The box is visible in the distance to the west of the station.*

BRAMPTON FELL

Above:- In April 1989, Class 43 No. 43108 passes Brampton Fell signal box with a diverted Edinburgh to King's Cross express. Opened in 1918, the box has a 20-lever frame slightly reduced from its original size and numbered 2–21. M. Rhodes
Location: *CA8 1HN*
Visibility: *From the level crossing on the B6413, which the box controls.*

BLAYDON

Above left & above:- The view of Blaydon signal box from the 1990s reveals several of the peculiarities of this signal box. It has faced away from the railway it controls since 1982, when the Scotswood route into Newcastle closed. It is also clear that the left half of the box is from different brick and this represents a 1911 extension to the late 19th century box. When the box was refurbished at the start of the 21st century the top half of this extension was removed leaving the right two-thirds of the box intact with a 43-lever frame. The box can be seen in the exhaust of 31242 as it passes with 6Z22, a Tyne Yard to Carlisle Kingmoor freight in 1983. D. Allen & M. Rhodes
Location: *NE40 4WS*
Visibility: *From the level crossing on Chain Bridge Road.*

CORBY GATES

Left:- The top half of the box at Corby Gates was constructed in 1955 on top of the 19th century North Eastern Railway brick base. The box has a 26-lever frame and is seen here in 1989 as HST No. 43070 passes with what the signalman kindly informed us was the 1S19, King's Cross to Edinburgh. M. Rhodes
Location: *CA4 8LH*
Visibility: *From Wetheral station platform.*

HALTWHISTLE

Above:- The 1901-built Haltwhistle signal box closed as a signal box in 2009 when it was replaced by a portable building at the other end of the station platform. It was, however, grade II listed in 1987 and remains in Network Rail ownership and preserved. In 1927 it was fitted with an 85-lever frame which was reduced to 61 levers in the 1970s when the branch line to Alston closed. In 1991, it was also fitted with an IFS panel controlling the nearby Melkridge coal loading facility, just two years before that closed. Our 1984 view shows quite a crowd of hikers about to board a Carlisle to Newcastle service made up of DMU Nos. 53233 & 54054. M. Rhodes

Location: *NE49 9HN*

Visibility: *From the station platform.*

HAYDON BRIDGE

Above:- The signal box at Haydon Bridge was built in 1877 but has a much younger mechanical frame dating from 1964 and with 31 levers. Here, in 1989, DMU Nos. 53690 & 54241 pause at the station with a Newcastle to Carlisle service. M. Rhodes

Location: *NE47 6HD*

Visibility: *From the end of the platform.*

HEXHAM

Top & above:- The striking North Eastern overhead signal box at Hexham opened in 1918 and contains a 60-lever frame. The box is seen here as Class 47 No. 47321 arrives with 6P74, a Speedlink trip from Tees Yard, bringing glue from Duxford for the nearby chipboard factory. Since the closure of Tyne Yard as a Speedlink centre, the wagons had tripped daily from Tees Yard. A second view, this time from the east, shows Class 156 No. 156454 slowing to enter Hexham station with a Newcastle to Carlisle train. Both M. Rhodes

Location: *NE46 1EZ*

Visibility: *Can be seen in the distance from the station footbridge at Hexham.*

MILTON

Above:- The tiny crossing box at Milton lies east of Brampton and opened in 1893. Originally fitted with a 6-lever frame, this was subsequently expanded to ten levers. Here, on 22 April 1989, a Newcastle to Carlisle service headed by DMU No. 53470 passes the box. M. Rhodes

Location: *CA8 1HX*

Visibility: *From the A689 level crossing, which the box controls*

PRUDHOE

Above:- The imposing signal box at Prudhoe bears testimony to more prosperous times at the station here. Built in 1872, the brickwork shows that it was extended in 1908. Fitted with a 45-lever frame in 1944, most of the levers are now out of use. Class 142 No. 142025 passes with a train from Hexham bound for Newcastle and on along the Durham Coast to Nunthorpe. M. Rhodes
Location: *NE42 6NR*
Visibility: *From the station platform.*

WYLAM

Above:- The second of the surviving North Eastern overhead signal boxes is at Wylam; it opened in 1897. Sadly the mechanical lever frame here was replaced with a IFS panel in 1969. Back in 1985, Class 37 Nos. 37077 & 37071 are seen passing under the box with 4E30, an empty steel train from Workington to Lackenby. M. Rhodes
Location: *NE41 8HR*
Visibility: *From the station platform.*

Blyth and Tyne & Tyneside

ALNMOUTH

Left:- The signal box at Alnmouth dates back to 1907 but the lever frame was removed some time ago when a small NX panel was fitted in 1976. This was replaced by a more extensive panel in 1990. Back in the summer of 1984, the box is seen with Class 47 No. 47307 disappearing north in the background with a Haverton Hill to Leith chemical train. M. Rhodes
Location: *NE66 3QF*
Visibility: *From the station platform.*

BEDLINGTON NORTH

Above & above right:- Built in 1912 and fitted with a 64-lever frame, the box at Bedlington North now has just levers Nos. 5–64 above the floor. Our interior view, taken in June 1980 shows the signalman watching Class 37 No. 37078 as it passes with a Tyne Yard to Blyth coal train. The external view, taken in May 1988, shows the view looking north from the station platform and Class 56 No. 56132 passing with 6B09, the afternoon trip from Cambois to Furnace Way Sidings. Both M. Rhodes
Location: *NE22 5AH*
Visibility: *From Barrington Road level crossing, which the box controls.*

BEDLINGTON SOUTH

Top & above:- The exact date of construction of Bedlington South signal box is not known although it is of an older design than the north box. It has 30 levers above the floor numbered 12–41. Back in May 1988, Class 56 No. 56132 is seen passing back north, having run round in Furnace Way Sidings to head to Widdrington Coal Disposal Point. Both M. Rhodes

Location: *NE22 7JD*

Visibility: *from Station Road level crossing, which the box controls.*

FREEMANS CROSSING

Top & above:- These two views of Freemans Crossing signal box are taken over 30 years apart. In summer 1980, Class 37 No. 37048 passes by the 1956-built structure with a Blyth Power Station to Butterwell trip. At this time the box had a lever frame and controlled semaphore signals installed at the time of the construction of Cambois Power Station (1955–56). In 1982 the mechanical frame was replaced by an IFS panel and the 2011 view shows Class 66 No. 66727 with the Blyth to Fort William alumina train, passing a greatly pared down track layout. Both M. Rhodes

Location: *NE24 1QQ*

Visibility: *From the Wembley Gardens level crossing, which the box controls.*

MARCHEYS HOUSE

Above:- The signal box at Marcheys House opened in 1895 and was fitted with a new mechanical lever frame in 1960, 15 levers from which are still in operation. Back in January 1990, Class 37 No. 37501 is see passing the box with 6N64, the daily Lynemouth to Tees Yard Speedlink trip freight. M. Rhodes

Location: *NE62 5XB*

Visibility: *From the crossing on Wansbeck Terrace, which the box controls.*

NEWSHAM

Above:- Called Newsham South back in 1985 when this view was taken, the signal box here has since been renamed simply Newsham. The box opened in the late 19th century but the exact date is not known. Originally the 1945 mechanical frame had 21 levers, but when the crossing gates were mechanised in the early 1980s, the frame lost lever No. 21 which had locked the gates. Here in 1985, Class 37 No. 37045 passes with a light engine movement from Gateshead depot to Cambois shed, headcode 0N25. M. Rhodes

Location: *NE24 3PR*

Visibility: *From the crossing on South Newsham Road, which the box controls.*

RYHOPE GRANGE

Top & above:- The 1905-constructed signal box at Ryhope Grange has survived, thanks to being used as an interim solution for the Durham Coast resignalling of 2011. Fitted with a 64-lever frame in 1950, 40 of the levers are still in use today. The £28 million project undertaken by Invensys in 2011 saw five flat screens installed with WestCad tracker balls and these control down the coast as far as Greatham. Back in June 1980 the box is seen looking from the north with Class 37 No. 37083 winding across the main line, onto the Sunderland Docks branch with a Murton Colliery to Sunderland train carrying coal for export. Over 30 years later, the box is seen from the new bypass, looking from the south and whilst the structure of the box is largely unchanged, as are the row of houses behind it, the new "grey box" related to the resignalling and the protective palisade steel fencing are very evident. Class 37 Nos. 37259 & 37602 pass with a Carlisle to Seaton nuclear flask train on 8 October 2015. Both M. Rhodes

Location: *SR2 7RD*

Visibility: *From the A1018 bypass road at this postcode.*

NORTH SEATON

Above left & left:- Dating back to 1872, the box at North Seaton contains a 21-lever frame installed in 1950. Here, in April 1988, Class 56 No. 56115 passes with 6B08, an afternoon trip from Lynemouth Colliery to Cambois Power Station.

Two young lads are dwarfed by Class 37 No. 37513 as it runs light engine from Blyth Cambois depot to the Lynemouth aluminium smelter in 1988. Taken from the "down" home signal at North Seaton (with permission), the view shows the viaduct over the River Wansbeck and then Marcheys House signal box and signals in the distance. Both M. Rhodes

Location: *NE63 0TB*

Visibility: *From the crossing on Newbiggin Road, which the box controls.*

WINNING

Above & above right:- *Looking east at Winning on an August evening in 1985, Class 56 No. 56132 is seen passing the 1895-built signal box. At this stage the bracket signals for the junction were still on a traditional signal post which, as can be seen from the 2011 view looking west, was to be replaced by an industrial strength steel signal frame early in the 21st century. In the second view Deltic No. 55022 passes the 16-lever box with a Lynemouth to Blyth Cambois empty alumina trip.* Both M. Rhodes

Location: *NE22 7LQ*

Visibility: *From the level crossing on Wansbeck Terrace, which the box controls.*

Teeside

BELASIS LANE

Right:- *By the time this book is published, the box at Belasis Lane may have closed. Opened in 1929, it has a 25-lever frame which has been made largely redundant since the closure of the chemical works at Haverton Hill. Back in 1983, the box is seen in its prime as Class 47 No. 47301 passes with 6O49, the daily Haverton Hill to Eastleigh Speedlink service. Just visible in the background is Class 08 No. 08867 with a Port Clarence to Tees Yard trip.* M. Rhodes

Location: *TS23 1LG*

Visibility: *From the overbridge west of the signal box on Belasis Avenue.*

BILLINGHAM

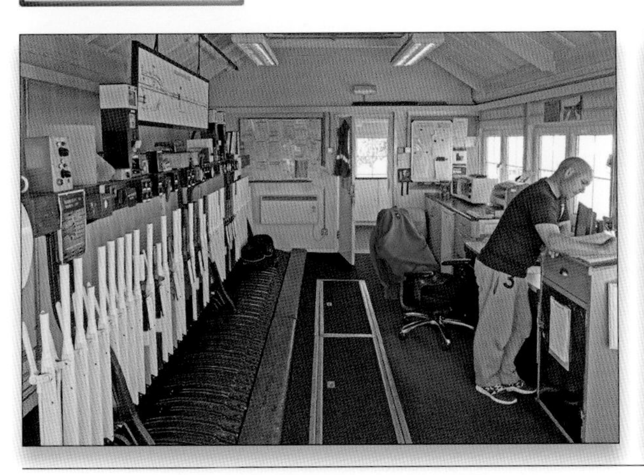

Above & above right:- *Relief signalman Danny Watcham fills in the TRB in Billingham signal box back in 2015. The 50-lever frame was installed in 1945 whilst the signal box itself dates back to 1904. In the external view, Class 66 No. 66065 is seen passing the box with 6P60, a trip freight from Hartlepool Pipe Mill to Tees Yard.* Both M. Rhodes

Location: *TS23 2RH*

Visibility: *From the crossing on Station Road, which the box controls.*

BOWESFIELD

Above:- At the time of this image, in 1983, the 1905-built North Eastern signal box at Bowesfield had a 45-lever mechanical frame as well as a 1969-installed IFS panel controlling the Eaglescliffe area. Subsequently in 1986, the IFS panel which controlled Stockton station, formerly in North Shore signal box (which burnt down), was moved in. Finally, in 1989, a third IFS panel replaced the lever frame and controlled Bowesfield itself. Class 47 No. 47349 passes the box with 6S66, the daily Tees Yard to Stranraer Speedlink working. M. Rhodes
Location: *TS18 3HD*
Visibility: *This is from a slip road off the eastbound A66 dual carriageway.*

CRAG HALL

Above, above right & below:- The signal box at Crag Hall was built in 1878 but in the early 1970s was decommissioned, only to be born again in 1974 when the new line to the Boulby potash mine opened. This is the reason for most of the windows being boarded up as only the minimum were reinstalled when the box was reopened. The interior view shows the 30-lever frame with relief signalman Jason Pipe on duty, whilst the first external view shows Class 20 Nos.20008 & 20122 slowing for the token exchange in charge of 6P03, a Tees Yard to Boulby trip freight, taken in January 1989. The image below shows Class 37 Nos. 37515 & 37516 shunting 9P61, a trip fright from Tees Yard at Skinningrove, with Crag Hall signal box to the right. All M. Rhodes
Location: *TS13 4EA*
Visibility: *From the A174, Broughton Road, across a small field.*

FERRYHILL

Top & above:- Two views of Ferryhill, first from the south in 1983 when a King's Cross to Edinburgh express is seen passing and then from the north with Class 20 Nos.20070 & 20028 shunting the yard at Ferryhill, having tripped up from Tees Yard on 14 November 1986. The box was built in 1952 and originally mechanically operated until an IFS panel was installed in 1971. This was superseded by a second IFS panel, dating from 1992 and this controlled just the freight line to Norton West Junction. Both M. Rhodes
Location: *DL17 0AR*
Visibility: *From the Lough House bank overbridge to the north of the box.*

GRANGETOWN

Above:- Class 37 No. 37509 passes the signal box at Grangetown with a Lackenby to Skinningrove trip in August 1991. The box here opened in 1954 and the mechanical frame was replaced by an NX panel in 1984. M. Rhodes
Location: *TS6 7RT*
Visibility: *In the distance from Tees Dock Road overbridge to the north east.*

GREATHAM

Above right & right:- Class 66 No. 66065 passes Greatham signal box with 6P60, the afternoon trip from Tees Yard to Hartlepool Pipe Mill. The box opened in 1889 and had a 21-lever mechanical frame fitted in 1941. This was replaced in 2004 by an IFS panel as our interior view of signalman Paul Betteney on duty in April 2015 shows. Both M. Rhodes
Location: *TS25 2HB*
Visibility: *From the crossing on Marsh House Lane, which the box controls.*

HEIGHINGTON

Above:- The signal box at Heighington has a much reduced 11-lever frame in 2019, but as this view shows, the 1872-constructed signal box was once much larger. M. Rhodes

Location: *DL5 6QG*

Visibility: *From the crossing on Heighington Lane, which the box controls.*

LONGBECK

Above:- Longbeck is a rather stylish LNER SB dating from 1932. The steeply pitched hipped roof is especially pleasing when one considers the then growing trend to use flat roofs. Longbeck SB's control area was extended in February 1970, when Saltburn West, Saltburn Station and Crag Hall SBs were decommissioned. At the time, except for a few semaphores near to Longbeck, most signals were replaced by colour lights and the route to Saltburn was fully track circuited. Concurrently, the number of platforms at Saltburn was reduced from four to two. In 1980, the lever frame was removed after the last of the semaphores were removed and the gates replaced by lifting barriers. D. Allen

Location: *TS11 6HD*

Visibility: *From the crossing on Longbeck Road, which the box controls.*

LOW GATES

Above:- Opened in 1956, Low Gates signal box had a 17-lever frame when this image was taken in May 1990. Class 47 No. 47018 passes with 4L64, the daily Wilton to Stratford freightliner. The signal box had IFS panels fitted in 1992 and 1997 and currently controls the track to Eaglescliffe and acts as a gate box for three local crossings. M. Rhodes

Location: *DL7 8EB*

Visibility: *From the High Street level crossing, which the box controls.*

MIDDLESBROUGH

Above:- Opened in 1877, the signal box at Middlesbrough had an IFS panel fitted to replace the mechanical frame in 1978, at the same time as the area was resignalled from semaphore to colour light signals. Here, on 7 March 1986, Class 56 No. 56122 passes with 6P73, a trip from Tees Yard to Lackenby. M. Rhodes

Location: *TS1 1ST*

Visibility: *From the western end of the station platform at Middlesbrough.*

NORTON EAST

Above, above right & right:- Dating back to 1870, the signal box at Norton East has only been open intermittently for the past 30 years. It is opened when trains use the west to east curve at Norton and is otherwise boarded up. Our black and white image, dating from July 1987, shows the half-hearted removal of the protective shutters as Class 47 No. 47304 passes with 6P62, a Thrislington to Cemetery North freight. Three decades later, a biomass train from Tyne Dock to Drax is seen passing behind Class 66 No. 66750 and this shows the overall context of the boarded up box well. The interior view is courtesy of a borrow key and shows the 25-lever frame which was installed in 1959. All M. Rhodes

Location: *TS20 1QE*

Visibility: *From the footpath over the line at the end of Kew Gardens.*

NORTON-ON-TEES

Above left, above & left:- *A Grand Central King's Cross to Sunderland express, powered by Class 43 Nos. 43084 & 43080 is seen passing the box at Norton-on-Tees. Opened in 1897, the box contains a 26-lever frame and a large wrought iron gate wheel to control the crossing over Calf Fallow Lane.* *All M. Rhodes*
Location: *TS20 1TT*
Visibility: *From Calf Fallow Lane crossing, which the box controls.*

NORTON SOUTH

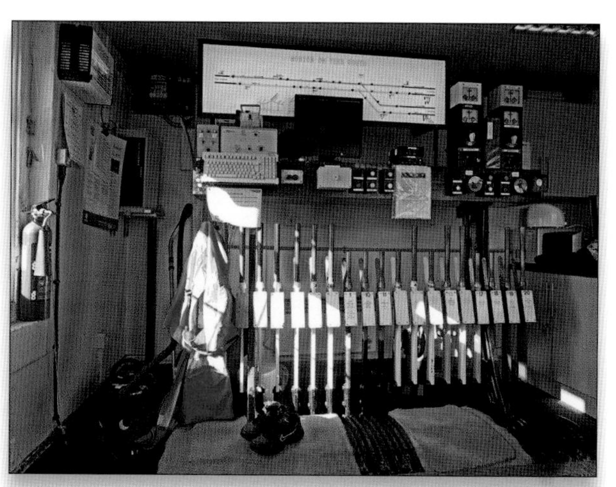

Right (upper & lower):- *The signal box at Norton South opened in 1870 and is fitted with a 1955-built 20-lever frame. The external view shows Class 66 No. 66144 passing with 6D83, a Tees Yard to Thrislington trip freight.* *Both M. Rhodes*
Location: *TS19 9HP*
Visibility: *The box is almost impossible to see from a public place but distant views are possible from the Junction Road overbridge to the north, but only when there are no leaves on the trees.*

NORTON WEST

Top & above:- Signalman Matthew Tyson is at repose, contemplating the 41-lever frame at Norton West signal box. The cabin was opened in 1910 and the frame dates from 1921. Class 66 No. 66557 is seen passing the box with 6H32, a Redcar Mineral Terminal to Ferryhill freight. Both M. Rhodes

Location: *TS19 9JX*

Visibility: *From the crossing on Blakeston Lane, which the box controls.*

NUNTHORPE

Above:- The 1903-constructed signal box at Nunthorpe contains a 16-lever frame but the signalman here also controls the line to Whitby. This line is operated on a "No Signalman Token Remote - NSTR" basis. The driver of a train unlocks the cabin to access the token machine at the end of the section, returns his token and then phones the signalman at Nunthorpe to request permission to remove the token for the next section of line. The system saves on manpower on lightly used branch lines. M. Rhodes

Location: *TS7 0BG*

Visibility: *From Guisborough Road crossing, which the box controls.*

REDCAR CENTRAL

Above:- Built by the LNER in 1937, Redcar Central signal box had an IFS panel fitted in 1970. A Salburn to Bishop Auckland train is seen passing the box in 1986. M. Rhodes

Location: *TS10 1DH*

Visibility: *From the crossing on West Dyke Road, which the box controls.*

SHILDON

Above:- The signal box at Shildon was constructed in 1887 and fitted with a 55-lever frame in 1928. This was reduced in size to 42 levers in 1984 when the wagon works and associated sidings closed. M. Rhodes

Location: *DL4 2DH*

Visibility: *From both the station platform and the Spout Lane overbridge to the east.*

TEES YARD

Left:- The line from Urlay Nook to Saltburn and Skinningrove is signalled by heritage and/or mechanical signal boxes, except for the section between Bowesfield and Middlesbrough, which is controlled by the Tees signal box located in the old "down" hump tower. In 1986, nearly two years after the "down" hump closed, the inside of the 1962-constructed NX panel is seen along with the greatly reduced track diagram. M. Rhodes

Location: *TS17 7BN*

Visibility: *Can be seen looking east from the Teesside Park Drive overbridge.*

URLAY NOOK

Above:- The box here was opened in 1896 and extended in 1943, at which stage a 41-lever frame was fitted. Most of the levers were rendered redundant with the closure of the Royal Navy Supply Depot here in 1997. Though NR's policy to eliminate level crossings can be justified on safety grounds, it doesn't always meet with public approval. Such is the case at Urlay Nook. Having failed to obtain permission to close the crossing, NR needed to retain Urlay Nook SB as a gate box when control of the signalling was transferred to Bowesfield SB in November 2013. D. Allen

Location: *TS16 0LA*

Visibility: *From the crossing on Urlay Nook Road, which the box controls.*

WHITEHOUSE

Above & above right:- Class 47 No. 47191 is seen passing Whitehouse signal box in March 1986 with 6Z21, an extra freight from Scunthorpe to Lackenby. The interior of the box shows relief signal woman, Carol Shutt (and her dog honey), with trainee James Buckley in front of the 40-lever frame which has been reduced in size from its original extent. Both M. Rhodes

Location: *TS3 6AR*

Visibility: *From the crossing on Cargo Fleet Road, which the box controls.*

York–Scarborough

BARTON HILL

Top & above:- Tony Gadd and his wife Tracy (who is resident signalwoman at Kirkham Abbey), pose for the photographer next to the gate wheel in Barton Hill signal box. The box here was built by the LNER in 1936 with a 16-lever frame and is shown with Class 185 No. 185122 passing with a Liverpool Lime Street to Scarborough service on 11 November 2015. Both M. Rhodes

Location: *YO60 7JZ*

Visibility: *From the level crossing on the un-named road just off the A64 at this postcode.*

KIRKHAM ABBEY

Above & right:- The newly-repainted signal box at Kirkham Abbey is seen here in November 2015. Built in 1873, the box had a 16-lever mechanical frame fitted in 1926. Both M. Rhodes

Location: *YO60 7JS*

Visibility: *From the crossing on Onhams Lane, which the box controls.*

HOWSHAM

Top & above:- The signalman at Howsham makes me a welcome cup of coffee during my visit in 2015. The tiny crossing box here opened in 1873 and had an 8-lever frame fitted in 1891. Just 5 of the levers remain in use today. Both M. Rhodes

Location: *YO60 7PQ*

Visibility: *From the crossing on Riders Lane, which the box controls.*

MALTON

Top & above:- *Built in 1873, the mechanical frame in Malton signal box was removed back in 1966 when the area was rationalised and the branch to Driffield closed. The panel was extended, as our internal view shows, in 1993 when the box took over control of the Helperton and Rillington area. Both M. Rhodes*
Location: *YO17 9DP*
Visibility: *From the level crossing on Castlegate, which the box controls.*

STRENSALL

Top & above:- *Built in 1901 the signal box at Strensall was originally fitted with a 40-lever frame which was still in use when our external view was taken in July 1984. Class 37 No. 37013 passes with the 15.22 Scarborough to Glasgow holiday extra. In 1988, the mechanical frame was replaced by an IFS panel, but the signal box remains largely externally unaltered since the 1984 view, although the windows next to the crossing have been changed and automated barriers have replaced the old wooden manual crossing gates. Both M. Rhodes*
Location: *YO32 5XD*
Visibility: *From the crossing at Lords Moor Lane, which the box controls.*

SEAMER

Left & above:- *Seamer signal box was known as Seamer East until 2000 when it had its 35-lever frame removed to make way for an NX panel controlling the tracks formerly signalled by Seamer East and Seamer West signal boxes. As our internal view shows, the reach of the NX panel is significantly larger now, after being extended to cover the Scarborough station area in 2010. Both M. Rhodes*
Location: *YO12 4LU*
Visibility: *From the station platform.*

WEAVERTHORPE

Top & above:- *Weaverthorpe signal box is strangely named in that it is on the other side of the A64 to the town and closer to the village of Sherburn, but as Chris Hill the resident signalman explained on my visit, the name was chosen by the North Eastern Railway to avoid confusion with Sherburn-in-Elmet. Opened in 1873, the box was fitted with a 16-lever frame in 1933.* Both M. Rhodes
Location: *YO17 8PS*
Visibility: *From the crossing on St.Hilda's Street north of Sherburn, which the box controls.*

Hull–Scarborough

BEVERLEY

Top, above & below:- *Beverley signal box (formerly Beverley Station) was opened in 1911 with a 36-lever frame. This has subsequently been reduced to 20 levers with Nos. 11–30 still present above the box floor.* All M. Rhodes
Location: *HU17 0HN*
Visibility: *From the crossing on Armstrong Way, which the box controls.*

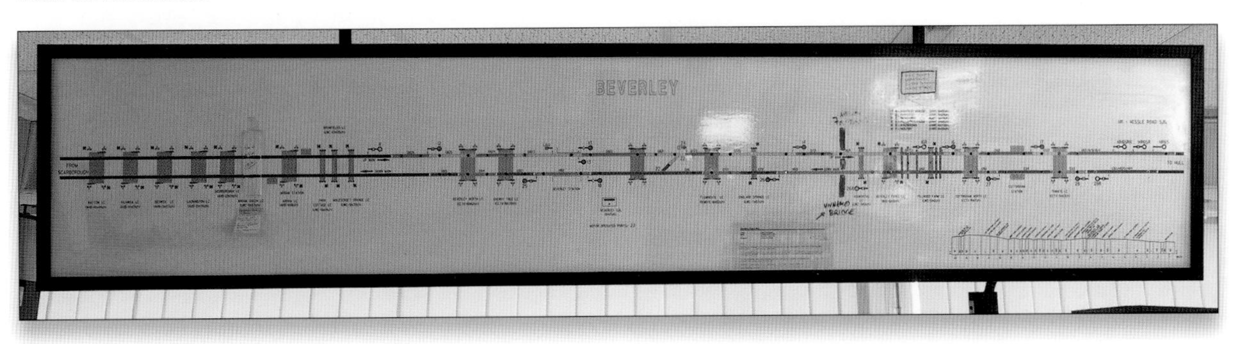

BRIDLINGTON

Top & above:- On 11 November 2015, resident signalman John Robinson has just 17 more working days at Bridlington. Having started on the railway at Wisley aged 15, John had a period away from the railway, until his unbroken 33 years as a signalman, working variously at Speighton, Carnaby, Driffield and then Bridlington (since 2000) signal boxes. The signal box at Bridlington was originally called Bridlington South and opened in 1893. In 1903 a 100-lever frame was installed and this was enlarged to 125 levers in 1912. Then in 1974, the box was rationalised down to its present 65 levers. Both M. Rhodes

Location: *YO16 4NT*

Visibility: *The box is best seen from the Station Road overbridge to the east.*

DRIFFIELD

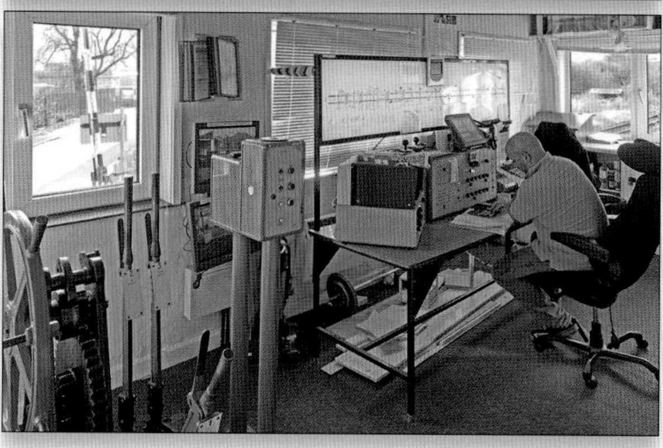

Top & above:- Signalman Phillip Walker fills in the TRB or "Train Record Book" at Driffield in November 2015. The internal view shows the remaining 3-lever frame which controls the mechanical crossing gates here. Built in 1875, the box had a 36-lever frame until 1987 when an IFS panel was installed to control the track between Beverley and Bridlington. Both M. Rhodes

Location: *YO25 6SP*

Visibility: *From the crossing on Skerne Road, which the box controls.*

GRISTHORPE

Left & above:- Opened in 1874, the signal box at Gristhorpe has a 15-lever frame. It is now reduced in size and missing seven of its levers, leaving just 8 levers in the frame. Both M. Rhodes

Location: *YO14 9PD*

Visibility: *From the crossing on an un-named road at this postcode.*

Hull–Selby

BARLBY

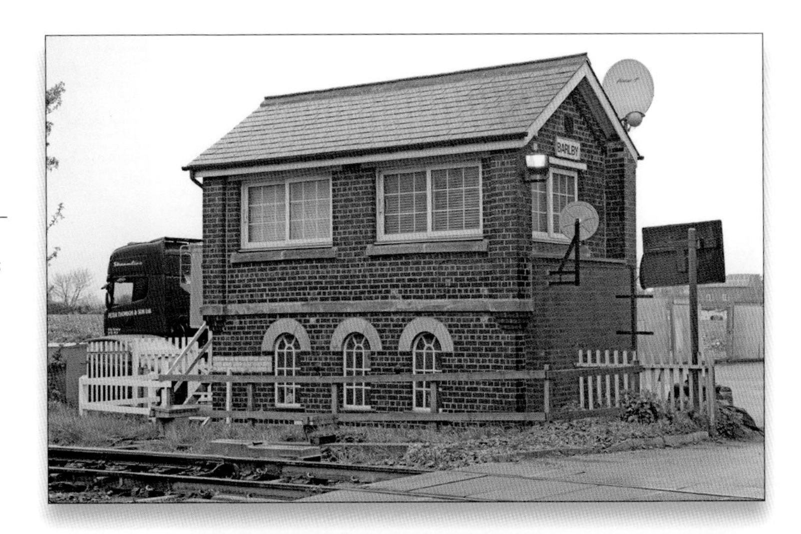

Right:- Opened in 1898, Barlby signal box was fitted with a new mechanical frame in 1932, which is now reduced to 7 levers. An IFS panel was added in 1972. M. Rhodes
Location: *YO8 5AF*
Visibility: *From the crossing on an un-named side road, south off the main Barlby Road.*

CRABLEY CREEK

Right & below:- Crabley Creek signal box is unusual in that the Nichols family who owned the local farmland insisted that there was a manned level crossing across the main line to Hull at the time the railway was built. The current signal box opened in 1891 and has a 14-lever frame, as shown in the internal view of signalman Bogg watching a Hull to Sheffield service pass the box in 2012. Both M. Rhodes
Location: *HU15 1RX*
Visibility: *From the crossing on Crabley Lane, which the box controls.*

GOOLE

Right:- Class 158 No. 158859 passes over the crossing on Boothferry Road past the signal box at Goole. Opened in 1909, the mechanical frame here was replaced by an NX panel in 1975. M. Rhodes
Location: *DN14 5DD*
Visibility: *From the station platform at Goole.*

GOOLE SWING BRIDGE

Above & above right:- *The Goole Swing Bridge and its signal box were given Grade II listing status in 1987. The signal box opened in 1869 and originally acted simply as a control point for the bridge with a simple 57-lever frame. In 1933 the bridge became a block point and a Westinghouse IFS panel was fitted. This was replaced in 2004 by a Henry Williams Domino IFS panel, with the original Westinghouse panel saved by the National Railway Museum. The bridge has suffered at least two serious collisions from passing ships, the most serious of which led to the complete closure of the line for seven months from December 1973. Class 60 No. 60001 is seen passing under the signal box (which was allegedly raised a couple of feet during the 1973 repairs, ready for electrification) with 6J94, a Rotherham to Hull Docks steel train in June 2014.* M. Rhodes & W. Halton

Location: *DN14 7RP*

Visibility: *This is limited but partial views of the bridge are possible from Sandhall Lane.*

HESSLE ROAD

Above & above right:- *Signalman Simon Vickers takes a "line block" at Hessle Road in November 2015. The box here was built in 1962 and fitted with an NX panel. A new NX panel was installed in 2008 on the original 1962 base. This was done to allow up to 12 trains per day along the Hull Docks branch which was refurbished for increased freight traffic.* Both M. Rhodes

Location: *HU4 6QQ*

Visibility: *From the south side of the dual carriageway Hessle Road overbridge.*

HULL PARAGON

Above left & above:- *Resident signalman and well known author, Mick Nicholson, takes a call from the station, at Hull Paragon signal box. Built in 1938, the box replaced two large miniature lever cabins that had controlled the station and was the first major colour light scheme in the country controlled by an OCS panel. During the Second World War, the eastern end of the box took a direct hit, but the robust concrete construction enabled it to keep working throughout the subsequent repairs. In 1984, there was what many call the "emergency resignalling" when Hull Paragon was reduced from 14 to 7 platforms. The original plan had been for control of the station to be handed to Hessle Road panel, but the project was £16,000 short of funds to do this and so a new NX panel was installed in Paragon box and continues to function largely unaltered to this day.* Both M. Rhodes

Location: *HU3 2JF*

Visibility: *In the distance from the station platform or from Park Street overbridge.*

OXMARDYKE

Left & below:- *Oxmardyke crossing box opened in 1901 and had a 16-lever frame installed in 1956. The gate wheel controlling the crossing dates back to 1901.* Both M. Rhodes

Location: *HU15 2UY*

Visibility: *From the crossing on Tongue Lane, which the box controls.*

SELBY SWING BRIDGE

Right- *The swing bridge at Selby was built between 1889 and 1891. In the 1970s the mechanical frame was replaced by two small panels, one to control the hydraulic mechanism of the bridge and the second for signalling of boats on the river. There is a single semaphore signal still in use for shipping. During 2014 the bridge was closed for three months, blocking the Selby to Hull route completely. £14 million of repairs were undertaken by Network Rail which should see the bridge through another 60 years of operation. Class 180 No. 180110 is seen passing over the refurbished bridge in 2014 with a King's Cross to Hull express.* M. Rhodes

Location: *YO8 4NW*

Visibility: *From the north end of the platform at Selby station.*

York–Harrogate

CATTAL

Above left, above & left:- *Cattal signal box opened in 1892 and in 1934 was fitted with a 15-lever frame.* All M. Rhodes

Location: *YO26 8DY*

Visibility: *From the station platform.*

BELMONT

Right:- *The tiny crossing box at Belmont opened in 1914 and has a 5-lever frame. The line between Harrogate and York has several manned level crossings as well as Belmont, at Hammerton Road and Whixley (both green portable buildings) and Hessay (with a ground frame). Class 150 No. 150205 passes Belmont with a York to Leeds service on 30 September 2013.* M. Rhodes

Location: *HG2 7EE*

Visibility: *From the crossing on Forest Lane, which the box controls.*

HAMMERTON

Above:- The signal box at Hammerton is unique in that the mechanical frame is in a cupboard on the station platform whilst the block token instruments are in the station office. With demolition of the original signal box in 1972, this unusual situation of a signal box in a lockable cupboard was introduced. The box has 10 levers as shown in our view taken in April 2012. M. Rhodes
Location: *YO26 8DN*
Visibility: *From the station platform.*

HARROGATE

Above:- Built in 1947, Harrogate signal box originally contained a 65-lever frame. In 2019 this is reduced to 45 levers with Nos. 21–65 still present above the box floor. In 2012 a small panel was added to the box to control much of the line to Leeds as the boxes at Rigton and Horsforth were closed. M. Rhodes
Location: *HG1 1AE*
Visibility: *From the end of the station platform.*

KNARESBOROUGH

Above:- Dating from when the Block Telegraph was first installed, Knaresborough SB is one of the oldest operational survivors on Network Rail, having opened in 1873. Externally the SB is aesthetically very pleasing and blends in well with the surrounding buildings. However, the inside is very cramped. Prominent in our view is the instrument for the AB section to Starbeck. In this direction all signals are semaphores. In contrast, the signals towards York were replaced by colour lights when the section to Cattal was singled in December 1973. The lever for No. 10 signal was shortened to remind the signalmen no physical effort is required to operate the colour light signal. D. Allen
Location: *HG5 9AA*
Visibility: *From the station platform*

MARSTON MOOR

Above right:- The signal box at Marston Moor was opened in 1910 with a 16-lever frame. It was reduced in importance in 1972 when the line between Hammerton and Poppleton was singled; it was downgraded to become a crossing box and no longer a block post. M. Rhodes
Location: *YO26 8JL*
Visibility: *From the crossing on Marston Lane, which the box controls.*

POPPLETON

Above:- The NER signal box at Poppleton dates back to the 1870s, but is little more than a glorified garden shed. An 11-lever frame was installed in 1941 and in 2007 a "domestic extension" provided a toilet to you and I! In 2011 Class 142 No. 142019 departs for Harrogate and Leeds as my father waits patiently on the platform for me to get my photograph. M. Rhodes
Location: *YO26 6QA*
Visibility: *From the station platform.*

STARBECK

Above:- A definitive opening date for the box at Starbeck isn't known, but it seem likely that it was around the turn of the 20th century. Originally the box had a 51-lever frame but this was drastically reduced in size in 1962 when the through route to Northallerton closed and just levers 2–27 survive today. Here in 1988, one of the first production Leyland railbuses approaches with a York to Leeds service. M. Rhodes
Location: *HG2 7JD*
Visibility: *From the station platform.*

South & West Yorkshire

BATLEY CROSSING

Left:- The crossing box at Batley dates back to 1878 and was originally called "Lady Anne's Crossing". Indeed, it wasn't even a block post until 1952. In 1966 the mechanical lever frame was replaced by an IFS panel. M. Rhodes
Location: *WF14 0QB*
Visibility: *From the foot crossing on Howley Street, which the box controls.*

BEIGHTON STATION

Right:- Opened in 1908, the box at Beighton had a 49-lever frame installed in 1962. This view, taken in 1992, shows Class 09 No. 09013, which was the permanent way yard pilot, partially hidden behind the box toilet. The yards here are long gone and replaced by woodland; most of the levers in the box are now white or out of use. M. Rhodes
Location: *S20 1AH*
Visibility: *From the crossing on Rotherham Road, which the box controls.*

GASCOIGNE WOOD

Right:- The 1908-vintage North Eastern Railway box at Gascoigne Wood had its lever frame replaced (along with that at Milford) in 1982 when extensive remodelling of the area was undertaken to provide new sidings for the Selby drift mine. M. Rhodes
Location: *LS25 5DL*
Visibility: *The box is almost impossible to see from a public place and lies down Common Lane on railway land.*

HORBURY JUNCTION

Left:- Opened in 1927, the signal box at Horbury Junction has a 65-lever frame. Here, back in 1985, Class 08 No. 08773 passes the box with a Healey Mills to Horbury wagon works trip freight. M. Rhodes
Location: *WF4 5DZ*
Visibility: *From Green Lane partial views are possible; this view is from the hard shoulder of the M1.*

KIVETON PARK

Right- Kiveton Park signal box was opened in 1916 by the Great Central Railway and had a 25-lever frame. This was replaced in 1980 by an IFS panel. M. Rhodes
Location: *S26 6NQ*
Visibility: *From the station platform.*

MILFORD

Left:- On 8 October 2012, Class 66 No. 66711 passes Milford signal box with 6H90, a Tyne Dock to Drax coal train. The box opened in 1958 and had its mechanical frame removed in 1982 when an NX panel was installed. M. Rhodes
Location: *LS25 5PP*
Visibility: *In the distance from Lumby Lane overbridge to the south.*

MALTBY COLLIERY SOUTH

Above, above right & right:- Back in 1986, Class 20 Nos. 20165 & 20150 are seen shunting wagons to form a train, before passing Maltby Colliery South signal box with 6Z29, a train of export coal from Maltby Colliery to Garston Docks. Ten years later in 1996, the signalman hides from view in the internal shot which shows the 36-lever frame, installed in 1912 - the year the box opened. Also visible above the frame, beyond the signal box diagram, is the IFS panel installed in 1984 to control the lines around Firbeck Junction. All M. Rhodes

Location: S66 8PE

Visibility: *Partial views possible from Scotch Spring Lane where it passes under the railway.*

PRINCE OF WALES COLLIERY

Left:- On 20 June 1986, Class 56 No. 56004 winds out of Prince of Wales Colliery with an MGR coal train to Drax Power Station. The box opened in 1912 and had a 36-lever frame at this time, as well as a 1968-installed IFS panel. In 1996 a further panel was installed leading to the removal of the mechanical frame. M. Rhodes

Location: WF8 1HX

Visibility: *From Skinner Lane crossing, which the box controls.*

SHIREOAKS STATION

Left:- The signal box at Shireoaks station has been almost permanently boarded up since 1997. It was built in 1874 and originally had 29 levers, reducing to 25 in 1950. Then, in 1979, these were removed and an IFS panel installed as well as an automated pedestal for the crossing barriers. M. Rhodes

Location: *S81 8LW*

Visibility: *From the station platform.*

WOODHOUSE JUNCTION

Above & above right:- In March 1992, Class 58 No. 58043 has just run round its train, the 6T30 Bolsover Coalite Plant to Shirebrook freight. The Great Central Railway signal box at Woodhouse was opened in 1926 and originally called Woodhouse East Junction. It contains an 84-lever frame, but closure of the sidings here and loss of freight traffic means most are now out of use. Both M. Rhodes

Location: *S13 7RP*

Visibility: *Partial rear views possible from Junction Road.*

The Midlands

The Midlands covers a broad area which, once completely resignalled, will come under the control of the new ROCs at York, Derby, and Rugby (assuming the West Midlands Signalling Centre at Saltley is eventually merged into Rugby). The closures predicted in the 2010 Network Rail plan ran roughly to schedule until 2013 but then, as in other areas, delays crept in, such that the Banbury boxes didn't close until 2016. In contrast other closures, such as that at Oddingley, were brought forward so that the crossing box here closed in 2016.

In the West Midlands, one of the two remaining major centres to be controlled by manual signalling in Worcester is down to remain unmodernised until 2048, which sounds good news for the historian and photographer alike. It is, however, difficult to believe such predictions as Network Rail has proven inaccurate in many of its short-term predictions, let alone looking two decades in advance. The author is reminded of a conversation with the resident signalman at Rauceby in Lincolnshire who recounted how when he had taken his job, three decades earlier, it had been on the understanding that the box was to close and be merged with Sleaford West and his was a one year long temporary post. Thirty years later he took great pleasure to stand in the sun on the box steps at Rauceby and contemplate his imminent retirement after an enjoyable career as the resident there for thirty years!

In the East Midlands where the Derby ROC will eventually control the area, the mechanical boxes along two major lines have survived beyond their predicted demise. Both Peterborough to Leicester and Derby to Stoke are yet to have new dates for resignalling. Again, there have also been closures earlier than expected with the boxes at Clipstone and Thoresby Colliery closing in 2016. Here closure was more related to the demise of the deep mine at Thoresby, rendering these two boxes surplus to requirement. Similarly the box at Tinsley Yard closed nearly two decades earlier than predicted in 2010.

Signal Boxes Scheduled to Close per Network Rail 2010 Masterplan

Saltley ROC (NB it is anticipated that this ROC will be merged into the Rugby ROC in 2018)	
Year	**Boxes to be transferred**
2012	Blakedown, Hartlebury, Kidderminster Jn, Kingswinford, Stourbridge Junction, Madeley Junction, Saltley PSB
2013	Bescot down tower, Bloxwich, Brereton Sidings, Hednesford, Walsall PSB
2014	Banbury North, Banbury South, Leamington Spa PSB, Wolverhampton PSB
2015	Aston SCC, Lichfield Trent Valley, Gloucester PSB
2016	Claydon LNE Junction, Saltley PSB (second part), Alrewas, Fine Lane, Rodige
2017	Birmingham New Street PSB
Should merger into the Rugby ROC take place in 2018 then the boxes below would be added to the Rugby ROC.	
2021	Oddingley
2025	Marylebone IECC
2047	Kingsbury shunt frame & Tyseley No. 1, Norton Junction
2048	Droitwich Spa, Henwick, Malvern Wells, Newland East, Worcester Shrub Hill Worcester Tunnel Junction
Rugby ROC	
2015	Rugby SCC, Wembley Mainline SCC, Wembley yard, Stafford No. 4, Stafford No. 5, Macclesfield
2018	Stoke on Trent
2019	Basford Hall Junction, Crewe Sorting Sidings North, Gresty Lane

Year	Boxes to be transferred
2021	Crewe SC, Winsford Junction
2030	Willesden Carriage Sheds Middle, North & South boxes
2032	Marston Vale SCC
2055	Beeston Castle & Tarporley, Crewe Coal Yard, Crewe Steel Works, Salop Goods Junction
Derby ROC	
2011	Croft, Kirkby Summit, Trent PSB, Leicester PSB
2013	Netherfield Junction, Rectory Junction, Sneinton GB
2014	Bingham, Bottesford West Junction, Fiskerton Station, Lowdham, Staythorpe Crossing
2015	Manton Junction, Fiskerton Junction, Rolleston Station
2016	Derby PSB, Caverswall, Eggington Junction, Foley Crossing, Hilton GC, Scropton, Sudbury, Tutbury Crossing, Uttoxeter
2017	Ashwell, Frisby, Ketton, Langham Junction, Melton Station, Oakham Crossing, Uffington, Whissendine, Wyfordby GC, Wymondham GC
2018	Sheffield PSB
2021	Bardon Hill, Mantle Lane, Moira West Junction
2022	Totley Tunnel East
2026	Kiveton Park, Worksop (part of)
2027	Clipstone, Elmton & Cresswell, Maltby Colliery, Norwood, Shirebrook Junction, Thoresby Colliery, Tinsley Yard

The East Midlands

ALREWAS

Above:- Alrewas signal box was built in 1899 by the Midland Railway and had its mechanical lever frame replaced by an IFS panel in 1982. The box was damaged by fire in 2005, hence the need for the new IFS panel which is still in use today. M. Rhodes
Location: *DE13 7BD*
Visibility: *From the level crossing on Croxall Road, which the box controls.*

ELMTON & CRESSWELL

Above:- The signal box here was opened in 1946 and installed with a 48-lever mechanical frame which had been built earlier, in 1938. This view, taken in 2009, shows Class 153 No. 153381 heading north past the box with a Nottingham to Worksop passenger service. Between the train and the signal box, the trackbed of the former branch line to Seymour Junction can clearly be seen. M. Rhodes
Location: *S80 4HB*
Visibility: *Best seen from the north end of the station at Elmton & Cresswell.*

BARDON HILL

Left:- In a snowy December 1981, a Class 56 awaits departure from Bardon Hill with 6V76, a Cliffe Quarry to Hayes and Harlington stone train. The signal box here was built in 1899 and had its lever frame replaced by an IFS panel in 1979. M. Rhodes
Location: *LE67 1TH*
Visibility: *From the crossing on Grange Road, which the box controls.*

LICHFIELD TRENT VALLEY JUNCTION

Right:- Opened in 1897, the signal box at Lichfield Trent Valley Junction was fitted with a 45-lever frame. Back in 1982 when this picture was taken, there was still a manual gated crossing on the Burton Old Road. In 2019, the road crossing has been replaced by a foot crossing and the wooden crossing gates are long gone. M. Rhodes
Location: *WS13 8LF*
Visibility: *From the foot crossing that the box controls.*

MANTLE LANE

Above:- *The 28-lever Midland frame is clearly visible in this view of Mantle Lane signal box taken in 1981. Two members of a permanent way gang cross to the loco holding sidings at Coalville. The box was modernised in 1979 by the addition of an IFS panel to control the west end of the yards at Coalville and then again in 1985 when a second IFS panel was added to control Coalville level crossing and Crossfields Farm sidings.* M. Rhodes
Location: *LE67 3DW*
Visibility: *From the level crossing on Mantle Lane, which the box controls.*

SHIREBROOK JUNCTION

Above:- *Class 58 No. 58033 passes Shirebrook Junction light engine, on its way back to base at Shirebrook depot. The signal box opened in 1899 and then in 1928 was extended northwards with an extra three window panes of new build. At this stage a 40-lever frame was installed. The steep branch to the left connects the W H Davies wagon works to the network, whilst the branch to the right heads off to Clipstone and Thoresby Colliery.* M. Rhodes
Location: *NG20 8TA*
Visibility: *Looking north from the Station Road overbridge, from where this image is taken.*

MOIRA WEST JUNCTION

Below:- *On 28 June 1983, Class 56 No. 56083 climbs up the incline caused as a result of mining subsidence at Swadlincote with 6T23, an empty MGR coal working from Drakelow Power Station to Rawdon Colliery. The box at Moira, built in 1896, had its mechanical frame removed by the time of this photograph and replaced by a 1986-vintage NX panel.* M. Rhodes
Location: *DE12 6ND*
Visibility: *Looking east from the road overbridge on Spring Cottage Road.*

WORKSOP EAST

Above:- *Worksop East signal box was opened by the Manchester, Sheffield & Lincolnshire Railway in 1880 and had a 22-lever frame, expanded to 23 levers in 1933 and then reduced to 20 levers in 1975. The disused frame has been retained in the box, even though since 1998 it has no longer been a block post and only serves as a gate box. Class 66 No. 66037 passes with an empty coal train from Cottam Power Station to the Humber Import Terminal at Immingham on 20 June 2014.* M. Rhodes
Location: *S80 1PS*
Visibility: *From Carlton Road crossing, which the box controls.*

The Joint Line & Lincolnshire

ALLINGTON

Right:- Perhaps not a heritage structure, but an example of the more sympathetic approach Railtrack and then Network Rail have sometimes taken when building new signal boxes, the structure at Allington is a 2005 build by Network Rail to the NR gabled design. It replaced the boxes at Allington Junction and Barkston East in 2005 and contains an NX panel. M. Rhodes
Location: *NG32 2EJ*
Visibility: *From the Allington Road crossing, which the box controls.*

ANCASTER

Left, below left & below:- Opened in 1873 the box at Ancaster had a 30-lever frame installed in 1887 which survives to this day. As the interior view shows, a new track diagram was installed in the 21st century but the frame remains, albeit with many white levers. All M. Rhodes
Location: *NG32 3QU*
Visibility: *From the west end of the station platforms.*

BARROW ROAD CROSSING

Above & right:- Signalman "Robbie" poses with the brown gate lever at Barrow Road Crossing in July 2012. Amazingly this was reclassified as a ground frame back in 1981 when the tracks to New Holland Pier were closed. Opened in 1885, the box originally had a 28-lever frame, which was reduced to 8 levers in 1981. The manual crossing gates remain on the busy Lincoln Castle Way crossing but fortunately for the road traffic, trains are only every two hours these days. Both M. Rhodes
Location: *DN19 7RT*
Visibility: *From the road crossing that the box controls.*

BATHLEY LANE

Left:- In 2011, Class 180 No. 180111 passes Bathley Lane, north of Newark, with a Hull to Kings Cross express. The signal box opened in 1930 with a 20-lever frame, which was replaced by an IFS panel in 1976. It was removed as a block post in 1998 and the crossing came under the control of Carlton Grove Road signal box using CCTV. The box is retained to control the crossing in emergencies. M. Rhodes
Location: *NG23 6HR*
Visibility: *From Bathley Lane level crossing.*

BECKINGHAM

Above (3 images):- Beckingham signal box dates back to 1876 and when it opened it contained a 32-lever mechanical frame. This was enlarged to 40 levers in 1940 and then replaced by an NX panel in 1977, which is illustrated in our interior view. Class 66 No. 66013 is seen passing the box on 1 May 2013 with 6D80, an empty fuel oil train from Neville Hill depot to Lindsey Oil Refinery. All M. Rhodes

Location: *DN10 4PX*

Visibility: *From the Old Trent Road level crossing, which the box controls.*

BELLWATER JUNCTION

Top & above:- One of the UK's more isolated signal boxes is at Bellwater Junction, where over 50 years ago the Great Northern line direct to Lincoln used to diverge from the main Skegness to Boston railway. Originally there had been a small 4-lever ground frame installed outside in 1904, but this was replaced by the current structure in 1913 and a larger 25-lever frame installed. Both M. Rhodes

Location: *PE22 8LH*

Visibility: *From Bellwater Drain Bank crossing, which the box controls.*

BRIGG

Above & right:- Originally known as Brigg East and opened in 1885, the signal box became simply Brigg in 1923. The box contains a 30-lever frame and in 2019 is often only manned for one shift per day. Back in November 2015, Class 66 No. 66705 is seen passing with loaded coal from Imingham Docks to Cottam Power Station. Both M. Rhodes

Location: *DN20 9EZ*

Visibility: *From Bigby High Road crossing, which the box controls.*

FINNINGLEY

Right:- Dating back to 1877, the signal box at Finningley was downgraded to a crossing box in 1979. Originally fitted with a 36-lever frame, the box was modernised with installation of an IFS panel in 1977. Class 66 No. 66703 is seen passing the box in August 2012 with 4R18, an empty coal train from Doncaster to Immingham Docks. M. Rhodes

Location: *DN9 3QD*

Visibility: *From Station Road crossing, which the box controls.*

GAINSBOROUGH CENTRAL

Below & below right:- Class 66 No. 66068 passes Gainsborough Central signal box in February 2013. Traffic past the heavily "fortified" box was increased at the time because of the Hatfield land slip between Scunthorpe and Doncaster. The box opened in 1885 and was originally called Gainsborough West, renamed Central in 1923. It still contains the original 1885, 26-lever frame and owes the steel bars on the windows to unwelcome visits from local youths who congregate on Gainsborough Central station of an evening. Both M. Rhodes

Location: *DN21 2AU*

Visibility: *From the south end of the platform at Gainsborough Central.*

GAINSBOROUGH TRENT JUNCTION

Right & below:- The interior view of Gainsborough Trent Junction signal box shows how not to pull a signal lever! The box contains several challenging pulls including No. 1 distant which is a 1647 yard pull with the signal located almost in Central station. The idiot pulling No. 8 distant (842 yards) is the author, carefully supervised and eventually successful! The signal box at Trent Junction is a relatively modern structure, built in 1964 and replacing older boxes at the location dating back to 1913 and 1880. The 40-lever frame in use today was relocated from the 1913 signal box. The external view shows Class 66 No. 66105 (with 66144 at the rear) with 6D74, a train of continuous welded rails from Doncaster to Scunthorpe (via a run round at Wrawby Junction). M. Rhodes & D. Whyles

Location: *DN21 1LG*

Visibility: *This is poor as the box is high above Carr Lane on an embankment, but can be partially viewed from this location.*

GODNOW BRIDGE

Right:- Class 66 No. 66184 passes Godnow Bridge signal box and crossing with coal empties from Drax to Immingham Docks in May 2012. The brick structure here was built in 2000 and contains the IFS panel from the old signal box. The original box at this location opened in 1886 and had a 10-lever frame, replaced by an IFS panel in 1981. M. Rhodes

Location: *DN17 4BN*

Visibility: *From Godnow Road crossing, which the box controls.*

GOXHILL

Left & above:- The classic Great Central designed box at Goxhill opened in 1910 and replaced an older structure dating back to 1884. The 36-lever frame is seen being inspected by the Local Operations Manager at the time (John Stocks) and Freight Shift Controller, James Skoyles. The wrought iron gate wheel is prominent in the view. Both M.Rhodes

Location: *DN19 7HL*

Visibility: *From Howe Lane level crossing, which the box controls.*

GREAT COATES NO. 1

Left & above- *Named simply Great Coates No. 1 in 2019 and often switched out of use, the signal box here was one of two which controlled the extensive sidings at West Marsh in Grimsby. Back in 1990, Class 08 No. 08388 is the yard pilot and the box is still called "Great Coates Sidings No. 1". No. 1 & No. 2 boxes opened in 1909 with 23 and 70 levers respectively, but No. 2 box, the larger of the two closed in 1966. Both M. Rhodes*

Location: *DN31 2UA*

Visibility: *Best viewed over the parapet of the Gilbey Road overbridge (seen in the black and white image).*

GROVE ROAD

Left- *The original 1871 signal box was replaced in 1887 by the structure in use today. The 20-lever frame was replaced by an IFS panel in 1976 and then in 1997 regular staffing of the box ceased, with control ceded to a CCTV monitor in nearby Ranskill box. M. Rhodes*

Location: *DN22 0RW*

Visibility: *From the level crossing at Grove Road.*

HECKINGTON

Right- *Class 47 No. 47739 passes Heckington station with a steel train from Boston Docks to Washwood Heath Yard. The signal box at Heckington opened in 1876 and contains an 18-lever frame installed second hand in 1925 after previous use in East Lincoln Junction box. M. Rhodes*

Location: *NG34 9GL*

Visibility: *From the level crossing on the B1394, Hale Road, which it controls.*

HOLTON-LE-MOOR

Above & above right:- Back in 2012, the signalman is at repose with his pipe in Holton-le-Moor signal box. The IFS panel shown in this view was installed in 1989, replacing the original 1890-vintage 23-lever frame. Class 60 No. 60011 is seen passing the box in 2012 with 6E54, the empty oil tanks from Kingsbury to the Humber Oil Refinery in Immingham. Both M. Rhodes
Location: *LN7 6AH*
Visibility: *From the busy level crossing on the A46, which the box controls.*

HUBBERTS BRIDGE

Right:- The unusual construction of the signal box at Hubberts Bridge is due to the small footprint available between the running lines and the adjacent A1121. The box was built in 1961, replacing an older 1879-vintage structure. It contains a 25-lever frame. Class 47 No. 47727 is seen passing on 24 February 2012 with a Washwood Heath to Boston Docks steel train. M. Rhodes
Location: *PE30 3QR*
Visibility: *From Hubberts Bridge Road crossing, which the box controls.*

IMMINGHAM EAST

Left:- The original Great Central signal box at Immingham East closed in 2012 and was replaced by a portable building half a mile to the east and no longer on dock land. This image is included because although the structure is a featureless temporary structure and there are no mechanical signals, the original 1912 block token instrument controlling access to the Immingham Light Railway has survived and is still in use today! M. Rhodes
Location: *DN40 1QY*
Visibility: *The box is down an unmade road to the south off Queens Road but is not visible from any public place.*

IMMINGHAM RECEPTION SIDINGS

IMMINGHAM WEST JUNCTION

Top & above:- Like the other signal boxes within the docks complex at Immingham, Immingham West Junction opened in 1912 and originally had a 48-lever mechanical frame. This was replaced with an IFS panel in 1972 when tracks were remodelled for the new iron ore import terminal. The current IFS panel dates from 2006 when track alterations were made for connections to the new Humber Coal Import Terminal, or HIT as it is known. Lying on the East Coast at a strategic location and within reach of German bombers, the box had a blast wall added in 1940, which is very obvious in our external view. Both M. Rhodes

Location: *DN40 2LZ*

Visibility: *The box is deep in dock property and not visible from a public place. It can be well seen from the overbridge on Humber Road in the western part of the docks.*

Above left, above middle & left:- Opened in 1912 when the docks were built by the Great Central Railway, Immingham Reception Sidings is the largest signal box in the docks complex. Originally fitted with a 92-lever electro-pneumatic miniature lever frame, it was extended with the addition of an NX panel controlling access to the Lindsey Oil Refinery in 1970 and then again with the addition of an IFS panel in 1970 for the Humber Road Junction and coal terminals. The 1967 NX panel was subsequently replaced and upgraded in 1980 to control access to both Lindsey and Humber oil refineries. Our first internal view shows long term resident signalman, Roy Kaminskie, on a sweltering day in July 2012 when the mercury nudged 32 degrees. Back in 2006, two coal trains are seen awaiting departure behind Class 66 Nos. 66033 and 66556, whilst two Class 08 pilot locomotives (since dispensed with) nestle behind the box. All M. Rhodes

Location: *DN40 2QN*

Visibility: *This is not possible from a public place but access to the box is a left turn off the eastbound A1173 into the docks area.*

KIRTON LIME SIDINGS

Left & below left:- The remarkable tall and narrow structure at Kirton Lime Sidings was built in 1886 and was constructed this way to allow the signalman views to the north and south. It has a 15-lever frame dating back to the date of opening. Both M. Rhodes

Location: *DN21 4JH*

Visibility: *From the Gainsthorpe Road West overbridge to the north-east of the box.*

LANGWORTH

Top & above:- All is not well at Langworth signal box in May 2012 as the buckets to collect leaks from the roof attest! Opened in 1890 with a 20-lever frame, the box was refitted with an IFS panel in 1990. Both M. Rhodes

Location: *LN3 5BB*

Visibility: *From Station Road crossing, which the box controls.*

MEDGE HALL

Above:- In September 2012 Class 66 No. 66551 passes Medge Hall signal box with a Bredbury to Roxby domestic waste train. The box at Medge Hall opened in 1886 with 11 levers. It gradually expanded until in 1955 the frame contained 14 levers. The box was downgraded to a ground frame in 1972 with the concomitant reduction in frame size to 7 levers. M. Rhodes

Location: *DN8 5SP*

Visibility: *From the crossing on Crook O'Moor Road, which the box controls.*

NORTHORPE

Left & above:- In 2019, the 1886-vintage, Manchester, Sheffield and Lincolnshire Railway designed box at Northorpe sees little traffic. Back in 2012, Class 66 No. 66109 passes with an Immingham to West Burton Power Station coal train. The box still contains the original 17-lever frame and a mechanical wheel to control the crossing gates. Both M. Rhodes

Location: *DN21 4AB*

Visibility: *From the crossing on the B1205, which the box controls.*

OXMARSH CROSSING

Left- The signal box at Oxmarsh Crossing was built in 1960 and contains a 30-lever frame inherited from the original 1885 construction on this site. The frame size seems excessive for a crossing box on such an infrequently used branch line, but reflects the more complex trackwork here when the freight sidings to New Holland Timber Dock were in use. M. Rhodes

Location: *DN19 7RE*

Visibility: *From Oxmarsh Lane crossing, which the box controls.*

PYEWIPE ROAD

Above, right & below right:- Back in 1996, Class 60 No. 60038 is seen passing Pyewipe Road signal box with a waste train from the Tioxide sidings to Roxby, one of few services to use the Immingham Light Railway. There was a signal box at this location between 1910 and 1948 but the current structure, with its 20-lever frame dates from 1958 and is often unmanned in 2019 as there is no regular traffic along the line here. All M. Rhodes

Location: *DN31 2SY*

Visibility: *Given the name of the box it is odd that it is visible from the level crossing on Gilbey Road, which it controls.*

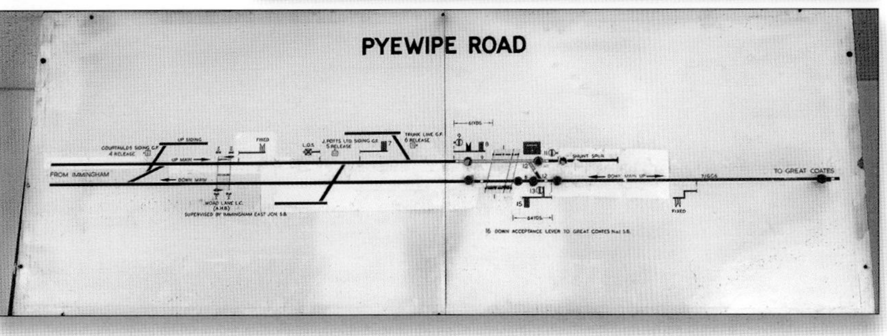

RANSKILL

Above:- Opened in 1875 and replacing an earlier construction dating from 1864, the box here contained a 50-lever frame at its largest extent in 1944. In 1975 this was replaced by an NX panel and a new NX panel was installed in 1997 when it took over control of Grove Road crossing. It was downgraded from a signal box or block post in 1980 when the power box opened in Doncaster, but still has the facility to control the East Coast Main Line here, should there be a failure in the Doncaster box. D. Allen

Location: *DN22 8LD*

Visibility: *From Station Road crossing, which it controls.*

RAUCEBY

Above:- During my visit in 2011, Sleaford relief signalman, Peter, took great delight in telling me the tale of his employment, signing on as a signalman at Rauceby 25 years earlier amidst dire warnings that the box only had one or two years to go until it would close and the crossing here become controlled by CCTV from Sleaford West signal box! As Class 47 No. 47739 passed with a Washwood Heath to Boston Docks steel train, he reflected that one shouldn't always believe closure plans! Rauceby signal box was opened in 1880 with a 20-lever frame which was reduced to just 5 levers in 1975 when colour lights were introduced, controlled by an IFS panel in the box. M. Rhodes

Location: *NG34 8PT*

Visibility: *From Willoughby Road crossing, which the box controls*

SIBSEY

Above & right:- The signal box at Sibsey opened in 1888 with a 15-lever frame which was expanded to 25 levers in 1907. In 1989 an IFS panel replaced the mechanical frame and the semaphore signals were replaced with colour light signals. Both M. Rhodes

Location: *PE22 0SB*

Visibility: *From the B1184, Station Road crossing, which the box controls.*

SKEGNESS

Above:- The current structure dates from 1882, although there are records suggesting a signal box existed here as early as 1870. The original box had a 50-lever frame but the popularity of the resort for holidays led to expansion in 1900 and a new 80-lever frame. Back in 1990, the station contained Class 150 No. 150105 and Class 114 "Derby Heavyweight" unit 53006 & 54010. M. Rhodes

Location: *PE25 3QN*

Visibility: *From the end of the station platform.*

SLEAFORD EAST

Top & above:- *Signalman Ray Hilliard explains about the new IFS panel installed just months earlier in Sleaford East box. Built in 1882, the box originally contained a 50-lever frame, 18 levers from which can still be seen behind the VDU on the new desk. Another feature not shown in our interior view was the mouse trap, essential because the warmth of the signal box had attracted some unwelcome guests!* *Both M. Rhodes*
Location: *NG34 8PF*
Visibility: *Both from the station platform and also the B1517 crossing, which the box controls.*

SLEAFORD WEST

Top & above:- *The semaphore signals at Sleaford West were replaced by colour light posts in 2011, just 18 months before our external view of a Skegness to Nottingham train was taken. The signal box here opened in 1882 with a 57-lever frame which was subsequently reduced to 46 levers as the interior view shows.* *Both M. Rhodes*
Location: *NG34 7UW*
Visibility: *From King Edward Street crossing, which the box controls with a manual gate wheel.*

SWINDERBY

Right:- *Class 153 No.153386 passes Swinderby signal box in 2011. The box here is an island of mechanical signalling, left stranded by the Lincolnshire resignalling of 2008 and the subsequent resignalling between Nottingham and Newark in 2016. The box was built in 1901 and has a 16-lever mechanical frame.* *M. Rhodes*
Location: *NG6 9HY*
Visibility: *From the Station Road level crossing, which the box controls.*

THORPE CULVERT

Left:- The original Thorpe Culvert signal box was opened in 1899 with a 22-lever frame, but had to be replaced by this Network Rail gabled brick structure containing an IFS panel in 2003, due to subsidence. M. Rhodes
Location: PE24 4NL
Visibility: *From Station Road crossing, which the box controls.*

THRUMPTON CROSSING

Above:- Officially called Thrumpton Road Crossing but with the name board "Retford Thrumpton", the box here opened in 1889 and originally contained a 33-lever frame. This was expanded to 54 levers in 1927 and then in 1965 the box was completely modernised with an NX panel as part of the opening of the power stations at Cottam and West Burton. In 2013 its control area was expanded as it took over West Burton Power Station where the signal box with its IFS panel closed. Back in 2010, Class 66 No. 66086 is seen passing with a Thoresby Colliery (sadly now closed) to Cottam Power Station coal train. M. Rhodes
Location: DN22 7HH
Visibility: *From Thrumpton Lane crossing, which the box controls.*

WEST STREET JUNCTION (BOSTON)

Above:- Dating back to 1874, West Street Junction signal box was extended from 50 to 60 levers in 1927. Belated rationalisation, after the direct route to Grimsby closed in 1971, was undertaken in 1974 with the frame reduced to its current 36 levers. Back in 1990, Class 150 No. 150105 heads west past the box with a Skegness to Nottingham service. M. Rhodes
Location: PE21 8EH
Visibility: *From Sleaford Road crossing, which the box controls.*

WAINFLEET

Top & above:- Wainfleet signal box opened in 1899 and our 2012 external view suggests it needed a bit of TLC at that stage. It was fitted with a 25-lever mechanical frame, just 5 levers from which were still in use in 2012. Both M. Rhodes
Location: PE24 4LQ
Visibility: *From High Street crossing, which the box controls.*

WICKENBY

Above & above right:- *Back in 2012, the signalman explains the workings of the 1990-installed IFS panel at Wickenby to me. The box here opened in 1890 and originally had a 20-lever mechanical frame. A Class 66 is seen passing the box with 6E82, a train of empty oil tanks from Rectory Junction to Lindsey Oil Refinery in January 2012. Both M. Rhodes*
Location: *LN3 5AW*
Visibility: *From Station Road crossing, which the box controls.*

Derby–Stoke

CAVERSWALL

Top & above:- *Caverswall signal box was built in 1942 and fitted with a 35-lever frame . It controls the now somewhat overgrown passing loops, just north-west of Blythe Bridge station. Our internal view shows signalman Russell Ashmore at work in June 2017. Both I. Stewart*
Location: *ST3 6HL*
Visibility: *From Caverswall Lane crossing, which the box controls.*

EGGINGTON JUNCTION

Top & above:- *Eggington Junction signal box dates back to 1877 when it was built by the North Staffordshire Railway. It originally contained a 37-lever frame but this was reduced to 14 levers some time after the direct route to Derby Friargate closed and the junction for which it is named disappeared. Signalman Phil Samson fills in the TRB in June 2017. Both I. Stewart*
Location: *DE65 6GU*
Visibility: *The box is not visible from a public place and is accessed down a lane off the A5132, Eggington Road.*

FOLEY CROSSING

Above, above right & right:- *Back in 1990, Class 37 No. 37510 is seen passing Foley Crossing on the outskirts of Stoke-on-Trent with 6E09, the 1552 Etruria to Tees Yard steel train. The box here was built in 1889 and has a 37-lever frame. Signalman Chris Wood watches a Class 153 single car unit pass the box with a Crewe to Derby train in June 2017. N. Allsop (2) and I. Stewart*
Location: *ST4 3FB*
Visibility: *From the foot crossing at the end of Sidings Place.*

SCROPTON CROSSING

Left:- *Scropton Crossing box was built in 1880 and contains a 22-lever frame. In 2009 it was refurbished with uPVC windows which quite realistically mimic the old sliding timber windows as this image shows. M. Rhodes*
Location: *DE65 5PN*
Visibility: *From the crossing on an unamed side road off Leathersley Lane, which the box controls.*

SUDBURY

Right:- *Dating from 1885, Sudbury signal box contains a 25-lever McKenzie & Holland mechanical frame. M. Rhodes*
Location: *DE6 5GX*
Visibility: *From the level crossing on the A515, which the box controls.*

TUTBURY CROSSING

Above:- Like Scropton Crossing, Tutbury Crossing signal box was refurbished in 2009. Sadly the new windows for this 1872 building were nowhere near as sympathetic as those fitted at Scropton. The box originally had a 10-lever frame which is now reduced to 9 levers. M. Rhodes
Location: *DE65 5DW*
Visibility: *From the level crossing on the A511, which the box controls.*

UTTOXETER

Above:- There is considerable debate as to which was the last mechanical signal box to be built in the UK, but one definite contender is Uttoxeter, having been opened in January 1981. A second contender is Porth, which also opened in 1981, but maybe a couple of months later? The 40-lever frame at Uttoxeter (which had to be reduced in size) and the wooden upper half of the box came from Carlton Road Junction signal box. The box is seen here in 2012 with Class 153 No. 153308 passing with a Crewe to Derby service. M. Rhodes
Location: *ST14 8JB*
Visibility: *From Charlton Lane level crossing, which the box controls.*

Worcester Area

ASCOTT-UNDER-WYCHWOOD

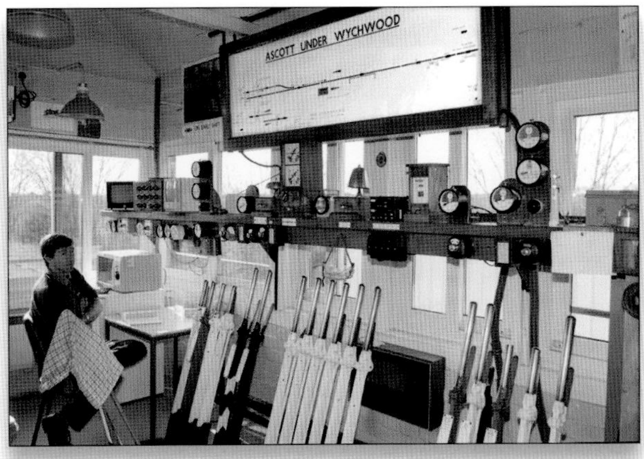

Above & above right:- The signal box at Ascott-under-Wychwood was built in 1883 and fitted with a 25-lever frame. Class 166 No. 166209 is seen passing the box in 2002 with a Worcester to Paddington service. The interior view confirms the lever frame has 7 empty slots since simplification of the trackwork here in the early 1970s. Both I. Stewart
Location: *OX7 6AJ*
Visibility: *From the level crossing on London Lane, which the box controls.*

DROITWICH

Top & above:- *Back in February 1985, Class 31 No. 31141 passes Droitwich signal box with the afternoon Curzon Street to Worcester parcels train. In 1985, the box still had its original sliding timber windows, but these have since been replaced. The box was built in 1907, replacing an older 1884-vintage structure; it contains 79 levers as well as an additional two for detonators. Our interior view shows resident signalman Alan explaining facets of the box operation to lifelong signalman Trevor Maxted.* Both M. Rhodes

Location: *WR9 9AZ*

Visibility: *Best viewed from the Acre Lane overbridge to the north of the railway station.*

EVESHAM

Above:- *There was an earlier signal box situated near to where the current Evesham signal box stands, dating back to 1883 (called Evesham South). This contained a 48-lever mechanical frame. It was replaced by the current structure in 1957 and a larger 72-lever frame was installed. This was then reduced to 42 levers in the early 1970s when the goods yard and sidings at Evesham finally closed, leaving just levers 31–72 above the floor in the box. In September 1984, DMU set No. L417 is passing with a Worcester to Didcot passenger service.* M. Rhodes

Location: *WR11 4RA*

Visibility: *From the Briar Close overbridge to the west of the station.*

HENWICK

Above & above right:- *In our interior view of the 1875-built Henwick signal box we see signalman George Galloway operating the crossing gates with the whole 25-lever frame in view. George had started on the railway in Bloxwich signal box back in 1999, but when it closed in 2013, he transferred to Henwick. Back in 1985, before the box was refurbished, DMU set No. L413 passes with a Hereford to Birmingham New Street service, working wrong line, as the sign at the crossing warns can happen.* Both M. Rhodes

Location: *WR2 5NP*

Visibility: *From Henwick Road crossing, which the box controls.*

LEDBURY

Left:- The signal box at Ledbury opened in 1885 with the brick-based structure replacing an earlier 1881 timber building. It has a 42-lever frame numbered 0–41 and also an additional 2-lever frame for activating detonators. Back in 1985, a Hereford to Birmingham New Street service is seen passing the box in the hands of a Pressed Steel Class 117 DMU. M. Rhodes
Location: *HR8 1BT*
Visibility: *From the end of the station platform.*

MORETON-IN-MARSH

Above:- Class 47 No. 47456 draws to a stop at Moreton-in-Marsh in the pouring rain on a dull day in October 1981 with its Paddington to Hereford service. The signal box at Moreton-in-Marsh was built in 1883 and installed with a 40-lever frame which still operates today. Like several other boxes in the area, it has an additional two levers to activate detonators. M. Rhodes
Location: *GL56 0AA*
Visibility: *From the south end of the "up" platform.*

MALVERN WELLS

Above:- Newly named Class 50 No. 50007 "Sir Edward Elgar" passes the box at Malvern Wells in 1985 with the 1600 Hereford to Paddington express. The signal box here opened in 1919 with a 40-lever frame. M. Rhodes
Location: *WR14 4AL*
Visibility: *The box can be seen in the distance looking south from the Peachfield Road overbridge.*

NEWLAND EAST

Above right:- A Class 116, Derby Suburban DMU passes the box at Newland East in February 1985 with a Hereford to Birmingham New Street service. The box here was built in 1900 and originally called Stocks Lane. It was renamed Newland in 1929 and then renamed again as Newland East in 1943. Much of the 33-lever mechanical frame has been out of use since the permanent way sidings at Newland closed in the late 1980s. M. Rhodes
Location: *WR13 5AZ*
Visibility: *From the level crossing on Stocks Lane, which the box controls*

NORTON JUNCTION

Above left, above & left:- *The interior view of Norton Junction signal box shows resident signalman, Wayne Edwards, chatting with Trevor Maxted. Wayne had started his career as a crossing keeper, graduating to signalman at East Usk which he fortuitously left six months before the box there was destroyed by fire. After stints in Ascott-under-Wychwood and Ledbury boxes, he settled at Norton. The box here was built in 1908 and had a 33-lever frame. This was reduced to 19 levers (numbers 8–26) in the early 1970s when the line to Evesham was singled. Our first external view, taken in 1963 by the late Dr.Anthony Vickers, shows Hymek No. D7067 coming off the Evesham line with a Paddington to Hereford express, well before rationalisation took place. The simplified junction is evident in the 1985 view of 56068 at the head of 6M14, a Severn Tunnel Junction–Bescot Speedlink service. M. Rhodes (2) & M. Rhodes Collection*

Location: *WR5 2QN*

Visibility: *Looking west from the Woodbury Lane overbridge.*

WORCESTER SHRUB HILL

Left & above:- *Resident signalman "Steve" has just taken a line block as there is a gang headed by Richard Arnott working at the foot of the signal box at Worcester Shrub Hill. The box here opened in 1935 when it replaced the 1882-constructed "Worcester Joint Station" signal box. Installed with an 84-lever frame, the box controls both Shrub Hill station and the goods sidings to the east of the station. In June 2016, a Class 66 is seen passing the box and some of its signals with a Round Oak to Margam empty steel train. Both M. Rhodes*

Location: *WR4 9EE*

Visibility: *From the south end of Shrub Hill station platforms.*

WORCESTER TUNNEL JUNCTION

Above, left & below:- As far as I can recollect, signalman Roger Goodhall spent most of our visit to Worcester Tunnel Junction discussing the complexities of the Network Rail pension scheme! The box here was built in 1905 with a 65-lever frame. This was enlarged to 77 levers in 1960 but today has just 58 levers after the rebuilding of the box in the 1970s caused by a train crashing into it. Class 172 No. 172221 is seen exiting the eponymous tunnel and passing the box with a Birmingham to Hereford service. Our 1985 view of a Worcester Shrub Hill–Birmingham service, formed of a 3-car Metropolitan-Cammell DMU, is now impossible to recreate due to the encroachment of lineside vegetation. All M. Rhodes

Location: *WR4 9GN*

Visibility: *The signal box is very difficult to see. Previous views from Tunnel Hill are obscured by foliage but glimpses of the box are possible from McKenzie Way which leads to the Worcester dialysis centre on land formerly occupied by the goods yard.*

Leicester–Peterborough

ASHWELL

Left & below:- *Class 66 No. 66739 passes Ashwell signal box with 6L28, the TThO Carlisle to Whitemoor Yard infrastructure service, as the signalman looks on. The box here opened in 1912 and was fitted with a 25-lever mechanical frame, most of which has white levers in 2019 as the goods yard at Ashwell closed in the 1960s.* Both M. Rhodes
Location: *LE15 7SP*
Visibility: *From the Whissedine Road level crossing, which the box controls.*

FRISBY

Left- *Perhaps a candidate for the least sympathetically renovated signal box in the UK, Frisby box was built in 1941 and originally contained a 10-lever frame. This was replaced by an IFS panel in 1987.* M. Rhodes
Location: *LE14 2NP*
Visibility: *From Washstones Lane level crossing, which the box controls.*

HELPSTON

Right:- *Built in 1898 by the Great Northern Railway, Helpston signal box controls several level crossings along the ECML and the Glinton Road crossing over the Peterborough to Leicester route. A panel was introduced there in 1976 replacing the mechanical frame and this was upgraded to a new IFS panel in 2000.* M. Rhodes
Location: *PE6 7DH*
Visibility: *From the Glinton Road crossing.*

KETTON

Left & below:- The classic Midland Railway signal box at Ketton was built in 1900 and has a 20-lever frame. Class 66 No. 66614 is seen passing the box with 6Z56, the ThFO aggregates working from Crewe to Chesterton Junction. Both M. Rhodes
Location: *PE9 3AY*
Visibility: *From Station Road crossing, which the box controls.*

LANGHAM JUNCTION

Above & right:- Langham Junction signal box has never controlled a "junction" as such, but rather the entrance to the "up" and "down" goods loops to the west of Oakham. Built in 1890, it has a 20-lever mechanical frame. The external view shows Class 37 No. 97301 passing with a special from the Railway Technical Centre in Derby to St. Pancras, running with the headcode 1Q52. Both M. Rhodes
Location: *LE15 7LG*
Visibility: *From Burley Road crossing, which the box controls.*

MANTON JUNCTION

Left & above:- *Opened in 1913, Manton Junction originally had a 35-lever frame. Back in 1983, the coal stove was still in operation as well as the frame, as our exterior view of Class 45 No. 45026 passing the box shows. The Peak is hauling 9T32, a trip freight from Toton Yard to Corby. The mechanical frame was replaced by an NX panel in 1988 and a second NX panel was added in 1998 to control the line to Corby.* *Both M. Rhodes*
Location: *LE15 8SZ*
Visibility: *Views from the tunnel mouth are no longer possible due to excessive vegetation and the box is not possible to see from a public place although it can be accessed from a lane off Wing Road in Manton.*

MELTON STATION

Right:- *Melton Station signal box was built in 1942 with a 45-lever frame. In 1978 an IFS panel was added to control the Brentingby Junction area and a second IFS panel was installed in 1986 to control the access to the Pedigree Petfoods sidings (now the goods loops to the east of the station). Here Class 20 Nos. 20227 & 20142 head a 7X09, Old Dalby to Amersham stock delivery train in 2012, with Class 20 Nos. 20905 & 20901 bringing up the rear.* *M. Rhodes*
Location: *LE13 0BG*
Visibility: *from the west end of the station platform at Melton Mowbray.*

OAKHAM

Above & right:- *Oakham has the distinction of acting as the prototype for the first Hornby OO model of a signal box. Built in 1899 it contains a 17-lever frame numbered A and 1–16. The interior view shows "Pinkie", Leicester relief signalman, chatting to Ashwell resident, Adrian Quine. Pinkie has used the same coffee pot and BSA motorbike for all his 40 years on the railway! Class 66 No. 66722 is seen passing the box with 4L22, the afternoon Hams Hall to Felixstowe container train.* *Both M. Rhodes*
Location: *LE15 6QE*
Visibility: *From the Barleythorpe Road level crossing, which the box controls.*

UFFINGTON

Left and above- *Uffington signal box, more correctly called Uffington & Barnack, opened in 1909 with a 16-lever frame. It controls the crossing on Uffington Road and has manually operated gates as the external view taken in 2012 shows.* *Both M. Rhodes*
Location: *PE9 3HW*
Visibility: *From the crossing on Uffington Road, which the box controls.*

WHISSENDINE

Above- *Opened in 1940 with a 20-lever frame, Whissendine signal box has been extensively modernised with uPVC windows etc. Here Class 222 No. 222104 passes with a Derby to St. Pancras (via Corby) express in 2011.* *M. Rhodes*
Location: *LE15 7HH*
Visibility: *From Station Road crossing, which the box controls*

East Anglia

The Norwich to Ely line in East Anglia was very much a trail-blazer for the Network Rail 2010 resignalling programme with nine signal boxes and a manual gated crossing being replaced by a single workstation in Cambridge power signal box. Since the Norwich to Ely resignalling however, there has been very little further modernisation work in the region with the planned replacement of the signal boxes along the Wherry lines from Norwich to Yarmouth and Lowestoft delayed. Seven signal boxes and four manned crossings boxes were due to be transferred to a new digital workstation in Colchester power box by the spring of 2019. These are listed below in the original Network Rail 2010 plans as closing in 2015.

The £29 million project undertaken by Atkins started with remodelling of Yarmouth station undertaken in October 2017. There are also two 1905-vintage swing bridges along the Wherry lines at Reedham and Somerleyton. Originally Network Rail predicted the survival of the signal boxes associated with these bridges until 2051, but wear and tear is taking its toll on these structures. The bridge at Reedham performs in excess of 1400 openings for river traffic each year and mechanical failures are increasing. It may be that both bridges will need replacement with modern Dutch-designed concrete swing bridges within the next decade.

As a consequence of the delays to the Wherry line work, the planned resignalling of the lines between Bury St. Edmunds and Peterborough and Ely to Kings Lynn has been deferred until the next Network Rail Control period at the very least.

Signal Boxes Scheduled to Close per Network Rail 2010 Masterplan

Romford ROC	
2015	Acle, Brundall Junction, Brundall XGP, Cantley, Chapel Road XGF, Lingwood XGF, Lowestoft, Oulton Broad North, Reedham Junction, Strumpshaw XG, Yarmouth Vauxhall
2016	Cambridge PSB, Foxton XGB
2017	Acton Canal Wharf, Acton Wells Junction, Dudding Hill Junction, Liverpool Street, Neasden Junction, Richmond, South Tottenham, Upminster IECC, Upper Holloway, Colchester PSB, Crown Point, Parkeston, Stowmarket XGB, Bury St. Edmunds, Chippenham Junction, Dullingham
2020	Downham Market, Kings Lynn Junction, Littleport, Magdalen Road, Kings Dyke, Manea, March East, March South, Stonea, Three Horse Shoes, Whittlesea, Whittlesea XGP
2022	Saxmundham
2024	Liverpool Street IECC A
2027	Liverpool Street IECC B & C, Ingatestone XGB
2030	Trowse Swing Bridge
2034	Deep Wharf XGP, Jurgens XGP, Upminster IECC
2038	Elsenham XGP, Lincoln Road XGP, Park Lane XGP, Trinity Lane XGP
2044	Clacton PSB
2051	Reedham and Somerleyton Swing Bridges (note this may change as both swing bridges are life expired and may need replacing before 2051).

Left:- Work started in 2017 to simplify the track layout at Great Yarmouth in preparation for resignalling and the demolition of the signal box and signals in this view. Back in the 1990s, one of the rarer locomotive substitutions on the Norwich to Yarmouth and Lowestoft services was by Class 50 No. 50050, which is seen here running round its train at Yarmouth. The track to platform 1 in the foreground was removed at the end of 2017 and all the signals were due to be gone by Easter 2019. M. Rhodes

East Anglia

CLACTON

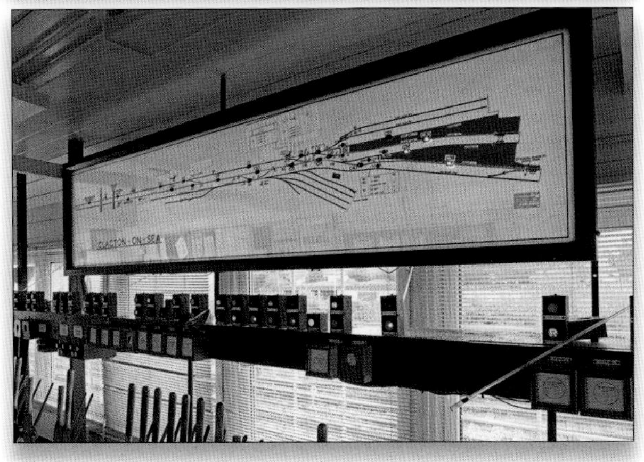

Above, above right & right:- Built in 1891, Clacton signal box originally contained a 52-lever frame. This was expanded to 64 levers in 1930 when the new enlarged passenger station opened. Further expansion took place to 69 levers in 1940 when the line to Thorpe-le-Soken was doubled and the box retains its 69 levers today. The semaphore signals were replaced by colour light posts in 1959/60 when the line was electrified and further major changes occurred in 1969 when the goods yard was closed. The box has been modernised with uPCV windows and cladding. All M. Rhodes

Location: *CO15 6PU*

Visibility: *From the end of the station platform at Clacton.*

FOXTON

Left & above:- Opened in 1878, the signal box at Foxton originally had a 21-lever frame which was enlarged to 30 levers in 1925. The box was downgraded to act as a crossing gate box in 1983, at which stage the mechanical frame was removed and replaced by an IFS panel with just four active switches. In June 2016, Class 66 No. 66848 is seen passing the box with the daily infrastructure train from Hoo Junction Yard to March Whitemoor Yard. Both M. Rhodes

Location: *CB22 6SH*

Visibility: *From Barrington Road crossing, which the box controls.*

SAXMUNDHAM

Above & above right:- Saxmundham signal box dates back to 1881 and had a 43-lever mechanical frame until RETB signalling was introduced along the East Suffolk line in 1986. At this stage the box was fitted with an IFS panel and Westcad VDUs as shown in the interior view of relief signalman Owen Bushell, taken in July 2017. The box has also been extensively rebuilt with uPVC cladding and revision of the brick base. Both M. Rhodes

Location: *IP17 1DX*
Visibility: *From Station Approach crossing, which the box controls.*

STOWMARKET

Right:- Class 66 No.66727 passes the crossing box at Stowmarket with the 0350 Hams Hall to Felixstowe container train. The box here dates back to 1882 and had its lever frame replaced by an IFS panel in 1985 as part of the overall modernisation and electrification of the line between Ipswich and Norwich. M. Rhodes
Location: *IP14 5AS*
Visibility: *Both from the station platform and Stowupland Road crossing.*

Bury St. Edmunds–Peterborough

BURY ST. EDMUNDS YARD

Right & below:- Between 1872 and 1888 there was a signal box called Bury St. Edmunds West End to the west of Bury station. This was replaced in 1888 by the current Bury St. Edmunds Yard signal box which has 51 levers today in a 54-lever frame which dates from 1943. In our interior view, Phil Mason, the resident signalman is seen on the phone, during a visit by the Local Operations Manager. The LOM was accompanied by Brandon resident "Dutchy" who was the local union representative responsible for checking on matters of concern for signallers in the West Anglia region. Class 60 No. 60050 is seen passing in front of the box back in October 1999 with a Peak Forest to Bury limestone train for the neighbouring sugar factory. Both M. Rhodes
Location: *IP32 6AJ*
Visibility: *The box can be seen in the distance from the west end of the station in the distance and also more closely from Sandy Lane which runs along the north side of the station.*

CHIPPENHAM JUNCTION

Right & below:- On the same day that Dutchy, the local trade union representative, visited Bury signal box, we also visited the box at Chippenham Junction. Dutchy is caught off guard as he chats to Kenny Mears (and his dog)! Chippenham Junction box probably opened in 1893, although there is debate about the exact date. It is fitted with a 16-lever mechanical frame. Class 66 No. 66714 is seen passing the box on 29 June 2011 with a Doncaster to Felixstowe intermodal service. Both M. Rhodes

Location: *CB8 7PH*

Visibility: *This is very difficult as the box lies half a mile down an access road which turns north off the A1304 at High Lodge.*

DULLINGHAM

Right & below:- Class 31 No. 31262 passes Dullingham box in June 1982 with the daily Cambridge to Newmarket trip freight. Built in 1883, the box here originally had a 22-lever frame. In 1978, when the line to Chippenham Junction was singled, it was fitted with an IFS panel and things were further simplified in 1983 when the line to Fulbourne was also singled. Both M. Rhodes

Location: *CB8 9UT*

Visibility: *From the Station Road crossing, which the box controls.*

EASTFIELD

Top, above & below:- *A most unusual survivor to the north of Peterborough is Eastfield signal box. Built in 1893 and with a 65-lever frame, the box controls some of the gooods sidings to the north of Peterborough as well as access to the GB Railfreight depot there. By the time of our internal view in 2012, when signalman Simon Barrett is seen surveying the frame, only levers 14–65 were in use , with Nos. 1–13 used as coat hangers as our image shows!* All M. Rhodes

Location: *PE3 9TN*

Visibility: *Looking north from the Westfield Road overbridge.*

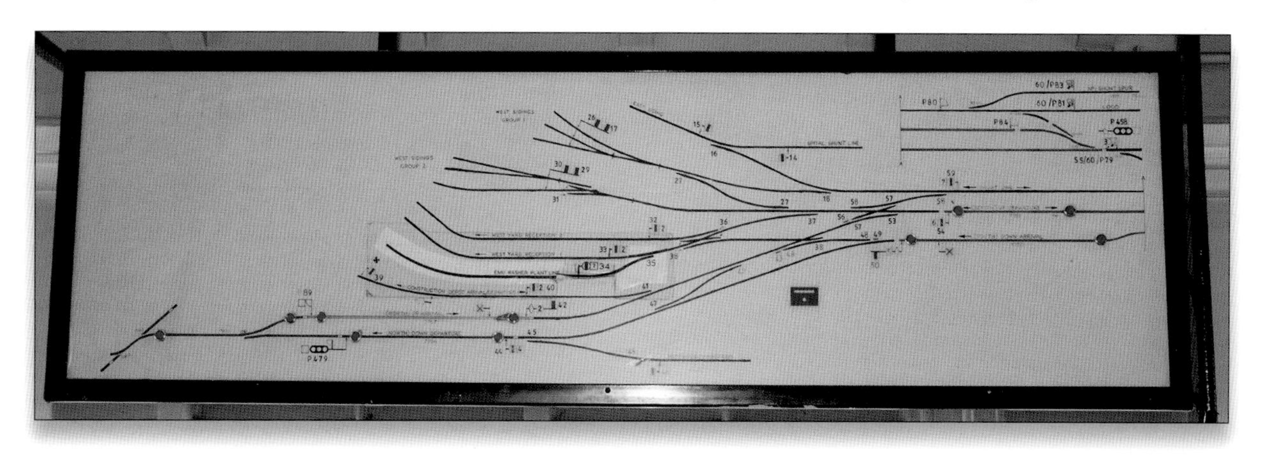

KINGS DYKE

Top & above:- *Opened in 1898 with a 19-lever frame, Kings Dyke signal box employed a "gate lad" until 1906 to open and close the crossing gates on the busy Peterborough Road. The manually operated gates were eventually replaced by automatic lifting gates in 1973. Class 66 No. 66564 is seen passing the box in 2011 with a Wakefield to Felixstowe freightliner service.* Both M. Rhodes

Location: *PE7 2JB*

Visibility: *From the Peterborough Road crossing, which the box controls.*

MANEA

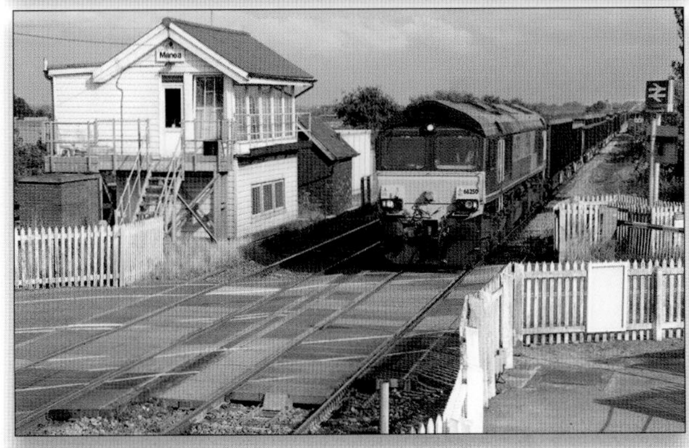

Above (3 images):- Signalman Ollie Robinson keeps an eye on things in Manea signal box where he was resident in 2013, having been persuaded to join the railway as a signalman by former West Anglia Operations Manager, Steve Ashling. The box here opened in 1883 with a 26-lever frame. The area controlled by the box extended to Chettisham in 1988, following the closure of Black Bank signal box, and then again as far as Ely North Junction (and the Cambridge power box) in 1992, when Chettisham signal box closed. Passing the box in October 2011 is Class 66 No. 66250 with 6Z47, an extra empty limestone train from Norwich to Peak Forest which had delivered limestone for Cantley sugar factory to Norwich Goods Yard. The bottom image well illustrates the semaphores at Manea as Class 66 No. 66305 passes with 4L87, a Leeds to Felixstowe container service on 18 July 2011. All M. Rhodes

Location: *PE15 0JA*

Visibility: *From the level crossing on the B1093, which the box controls.*

MARCH EAST JUNCTION

Top & above:- Class 66 No. 66581 passes March East signal box with 4E33, a Felixstowe to Doncaster intermodal service. In the loop behind it is Class 66 No. 66104 with 6Z74, a Hoo Junction to March Whitemoor Yard infrastructure service. The signal box at March East was subjected to one of the longest over-running refurbishments on Network Rail during 2011. A job on the 1885-vintage box to lower the ceiling and replace the windows, which was supposed to take ten weeks ended up taking several times this duration. The frame in the box was expanded to 55 levers in 1897 and reached its largest extent in 1973 with 61 levers. Today the frame is 59 levers. Both M. Rhodes

Location: *PE15 8NZ*

Visibility: *From the level crossing on the B1101, which the box controls.*

MARCH SOUTH JUNCTION

Above, above right & below:- March South Junction signal box was called Nene Junction when constructed in 1876 and was renamed March South in 1928. Equipped with a 51-lever frame numbered 1–50 with an extra lever labelled "A", it is called a junction as it used to control the junction with the branch line to Wimblington and Chatteris. Taken from March South signal box in 1991, the busy view below shows Class 156 No. 156405 with a Birmingham to Cambridge service whilst Class 31 Nos. 31181, 31186 and celebrity 31165 shunt in March east sidings. All M. Rhodes

Location: *PE15 8RY*

Visibility: *From the crossing on Creek Road, which the box controls.*

STONEA

Above & above right:- Signalman Keith Flynn is seen filling in the TRB in Stonea signal box back in October 2011. The original heritage structure at Stonea opened in 1883 with a 20-lever frame and was demolished in 1984, to be replaced by the portable building in use today. The box was fitted with an IFS panel. Class 66 No. 66062 is seen passing the modern building and ancient wooden crossing gates with a Peak Forest to Ely Potters Sidings limestone train. The limestone is bound for the sugar factory at Whissington. Both M. Rhodes

Location: *PE15 0DX*

Visibility: *From the crossing on the B1098, which the box controls.*

THREE HORSE SHOES

Top & above:- *Class 66 No. 66723 is seen passing Three Horse Shoes signal box in October 2011. The derelict goods shed and land around the box are a reminder of the extensive goods facilities which used to exist here. Their closure means that much of the 30-lever frame in the 1901-constructed signal box is white or out of use as our interior view shows.* Both M. Rhodes
Location: PE7 2DW
Visibility: *From the level crossing on March Road, which the box controls.*

WHITTLESEA

Top & above:- *Resident signalman, Andrew Heathmoss, chats with Local Operations Manager, Andrew Frost, during one of Andrew's regular visits to the boxes in his patch between Ely and Peterborough. The box at Whittlesea dates back to 1887 and saw a gradual expansion of its frame because of the goods sidings at Whittlesea; a frame of 27 levers was in place by 1940. Class 66 No. 66728 is seen passing the box with 6E88, a Middleton Towers to Barnby Dun sand train in April 2011.* Both M. Rhodes
Location: PE7 2EU
Visibility: *From the east end of the station platform.*

WHITTLESEA CROSSING

Right:- *The manual wooden crossing gates to the west of Whittlesea station are controlled by a crossing box located in a portable building. The signals, however, are under the control of the main Whittlesea signal box as can be seen from the W25 label on the left hand signal in this image. In 2012 Class 47 No. 47580 and out of sight Class 57 No. 57006 top-and-tail an empty coaching stock working from Carnforth to Norwich for a charter train from Norwich the next morning.* M. Rhodes
Location: PE7 2EU
Visibility: *From the level crossing on the B1093, which the box controls.*

Ely–Kings Lynn

DOWNHAM MARKET

Above & above right:- The box at Downham Market dates back to 1881 and was originally fitted with a 28-lever frame. This reached 34 levers and remained so until 1964 when rationalisation began. The biggest changes occurred in 1995 and 1996 when many redundant levers (caused by the closure of the grain sidings at Downham Market) were removed, reducing the frame to its current size of 19 levers. Class 365 No. 365510 is seen arriving at Downham Market with a King's Cross to King's Lynn service in 2014. Both M. Rhodes

Location: *PE38 9EP*

Visibility: *From the level crossing on Railway Road, which the box controls.*

KING'S LYNN JUNCTION

Above, above right & right:- Class 66 No. 66175 is seen passing King's Lynn Junction on 6 May 2014 with 6L85, a Warrington Arpley Yard to Middleton Towers empty sand train which will load for Ellesmere Port and the Quinglass factory. The box here opened in 1879 with a 62-lever frame which was enlarged to 82 levers by 1940. In 1971 and 1972, with rationalisation of the goods facilities and junction to Middleton Towers, the frame was reduced to its current size of 49 levers. In 2004 the connections to King's Lynn Harbour were placed permanently out of use and the modern "tiled" track diagram reflects these changes. All M. Rhodes

Location: *PE30 2QJ*

Visibility: *From Tennyson Avenue crossing, which the box controls.*

LITTLEPORT

MAGDALEN ROAD

Top & above:- Magdalen Road signal box is in fact at Watlington station. Opened in 1928 and replacing an older 1880 structure, it originally had a 40-lever frame. This was replaced in 1992, at the time of electrification of the route to King's Lynn, with an IFS panel. Rest day relief or "Flexisignaller" (as modern terminology describes him), David Murdoch is chatting with March LOM Andrew Frost in 2014 during my visit. Class 66 No. 66171 is seen passing a year earlier in February 2013 with a Middleton Towers to Goole sand train. Both M. Rhodes

Location: *PE33 0JQ*

Visibility: *From Station Road crossing, which the box controls.*

Top, above & below:- The signal box at Littleport opened in 1882 in conjunction with the doubling of the line from Ely North Junction. It has a 25-lever frame and controls the manually-operated crossing gates to the south of the station. In the summer of 1981, newly-repainted Class 47 No. 47005 approaches the signal box at Littleport with the 10.36 Liverpool Street–King's Lynn express. All M. Rhodes

Location: *CB6 1JL*

Visibility: *From Station Road crossing, which the box controls.*

Wherry Lines

ACLE

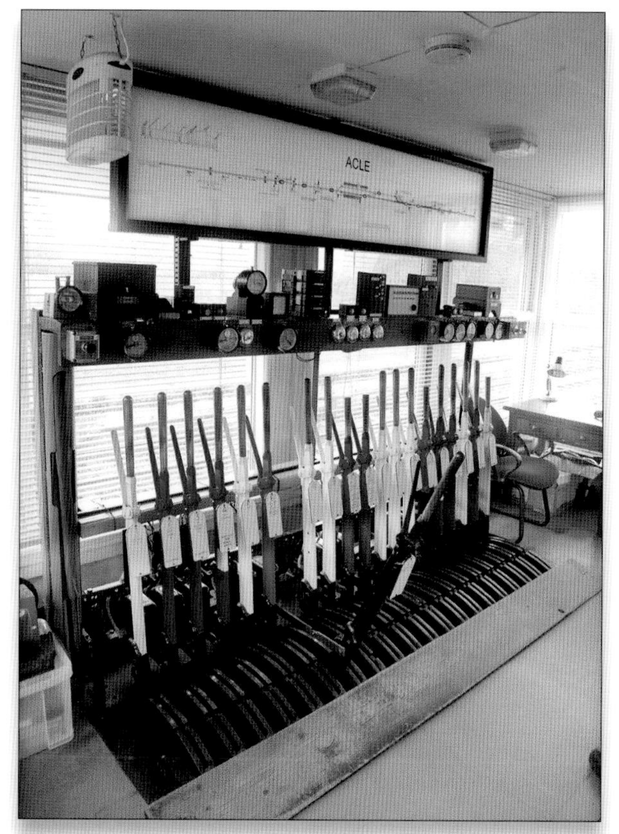

Top & above:- The signal box at Acle dates back to 1883 and was built to a GER design which, as the view of Class 68 Nos. 68004 & 68024 shows, has been extensively modernised by the addition of new windows and modern double glazing. The Class 68s are top-and-tailing a Norwich to Yarmouth service in September 2016. The box is fitted with a 20-lever Saxby & Farmer frame which also dates to 1883 and has relatively few white or redundant levers. The signal box diagram above the frame has recently been modernised from the original paper representation of the tracks to a new plastic laminated diagram. Both M. Rhodes

Location: *NR13 3BZ*

Visibility: *From the Norwich end of the "down" platform at Acle station and also the station footbridge.*

BRUNDALL JUNCTION

Top & above:- One longstanding feature of the Wherry lines during the 21st century is the use of locomotives on both local and summer Saturday passenger traffic. During 2017 there were two locomotive-hauled passenger sets employed on local passenger turns; one with two Class 37s and the other, seen here with two Class 68 locomotives. Nos. 68016 and 68021 pass Brundall Junction with a morning Yarmouth to Norwich service, packed with commuters. Signalman, Owen Bushell, watches from the signal box as the sun pops up over the horizon on 3 February 2017. The signal cabin is relatively unaltered and retains many original features.

In our interior view, we see signalman Robert Norman on duty at Brundall Junction on 15 May 2013. Robert started on the railway aged 15, having initially wanted to work in farming. He went to the job centre in Norwich who suggested he tried a post as a "box lad". Thus he started at Thorpe Junction in Norwich where he worked for three years. He then spent 6 months as a lad messenger at Norwich, responsible for cycling out to call drivers and guards in for work (a historical role dating back to the days when most homes did not possess a telephone). Then, at 18 he passed out as a signalman in Hethersett signal box where he stayed for 10 years. There followed promotion to "relief signalman" at Brundall for three years and finally 33 years as a resident signalman at Brundall. His younger brother Alan also ended up joining the railway and was for many years a resident signalman at Spooner Row until that box closed in 2012 and Alan retired. This view shows 34 of the 35 levers in the 1927-vintage Stevens 35-lever frame. Both M. Rhodes

Location: *NR13 5PJ*

Visibility: *Located at the Lowestoft end of the "up" platform at Brundall, the box is best observed from the station car park.*

BRUNDALL CROSSING

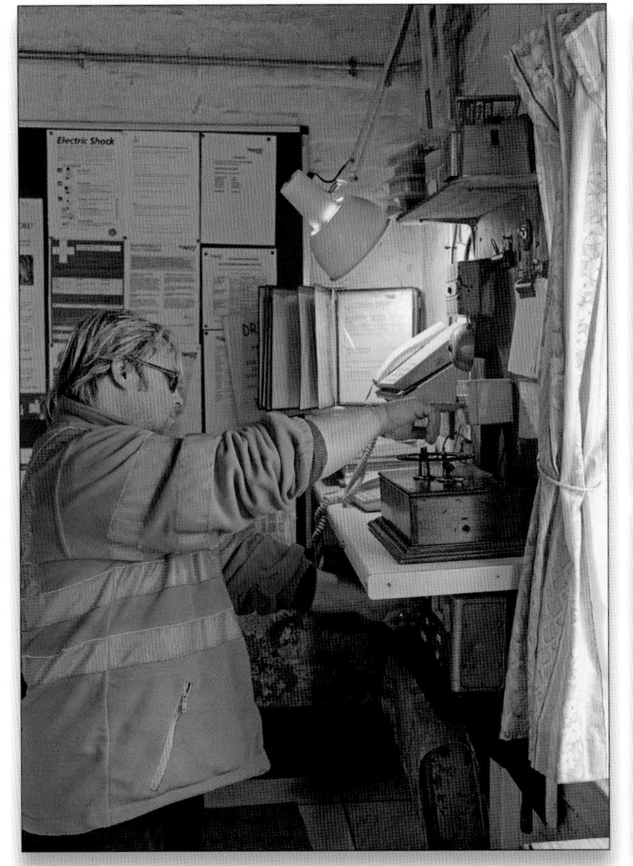

Top & above:- Andy Soltan presses the release for the manual crossing gates at Brundall station. His cabin is at the Norwich end of the "down" platform at Brundall station, under the footbridge. Andy had been a resident signalman at Spooner Row until it closed in 2012 and took the new post at Brundall Crossing, which fitted in well with his other interests as a rock musician! The manual-gated crossing at Brundall controls access to the marina and the Broome Boatyard. Both M. Rhodes

Location: *NR13 5PJ*

Visibility: *The manually-operated gates and small gate keepers hut are best seen from Station Road crossing, which they control*

CANTLEY

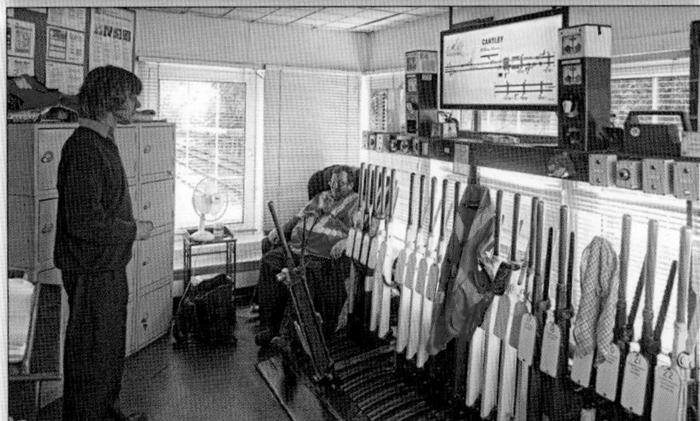

Above (3 images):- The signal cabin at Cantley dates back to 1887, whilst the 22-lever frame is more modern, installed in 1913. Signalman Paul Young is "learning" the box on 4 June 2016 under the watchful eye of Phil McCabe. Until 2012 Paul worked on the Norwich to Ely line and during this visit was training as part of his new role of Yarmouth relief signalman. On 1 September 2015, Class 37 Nos. 37425 & 37422 pass Cantley signal box with a Norwich to Lowestoft service. As can be seen from this view, the box has been extensively modernised with uPVC windows and double glazing. It is hard to imagine that back in the 1960s, the sleepy little station at Cantley used to receive four daily trains, each made up of fifty 11-ton vanfits loaded with sugar beet! The bottom image shows Class 47 Nos. 47813 & 47805 top-and-tailing a Lowestoft to Norwich service past the semaphores at Cantley. All M. Rhodes

Location: *NR13 3SP*

Visibility: *From the east end of the station or the crossing on Station Road, which the box controls.*

LINGWOOD

Top & above:- The Wherry Lines have four sets of manual crossing gates and whilst the crossing keepers' accommodation at these is most often a simple portable building, the crossing gates and ground frames date back to the late 1880s when the line was first signalled. Here, the gates and ground frame at Chapel Road crossing are seen in 2011 whilst Class 47 No. 47802 (with 47841 at the rear) brings a morning Yarmouth to Norwich service across Lingwood MCG as it draws to a halt at Lingwood station. Maintenance of the timber crossing gates is an ever increasing problem as the wood used in recent years seems to rot more quickly than in previous decades. Both M. Rhodes

Location: *Chapel Road - NR13 4NZ, Station Road - NR13 4AZ.*

Visibility: *From the respective level crossings.*

LOWESTOFT

Top, above & below- Morning sun highlights the splendid 61-lever frame in Lowestoft signal box. The frame built by Saxby & Farmer, was installed in 1905, whereas the signal box building was built in 1885. Our external view was taken in 1996 from a footbridge over the running lines and goods yard at Lowestoft. This has sadly been demolished because it became unsafe and the signal box has since been repainted in Great Eastern colours and refurbished. Two Class 150 units await with trains for Norwich and Ipswich respectively. In the view below, Class 47 Nos. 47813 & 47805 depart from Lowestoft with a service for Norwich on 1 June 2015. All M. Rhodes

Location: *NR2 2EL*

Visibility: *The box lies a couple of hundred yards west of the station and can be seen in the distance from the end of Lowestoft station platform, or partially from Denmark Road which runs alongside it.*

OULTON BROAD NORTH

Above & above right:- *On 10 March 2017, signalman Owen Bushell cooks up a delicious vegan breakfast featuring "tofu sausages" complemented by our home baked bread! The signal box at Oulton Broad North was built to a GER design in 1901 and then extended with a new 35-lever frame in 1928 when the Oulton Broad Junction signal box was closed. The signal box not only controls traffic on the Norwich line and the junction with the East Suffolk line, but also houses the release that allows Oulton Broad Swing Bridge to open. Class 68 No. 68003 (with 68016 at the rear of the train), arrives at Oulton Broad North with 2D70 from Norwich to Lowestoft, with Oulton Broad North signal box seen in the background behind the brand new "up" starting signal, installed just weeks earlier.* Both M. Rhodes

Location: *NR32 3LT*

Visibility: *From the Bridge Road level crossing, which the box controls.*

OULTON BROAD SWING BRIDGE

Above- *The swing bridge over Oulton Broad dates back to 1907 and the old signal cabin on the bridge is now boarded up. Control is now from a 2005-vintage portable building which contains an IFS panel. As mentioned earlier, the release to allow the swing bridge to open for river traffic is in Oulton Broad North signal box. Here the bridge is just closing after the passage of a boat on 10 March 2017.* M. Rhodes

Location: *NR32 3LW*

Visibility: *From Bridge Street across the waterway.*

REEDHAM JUNCTION

Right & above right- *Signalman Bob Howard fills in the train register at Reedham Junction on 27 July 2013, just days before he retires on 2 August 2013. After first joining the railway in 1964, Bob had worked in many roles and dozens of signal boxes all over the former Great Eastern area, but was looking forward to spending more time on his hobby - O gauge North American model railways! The signal box at Reedham Junction was built in 1904 and contains a 60-lever, 1904-vintage McKenzie & Holland mechanical frame. Class 47 No. 47813 brings up the rear of a Norwich to Lowestoft service, headed by 47805. The formation is seen passing Reedham Junction on 10 June 2015.* Both M. Rhodes

Location: *NR13 3EZ*

Visibility: *From the east end of the station platform or from the Wilton Green overbridge which looks directly down onto the box.*

REEDHAM SWING BRIDGE

Above, right, below right & below:- *Reedham Swing Bridge was opened in 1904 and controls the "new" swing bridge which opened in 1905. There was an older fixed iron bridge to the east of the current alignment, which is why the tracks approaching the bridge from Reedham Junction slew to the west just before the river. The signal box was equipped with a 1904, McKenzie & Holland 12-lever frame seen here on 16 May 2013.*

With the bridge open for river traffic at Reedham, this view shows the east side of the signal box with the helpful black sign board which allows the signalman to inform river traffic when the bridge will open for them. He has signs for 10, 20 and 30 minutes which helps sailing boats decide how much they need to tack to time their approach to the bridge correctly. Our second external view shows Class 57 No. 57310 bringing up the rear of the 2012 season railhead treatment train, which was headed by 57306.

Resident signalman Alan English is seen "putting back" after a train has passed in May 2013. Alan had previously worked in London before settling for the last 18 years in the comfort of the resident position at Reedham Swing Bridge. Mind you, the job has its highlights as Alan starred alongside Michael Portillo when Portillo visited the railways of East Anglia!

All M. Rhodes

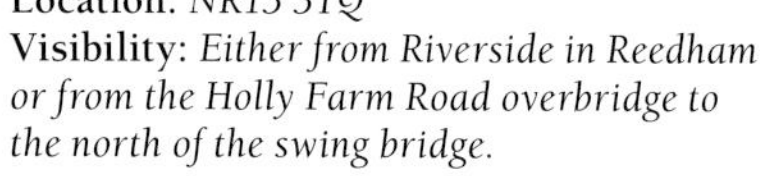

Location: *NR13 3TQ*

Visibility: *Either from Riverside in Reedham or from the Holly Farm Road overbridge to the north of the swing bridge.*

SOMERLEYTON SWING BRIDGE

Above, above right & right:- *Dean Hayman, the No. 2 Mobile Operations Manager (MOM) chats to resident signalman Carl King inside Somerleyton Swing Bridge signal box. The control gear for the swing bridge is seen behind the pair whilst the 1904-vintage 14-lever frame controlling passing rail traffic is on the right of the image. Looking east, the black sign for shipping is prominent in the close up view of the 1904 GER signal box at Somerleyton. Taken from Somerleyton station, a Lowestoft to Norwich service in the hands of Class 156 No. 156407 shimmers in the June heat haze as it climbs to cross the River Waveney. Two of the increasingly scarce concrete signal poles are well seen in this view. All M. Rhodes*

Location: *IP19 8RT*

Visibility: *Can be seen in the distance from Somerleyton station which is found at NR32 5QN.*

YARMOUTH

Above left, above & left:- *Class 47 Nos.47813 & 47805 are seen leaving Yarmouth on 10 June 2015 with a service to Norwich, passing Yarmouth signal box. The box was built by the Great Eastern Railway in 1884 and along with Acle, Brundall and Lowestoft was one of the four original boxes to control the Wherry Lines. It contains a 1905, Saxby & Farmer mechanical frame with 63 levers, seen here during a visit on 31 January 2017. The signal box at Yarmouth has had new windows fitted but retains much of it's original character. Seen here in January 2017, there is a panoply of signalling talent posing on the box veranda. From left to right are James, a resident in the box, Paul Young (Yarmouth relief) and Owen Bushell , also a relief signalman, but covering as far afield as Saxmundham. Finally on the right is their former mentor, Steve Ashling, previously West Anglia Operations Manager, but now retraining as a driver for Abellio Greater Anglia. All M. Rhodes*

Location: *NR30 1SD*

Visibility: *The box is well seen from the end of the station platforms or the A47 overbridge to the north of the station.*

Southern England

At the time of writing this chapter, most of the mechanical signal boxes on the Southern Region have been decommissioned. The Gillingham to Exmouth resignalling scheme, scheduled for 2012, took place on time and the schemes at Aldershot and Ash Vale, Snodland, Horsham to Arundel and Poole to Dorchester were all completed within 12–18 months of their originally planned schedule. The resignalling between Lewes and St.Leonards was a little later than planned, completed in 2015 rather than 2013 as originally envisaged. The North Kent resignalling around Gillingham was however almost on time, completed in 2016 as compared to the target of 2015. All this investment means that only small pockets of mechanical and heritage signalling remain on the Southern Region and dates and times for its replacement are uncertain. Certainly the definitive statement from Network Rail in 2010 that Maidstone West signal box will survive until 2055 seems somewhat far fetched!

Signal Boxes Scheduled to Close per Network Rail 2010 Masterplan

Three Bridges ROC	
2013	Berwick, Eastbourne, Hampden Park, Pevensey, Polegate, Havensmouth, Amberley, Billingshurst, Pulborough, Plumpton XGB, Bexhill
2015	Arundel, Barnham, Chichester, Littlehampton, Lewes, Newhaven Harbour, Newhaven Town
2016	Lancing, Victoria SCC (part of)
2017	Lovers Walk depot panel, Three Bridges PSB (part of)
2018	London Bridge PSB, Angerstein
2019	Whyteleaf South XGB, Bounds Green North shunt box, Bounds Green South shunt box, Kings Cross PSB (transfer over 3 years)
2020	Victoria SCC
2021	Cricklewood shunt box
2022	Oxted, West Hampstead PSB
2023	Selhurst depot panel
2057	Bognor Regis
Basingstoke ROC	
2012	Chard Junction, Gillingham Dorset, Honiton, Templecombe, Yeovil Junction, Feniton XGP, Sherborne XGP
2013	Aldershot, Farnham, Ash Vale Junction, Dorchester South, Hamworthy Junction, Poole, Wareham, Wool, Stoke XG
2014	Yeovil Pen Mill
2016	Eastleigh PSB, Farncombe, Guildford PSB
2017	Feltham, Baingstoke ASC, Woking
2018	Wimbledon SCC, Salisbury
2019	Wimbledon Top Yard depot panel, Clapham Yard
2023	Brockenhurst
2029	Bournemouth
2035	Havant ASC
2040	Dorking
2051	Haslemere, Petersfield
2056	Wokingham
2057	Marchwood, School Road MGH
Gillingham ROC (NB it is anticipated this ROC will be merged into Three Bridges ROC)	
2011	Canterbury East, Shepherds Well, Faversham, Margate, Ramsgate
2012	Snodland
2015	Gillingham, Rainham, Rochester, Sittingbourne
2017	Deal, Minster, Sandwich
2019	Ashford IECC (north kent), Slade Green depot panel, Ashford-Hoo Junction, Ashford-Dartford West

Ashford ROC	
2016	Maidstone East
2017	Folkestone East
2018	Tonbridge
2019	Wye area control centre
2047	Canterbury West, Sturry
2048	Bopeep Junction
2053	Hastings, Robertsbridge, Rye
2055	Aylesford, Cuxton, East Farleigh, Wateringbury, Maidstone West

Southern Region

AYLESFORD

Above:- Built in 1921, the box at Aylesford was originally fitted with a 26-lever frame, as seen in this view. In 2005 the mechanical frame was replaced by an IFS panel. T. Maxted
Location: *ME20 7GB*
Visibility: *From the level crossing on Mill Hall, which the box controls.*

BOPEEP JUNCTION

Above- Apparently, in the mid-19th century, Bopeep Junction was a remote spot and was named after an inn visited by shepherds. The signal box here opened in 1912 and has a 24-lever frame which dates from 1973. With the closure of St. Leonards West Marina signal box in 1997, it acquired an IFS panel to control this section of track.. This internal view was taken in 2001. Following the delayed West Sussex Resignalling in February 2015, Bopeep Junction SB became a fringe to Three Bridges ROC East Sussex workstation in one direction and Hastings signal box in the other. D. Allen
Location: *TN38 0AB*
Visibility: *From the end of the platform at West St. Leonards station.*

BOGNOR REGIS

Top & above:- Opened in 1938, the box at Bognor Regis was installed with a 66-lever frame. Our internal view shows Local Operations Manager, Brian Anderson, discussing the merits of the speed restriction for shunting at Bognor, which in June 2013 stood at 5 mph. Staff wanted to allow up to 15 mph and whilst the discussion rages, resident signalman Nick St. Croix looks on as signalling veteran Trevor Maxted makes the case for higher speeds. The external view shows Class 377 No. 377464 with a mid-morning express to Waterloo. Both M. Rhodes
Location: *PO21 1AE*
Visibility: *The best position to observe the box is from the footbridge between the B2166 and Upper Bognor Road.*

CANTERBURY WEST

Above:- Built in 1928, Canterbury West signal box is one of very few surviving boxes which straddle the tracks they control. It was initially fitted with a 96-lever frame but this has now been reduced to 72 levers, two-thirds of which are white or out of use. Our external image is one of the author's earliest signal box shots, taken in 1974. M. Rhodes

Location: *CT2 8AN*

Visibility: *From the end of the platform at Canterbury West station.*

CHARLTON LANE CROSSING

Above:- Opened in 1894, Charlton Lane Crossing signal box is really nothing more than a small garden shed! Fitted with a 7-lever mechanical frame it ceased to be a block post as long ago as 1970 and has operated since then as a "gate box". Class 465 No. 465250 passes in 2017 with a North Kent service. D. Haywood

Location: *SE7 8LF*

Visibility: *From Charlton Lane level crossing, which the box controls.*

CHICHESTER

Above:- The signal box at Chichester was opened in 1882, replacing an older 1875-vintage structure on the same site named Chichester West. Originally it was fitted with an 87-lever mechanical frame, but this was reduced to 46 levers in 1944. As the railway around the station was rationalised the box was renamed simply "Chichester" in 1973. The mechanical frame was replaced by an NX panel in 1985 and a second panel was added in 1992. D. Hill

Location: *PO19 1RJ*

Visibility: *From the Waitrose access road off the A259 from where this image was taken.*

DEAL

Above:- Deal, opened in 1939, is one of the smallest examples of the Southern Railway's Art Deco signal boxes and was the last to be commissioned before the outbreak of World War II. Unlike the similar structure at Dorking, it didn't require any end sections. It opened in May 1939 when the roles of the former signal box and gate box were amalgamated. The layout is presently controlled from the 42-lever frame and includes a mix of colour lights and semaphores. D. Allen

Location: *CT14 6PS*

Visibility: *From the Albert Road level crossing, which the box controls.*

DORKING

Left- The large Art Deco signal box at Dorking opened in 1938 and was equipped with a 44-lever mechanical frame. Back in 1997, Class 455/8 No. 5820 is seen passing the box with a Victoria to Littlehampton service. M. Rhodes

Location: *RH4 1QP*

Visibility: *From either the station platform or the London Road overbridge (from where this view is taken).*

EAST FARLEIGH

Above & right:- The signal box at East Farleigh opened in 1892 with a 25-lever frame. This has subsequently been reduced to just 11 levers. Both T. Maxted
Location: *ME16 9NB*
Visibility: *From the level crossing on Farleigh Lane, which the box controls.*

FOLKESTONE EAST

Left:- On the cusp of heritage and modern, the signal box at Folkestone East opened in 1962 with a small NX panel. This was expanded in 1998, when the box took over the control of traffic through Dover. Here in the early 1990s, 3-Cep No. 1108 passes the box. T. Maxted
Location: *CT19 6NL*
Visibility: *Partial views are possible from the end of Stuarts Road.*

FOLKESTONE HARBOUR

Right:- It is a moot point as to whether the signal box here should be included amongst the closures section or here, because it has been listed as out of use since 2006 but as far as can be found, no official closure notice has been issued (apologies if readers know better - please let me know). Built in 1933, the box had a 36-lever frame reduced to just 22 levers by the time of our image. T. Maxted
Location: *CT20 1QH*
Visibility: *From the level crossing to the east of Folkestone Harbour station, which the box controls.*

HASTINGS

Top & above:- When opened in 1891, this signal box was originally called Hastings East Yard. It was renamed simply "Hastings" in 1930 and contains an 84-lever mechanical frame. Our internal view, taken in June 2013, shows resident signalman Richard Conolley on duty. Both M. Rhodes

Location: *TN34 1BA*

Visibility: *Either from the end of the station platform or from the overbridge on South Terrace (beware psychopathic seagulls!).*

LEWES

LITTLEHAMPTON

Top & above:- Signalman Mark Crouch is on duty during our official visit to Littlehampton signal box in 2013. The box was built in 1886, replacing an earlier structure on the site that dated back to 1863. Fitted with a 44-lever frame it is unusually compact measuring just 21 x 9 feet! Class 377 No. 377145 is seen passing the box with a mid-morning service to London. Both M. Rhodes

Location: *BN17 7EL*

Visibility: *Partial from the end of the station platform and also from Gloucester Road.*

Above:- Opened in 1889, the signal box at Lewes was originally called Lewes Main Junction. This was changed to Lewes Junction in 1922 and then Lewes 'B' in 1963. Finally the signal box was named simply "Lewes" in 1972. Originally it had been equipped with a 104-lever frame but this was replaced by an NX panel in 1976. Class 313 No. 313021 passes on a dreary Sunday afternoon in 2017 with a service to Seaford. M. Rhodes

Location: *BN7 2SA*

Visibility: *Both from the station platform and also from the footbridge off Court Road, from where this image is taken.*

MAIDSTONE EAST

Top & above:- Resident signalman Phil Price chats to Trevor Maxted in Maidstone East signal box. The signal box here was built in 1962 and contains one of very few surviving miniature lever frames with 47 levers. The box had NX panels added in 1983 and 1984 to control the lines towards Wrotham. Both M. Rhodes
Location: *ME14 1RE*
Visibility: *From the platform at Maidstone East station.*

MAIDSTONE WEST

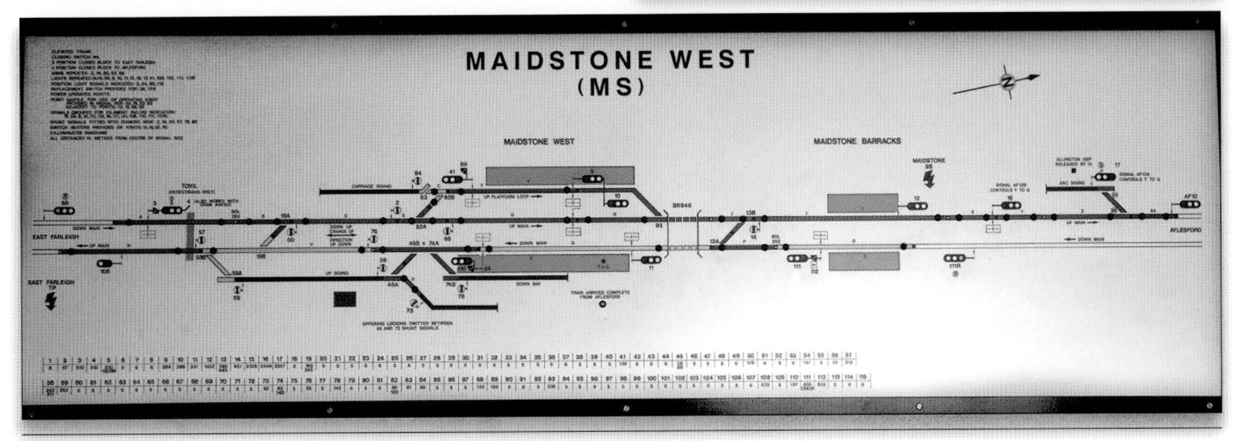

Top right, above right & above:- The largest mechanical signal box on the southern region, by some margin, is at Maidstone West. Our internal view emphasises the situation with over 75% of levers coloured white or out of use. Signallers Dave Peters and Reg Stevens are chatting in front of the 115-lever frame, installed in 1899 in the 1892-built signal box. All M. Rhodes
Location: *ME16 8LZ*
Visibility: *The box is hard to see from the station but can be glimpsed from the parking spaces on Bodiam Court.*

MARCHWOOD

Below & right:- Class 66 No. 66163 arrives at Marchwood station in 2000 running as 0B05, a light engine from Eastleigh. The signal box here opened in 1925 and was fitted with a 17-lever mechanical frame which was further expanded to 24 levers in 1960 as our internal view shows. Both M. Rhodes
Location: *SO40 0XG*
Visibility: *From either Plantation Drive or the Main Road level crossing, which the box controls.*

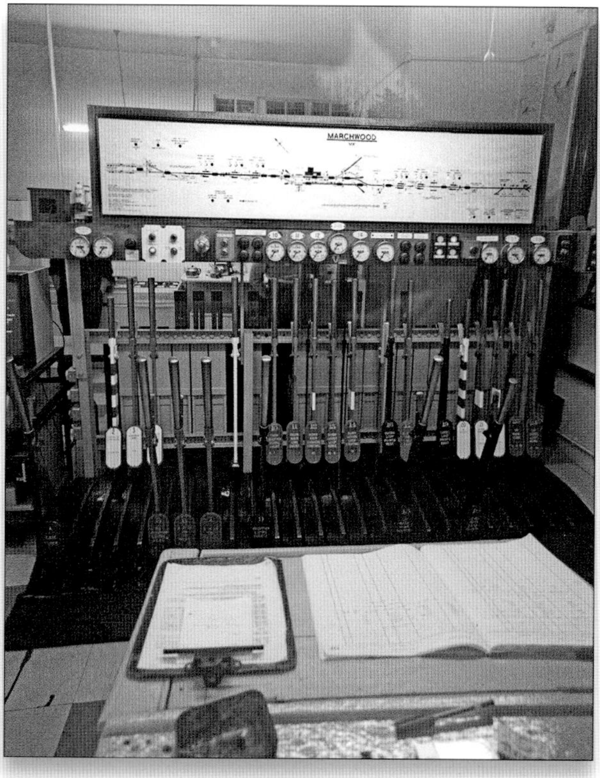

NEWHAVEN HARBOUR

Left:- The signal box at Newhaven Harbour opened in 1886, replacing an older structure dating back to 1865. It is fitted with a 42-lever frame. T. Maxted
Location: *BN9 0BH*
Visibility: *From the level crossing off Beach Road, which the box controls.*

PETERSFIELD

Right:- Opened in 1890, the signal box here was originally known as Petersfield North but was renamed simply "Petersfield" in 1902. Initially it had a 48-lever frame but this had expanded to 53 levers by 1958. Rationalisation then occurred as a result of Beeching and in 1974 it was reduced to 11 levers, but with the addition of an IFS panel to control track further afield. T. Maxted
Location: *GU32 3EE*
Visibility: *From the Station Road crossing, which the box controls.*

REIGATE

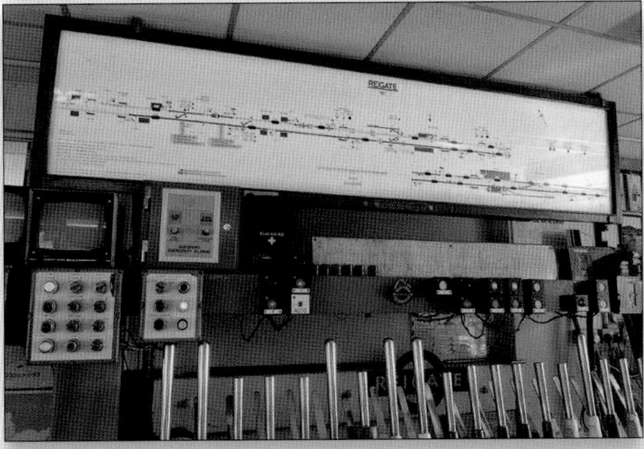

Top & above:- *Replacing a previous structure dating from 1892, the signal box at Reigate opened in 1929 with a 24-lever frame. An IFS panel was added in 1983, controlling the lines to Gomshall.* *Both T. Maxted*

Location: *RH2 9PY*

Visibility: *From London Road level crossing, which the box controls.*

ROBERTSBRIDGE

Above:- *Robertsbridge SB lever frame has controlled the 14 route miles of the so-called '1066 Route' between Stonegate and Battle ever since Etchingham SB was decommissioned in 1985. The whole route is track circuited and the last semaphores at Robertsbridge were replaced by colour lights in March 1986. The SB now controls four level crossings remotely by means of CCTV. The previous manually-controlled barriers at Robertsbridge itself were replaced by automated gates in 1974.* *D. Allen*

Location: *TN32 5DD*

Visibility: *From the Station Road overbridge.*

RYE

Above:- *The impressive classical-style station buildings contrast with the rather plain South Eastern Railway signal box which dates from when the station was rebuilt in 1893. The box has 30 levers and was retained to control the only crossing point and the tokenless block sections toward Hastings SB (Ore) and Appledore. Class 207 No. 207103 passes the box with an Ashford to Hastings passenger service in 2001.* *D. Allen*

Location: *TN31 7AB*

Visibility: *From the station platform.*

RYDE IOW

Left:- *Opened in 1928 and replacing an older structure on the site, dating back to 1875, Ryde signal box is equipped with a 40-lever frame. An NX panel was added in 1988 to control the tracks to Brading and Sandown. Here, in 2010, a former London Underground unit passes the box.* *T. Maxted*

Location: *PO33 2BA*

Visibility: *From the station platform at Ryde St. Johns.*

SANDWICH

Right:- Although opened in 1938, during the era of the Art Deco 'glasshouse' signal boxes, the Southern Railway built a conventional signal box at Sandwich. The box replaced an older 1893 structure at the site and contained a 27-lever frame. This was replaced by an IFS panel in 1977 when Woodnesborough gate box was decommissioned and the level crossing converted to remote operation by means of CCTV supervised by Sandwich. At the same time, the remaining semaphores at Sandwich were replaced and the lever frame removed. The level crossing adjacent to the SB had the gates replaced by lifting barriers in 1973. This view, taken on 1 August 2001, isn't very flattering; not helped by faded and flaking paintwork and the bricked-up locking room windows. D. Allen

Location: *CT13 0BT*

Visibility: *From the level crossing on Dover Road, which the box controls.*

WATERINGBURY

Left:- Occupying a delightful position alongside the river, Wateringbury is the southernmost of the surviving Medway Valley SBs. In common with the station building and goods shed, the SB, built in 1893, is Grade II Listed. Initially fitted with a 27-lever frame, this was reduced to 9 levers in the 1960s. Further changes came in 2005 when resignalling resulted in the replacement of the remaining five semaphores by colour lights. The lever frame remains in use but only six of the nine levers are required. This view, dating from 28 July 2001, shows 4CIG No. 1808 departing with the 1700 Maidstone West to London Bridge service. D. Allen

Location: *ME18 5GA*

Visibility: *From the crossing on Bow Hill, which the box controls.*

WOKINGHAM

Above & right:- Wokingham signal box was built in 1933 and replaced an older signal box at the location originally erected in 1871. The interior view of the box, which contains 40 levers, shows resident signalman Nigel Bassett chatting with relief signalman Trevor Maxted. Nigel had started his signalling career as "box boy" under Trevor's direction in the old Guildford signal box, which closed in 1999 to be replaced by the Guildford area signalling centre. Both M. Rhodes

Location: *RG41 2XS*

Visibility: *From the crossing on Station Road, which the box controls.*

Greater London

ACTON CANAL WHARF

Left & above:- Acton Canal Wharf signal box, like that at Dudding Hill, is a modern (2004) Network Rail construction but on the base and template of the original box at this location. Our external view, taken in 1990, shows the original 1894 Midland Railway structure which contained a 1965-vintage 35-lever frame, which is retained in the newer structure. Both FFP Media

Location: *NW10 6DN*

Visibility: *Partial views of the box are possible from the west end of the Discount Vehicle Hire car park off Atlas Road.*

ACTON WELLS JUNCTION

Above (3 images):- Class 25 No. 25050 is seen passing Acton Wells Junction back in February 1981 with a Willesden Yard to Acton Yard transfer freight. On the same day, Class 33 No. 33204 passes the box with a Hoo Junction–Acton Yard empty china clay train. The box here dates back to 1892 and the interior image shows the cabin at a time of transition from mechanical to electrical control. Originally fitted with a 60-lever frame, the 1990 image shows the new IFS panel standing over the lever spaces from 50 to 60 whilst Mike Lane, the resident signalman, takes a call from a neighbouring box. M. Rhodes (2) & FFP Media

Location: *NW10 6EA*

Visibility: *The box lies to the west of Wells House Road but good views from a public place are not possible.*

DUDDING HILL

Above & right:- Originally built by the Midland Railway in 1902, Dudding Hill box was completely rebuilt by Network Rail in 2004 because the older structure was falling down. The 1954 brick base, used half a century earlier to shore up the Midland box, was used for foundations and the 16-lever mechanical frame, dating back to 1902, was kept in use. Both M. Rhodes

Location: *NW2 6RW*

Visibility: *The box is well observed from a footpath overbridge on a path at the end of Park Side, running south east into Gladstone Park.*

GREENFORD EAST

Top & above:- Signalman Ian Scott, a new signalling recruit in his first post as resident at Greenford East, chats to signalling veteran Trevor Maxted. The box here was built in 1904 with a 41-lever frame but extended in 1938 to 55 levers and then again in 1956 to its current 76-lever frame. The join in the brickwork from the 1956 extension can clearly be seen in our external view. Both M. Rhodes

Location: *UB6 0UW*

Visibility: *Access is from a lane off Rockware Avenue, but good views of the box from a public place are not possible.*

NEASDEN JUNCTION

Top & above:- The signal box at Neasden Junction has been converted into a fortress with metal grilles on all the windows and palisade fencing around the perimeter. Built in 1899, the box contains its original 24-lever frame. Both M. Rhodes

Location: *NW10 2UE*

Visibility: *The box can be glimpsed through trees from Wharton Close, but good views from a public place are not possible.*

SOUTH TOTTENHAM STATION

Right:- Opened in 1894 by the Great Eastern Railway, South Tottenham Station Junction (as it was originally known) was fitted with a 54-lever frame numbered 1–53 + A. This was replaced by an NX panel in 1977 and then a more modern panel in 2009. Back in 1990, Class 58 No. 58038 is seen passing with an empty oil train returning to Ripple Lane. FFP Media
Location: N15 6UJ
Visibility: From the end of the station platform at South Tottenham.

WILLESDEN - CARRIAGE SIDINGS NORTH & SOUTH

Left & below:- The two remarkable survivors within the Willesden carriage sidings complex date back to 1946 when they were built by the LMS for the planned carriage sidings. The carriage depot didn't open until 1953 and this is when the two boxes were commissioned. Willesden Carriage Sidings North is the larger of the two cabins with a 42-lever frame and also a small panel added a few years after commissioning in connection with the construction of the new carriage shed No. 5/6. The box is unusual in that it is closed each day between 1330 and 2000, presumably because most carriages are out at work between these times. Both I. Stewart
Location: NW10 0RW
Visibility: As might be expected views of the box are not possible from a public place although the cabin can be seen clearly from the West Coast Main Line to the east at the north end of the carriage depot at Willesden, just before reaching Wembley station.

Above (2 images) & right:- Built and commissioned at the same time as the North box, the South cabin has a 30-lever frame. It is more easy to see than it's northern cousin as it lies close to the North Circular Road. There is a small locomotive stabling point adjacent to the box which is still in use in 2019 and is seen here back in 1977 when Class 82 No. 82008 and Class 83 No. 83011 stand behind the box. I. Stewart (2) & M. Rhodes
Location: NW10 0RW
Visibility: Partial views are possible from Blackmore Drive which turns directly off the North Circular Road.

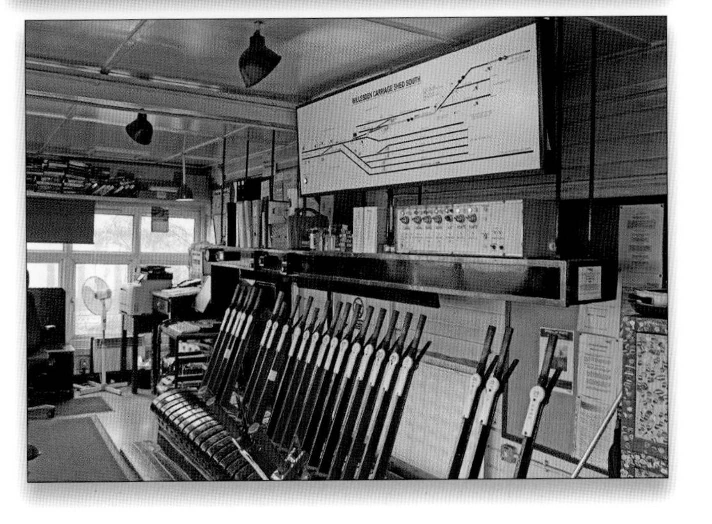

South West England

With resignalling along the former Great Western main lines all but completed as far as Cornwall during the 1980s and the last gaps in the south-western lines of the Southern Region losing their semaphores in 2014, there are very few mechanical signal boxes left in the South West. As yet there are no firm dates for the transfer of the remaining heritage signalling in Cornwall into the Thames Valley ROC at Didcot.

Signal Boxes Scheduled to Close per Network Rail 2010 Masterplan

Year	Signal boxes
2011	Slough panel
2012	Causeway, Swindon panel
2013	Colthrop, Kintbury
2014	Swindon panel (second part), Minety LC
2015	Gloucester PSB, Bristol PSB, Puxton & Worle, Oxford panel
2017	Slough (second part)
2018	Greenford
2019	Goonbarrow Junction, Liskeard, Lostwithiel, Par, Penzance, Roskear Junction, St. Blazey, St. Erth, Truro
2021	Alston, St. Marys,
2022	Plymouth PSB
2025	St. Andrews Junction
2026	Crediton, Exeter PSB, Paignton, Oxford (second part), Westbury panel

CREDITON

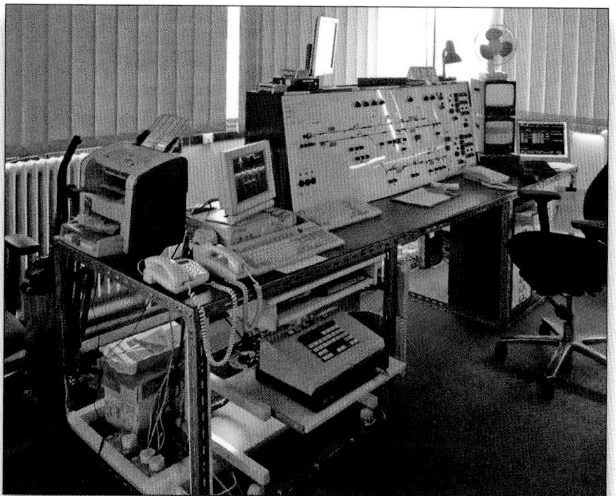

Above:- Dating back to 1875, the signal box at Crediton was originally called Crediton West and renamed simply "Crediton" in 1913. Its 22-lever frame was replaced by an OCS panel in 1984 and as the only signal box along the Barnstaple branch it controls trains as far as the end of the line by NSTR, or No Signalman Token Remote. G. Bowden

Location: *EX17 3PP*

Visibility: *From the level crossing on an unnamed road to the west of the station.*

Above right & right:- Built in 1959, the signal box at Exmouth Junction replaced an older 1875-vintage structure. It was fitted with a 64-lever frame, which was replaced in 1988 by an OCS panel. Both M. Jamieson

Location: *EX4 7AQ*

Visibility: *Partial views are possible from Priory Park, but the access gate to the box is out of view of the box itself so it is hard to view the box from a public place.*

GOONBARROW

Above, above right & right:- There has been a signal box at Goonbarrow since 1893, but the current structure was built in 1909. It was fitted with a 23-lever frame which had been used between 1904 and 1908 in Wearde signal box near Saltash, which closed in 1908. A 24th lever was added in 1924 and the frame remains pretty much unchanged today as our internal view of signalman Craig Munday shows. The line controls the only passing loop on the Newquay branch and the driver of Class 153 No. 153380, with a Newquay to Par service, pauses for a little chat as well as the token exchange with Craig Munday on 19 September 2015. All M. Rhodes

Location: *PL26 8SE*

Visibility: *Access to the signal box is through the English China Class plant at Bugle, just off the B3374. The box is best seen from a passing train along the Newquay branch.*

LISKEARD

Above & above right:- Built in 1915 and replacing an older (1892) box, Liskeard has a 36-lever frame. M. Rhodes & C. Munday

Location: *PL14 4DZ*

Visibility: *From the end of the station platform*

LOSTWITHIEL

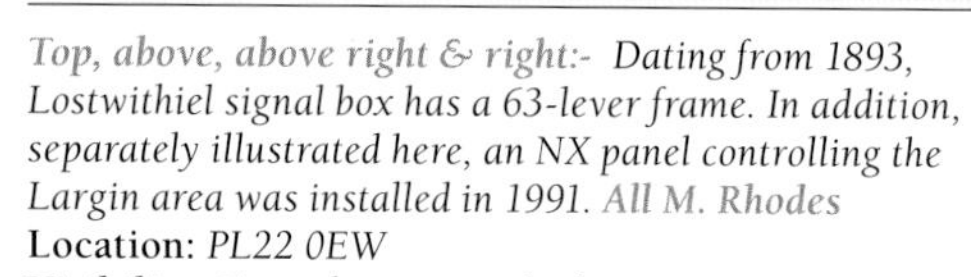

Top, above, above right & right:- Dating from 1893, Lostwithiel signal box has a 63-lever frame. In addition, separately illustrated here, an NX panel controlling the Largin area was installed in 1991. All M. Rhodes
Location: *PL22 0EW*
Visibility: *From the station platform.*

PAR

Left & below- Par signal box opened in 1879 and was extended in 1893. Its 57-lever frame dates from 1913; an OCS panel was added in 1986 to control the Burngullow area. Our external view shows the exceptionally rare sight (these days) of two freight trains alongside the signal box. Class 66 No. 66053 has just run round its train, the 6B03 St. Blazey to Burngullow trip whilst Class 66 No. 66096 is passing with 6G08, a china clay train from Goonbarrow to Fowey Docks. Both M. Rhodes
Location: *PL24 2LT*
Visibility: *From the station platform.*

PENZANCE

Left & above:- *There has been a signal box at Penzance since 1880 and the current structure, built in 1938 is the third and largest box to control the station. It is installed with a 75-lever mechanical frame; the majority of levers are still in use.* M. Rhodes & C. Munday
Location: *TR18 3LQ*
Visibility: *From Chyandour Cliff which runs behind the box.*

ROSKEAR JUNCTION

Left:- *Roskear Junction box opened in 1895 and originally had a 29-lever frame. This was replaced in 1970 by an IFS panel at the same time as the signal box at Camborne closed and Roskear Junction took over control of this area.* C. Munday
Location: *TR14 7TE*
Visibility: *From the crossing on Stray Park Road, which the box controls.*

ST. BLAZEY

Above & right:- *The 1908-built signal box at St. Blazey replaced an older 1880 building. It contains a 41-lever mechanical frame.* Both M. Rhodes
Location: *PL24 2JA*
Visibility: *The box is hard to see from a public place but access is from a gate on the A3082 St Blazey Road. The best way to observe the box is from a Par to Newquay passenger train.*

ST. ERTH

Above:- Class 50 No. 50033 passes St. Erth with a Manchester to Penzance express in 1982. The signal box at St. Erth opened in 1899 replacing a temporary structure erected in 1894. Originally it was fitted with a 55-lever frame and this was expanded to the current 69 levers in 1929. M. Rhodes
Location: *TR27 6JW*
Visibility: *From the end of the station platform.*

YEOVIL

Above:- Opened in 1937, the signal box at Yeovil Pen Mill is an island of mechanical signalling now surrounded by the power boxes at Westbury, Salisbury, Dorchester and Exeter. It contains a 65-lever frame. Here, Class 150 No. 150106 passes with a Weymouth to Bristol service. M. Rhodes
Location: *BA21 5DD*
Visibility: *From the station platform.*

TRURO

Above & above right:- Class 50 No. 50037 arrives at Truro station passing the signal box with a Plymouth to Penzance local service. Remarkably, the train had extra carriages added because our church youth camp at Truro School had block booked over 100 tickets for a day out to St. Ives, resorting to rail rather than road coaches at the suggestion of the author! The box here was opened in 1899, replacing two previous buildings and was called Truro East. Originally fitted with a 45-lever frame, this was enlarged to 51 levers in 1971 when Truro West signal box closed and Truro East was renamed simply "Truro" and controlled both ends of the station. Both M. Rhodes
Location: *TR1 3HH*
Visibility: *From the unnamed road crossing to the east of the station, which the box controls.*

Wales & The Borders

The entire railway network in Wales will eventually be controlled from the Cardiff ROC, built on the site of the old Cardiff Canton parcels depot. There have been significant delays to the planned migration of routes into the ROC when compared to the 2010 Network Rail plan for the area. The resignalling of the Shrewsbury to Crewe line ran over a year late and the proposed resignalling of the North Wales main line has both been delayed and significantly scaled back. During 2018 the line between Shotton and Colwyn Bay was resignallled with closure of the signal boxes at Rockcliffe Hall, Holywell, Talacre, Prestatyn, Rhyl and Abergele. As yet there are no definite dates for the resignalling of the Llandudno branch or the main line further west.

Similar uncertainty exists as regards the manually-signalled line from Newport to Shrewsbury, which was to have been resignalled in 2017 but as yet is deferred, at least until the next Network Rail five year control period.

In South Wales, mechanical signalling has been eradicated from the valley lines north and south of Cardiff, but still exists at Park Junction and Tondu. Another anachronistic survivor is the crossing box at Bishton, west of Newport, still open in 2019. Electrification from Paddington to Cardiff is the main area of investment for Network Rail in South Wales and will also be linked to resignalling of the line to Swansea with the closure of the Port Talbot power signal box. Further resignalling to the west has not yet been given a firm date by Network Rail.

Signal Boxes Scheduled to Close per Network Rail 2010 Masterplan

Cardiff ROC	
Year	**Boxes transferred**
2011	Newport PSB
2012	Caldicot, Lydney and second part of Newport PSB
2013	Crewe Bank, Harlescott, Nantwich, Prees, Wem, Whitchurch, Wrenbury, Llanelli West, Bargoed, Cardiff PSB, Aberthaw, Barry, Cowbridge Road
2014	Abergele, Deganwy, Holywell Junction, Llandudno Junction, Llandudno station, Mostyn, Prestatyn, Rhyl, Rockcliffe Hall, Talacre, Tal-y-Cafn, Tyn-y-Morfa, Heath Junction, Ystrad Mynach South, Cardiff PSB (second part)
2015	St. Fagans, Pembrey
2017	Abercynon, Radyr, Abergavenny, Bromfield, Craven Arms, Dorrington, Hereford, Leominster, Little Mill Junction, Marsh Brook, Moreton-on-Lugg, Onibury, Pontrilas, Tram Inn, Wooferton Junction, Park Junction
2018	Carmarthen Junction, Clarbeston Road
2019	Kidwelly
2020	Port Talbot PSB, Bangor, Gaerwen, Holyhead, Llandudno Junction (second part), Llanfair PG, Llanwrst, Penmaenmawr, Ty Croes, Valley
2025	Gobowen North, Croes Newydd North, Penyffordd
2043	Tondu
2045	Whitland, Pantyffynnon & LC, Machynlleth, Bishton
2048	Ledbury
2050	Abbey Foregate, Severn Bridge Junction, Sutton Bridge Junction, Crewe Junction
2053	Hereford (second part), Ferryside, Clarbeston Road and Whitland (second parts)
2055	Neath & Brecon Junction

North Wales

BANGOR

Right:- Originally opened as Bangor No. 2 in 1923, the box has subsequently become simply "Bangor". It currently has a 60-lever frame which has been reduced in size since the box was opened. M. Rhodes
Location: *LL57 2TX*
Visibility: *From the station platform.*

DEGANWY

Below & below right:- Idyllically situated on the River Conwy estuary, the box at Deganwy opened in 1914. It has an 18-lever mechanical frame. Both M. Rhodes
Location: *LL31 9EJ*
Visibility: *On the station platform.*

GAERWEN

Above & right:- *Opened in 1882, the signal box at Gaerwen which controls the junction to the former branch to Amlwch has a 20-lever mechanical frame.* *Both M. Rhodes*

Location: *LL60 6DP*

Visibility: *From the level crossing on Chapel Street, which the box controls.*

HOLYHEAD

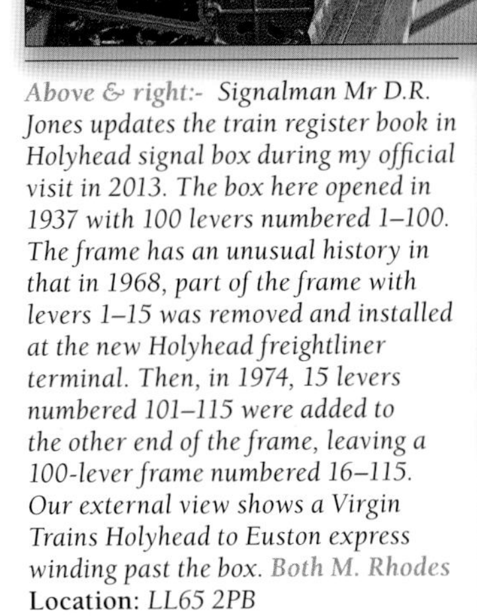

Above & right:- *Signalman Mr D.R. Jones updates the train register book in Holyhead signal box during my official visit in 2013. The box here opened in 1937 with 100 levers numbered 1–100. The frame has an unusual history in that in 1968, part of the frame with levers 1–15 was removed and installed at the new Holyhead freightliner terminal. Then, in 1974, 15 levers numbered 101–115 were added to the other end of the frame, leaving a 100-lever frame numbered 16–115. Our external view shows a Virgin Trains Holyhead to Euston express winding past the box.* *Both M. Rhodes*

Location: *LL65 2PB*

Visibility: *From the footbridge linking Penllech Nest and Morrison Crescent.*

LLANDUDNO

Top & above:- My visit to Llandudno signal box was at the end of the day in the gathering gloom and signalman Paul Wild is reduced to a blur by the shutter speed needed to capture the interior of the box. Built in 1891 the box now has a 34-lever frame, reduced considerably from its extent in the 1970s when Llandudno had extensive carriage sidings and a busy summer Saturday excursion timetable. Both M. Rhodes

Location: *LL30 2AF*

Visibility: *From the end of the station platform.*

LLANFAIR PG

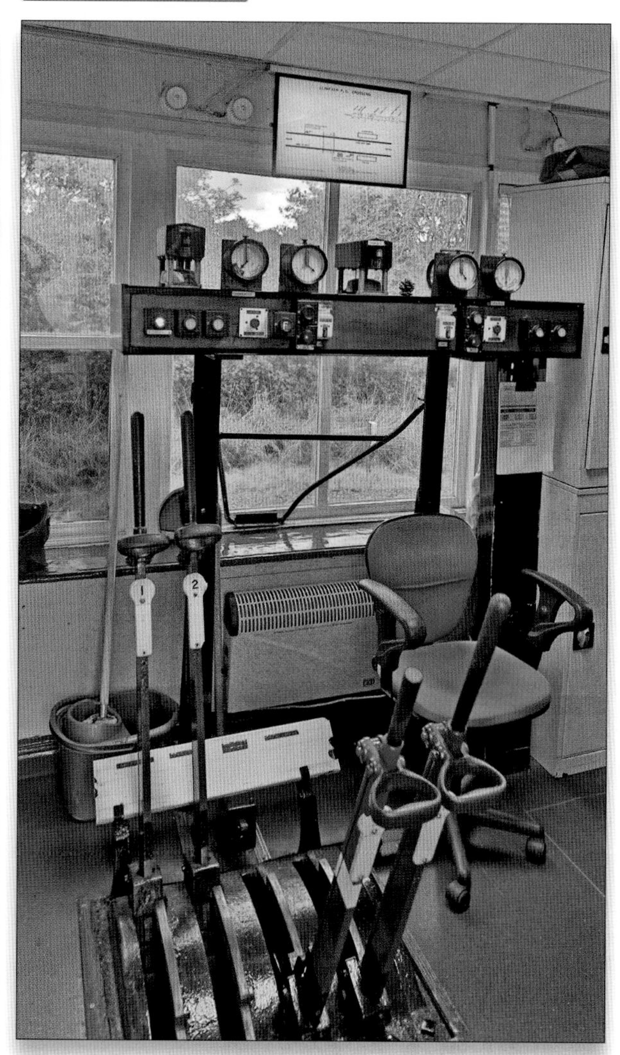

Top & above:- Much of the reference material that has aided the compilation of this illustrated encyclopaedia has been produced by the Signalling Record Society and has been excellent. Llanfair PG signal box is, however, one of very few sites where my visit revealed that the information on record was not correct. The box is one of the oldest in Wales, opened in 1871. It has a 4-lever mechanical frame as illustrated. Both M. Rhodes

Location: *LL61 5UQ*

Visibility: *From the station Road level crossing, which the box controls.*

LLANWRST

Top & above:- *Opened in 1880, the box at Llanwrst has a 20-lever frame. The current frame is thought to be second hand, having been observed in a signal box at Brundritts Sidings in 1909. In 2019 only four of the levers remain active with the points at Llanwrst being train-operated.* *Both M. Rhodes*

Location: *LL26 0EG*

Visibility: *In the distance from the station platform at North Llanwrst.*

PENMAENMAWR

Top & above:- *Perhaps one of the ugliest mechanical signal boxes on the network is at Penmaenmawr. Opened in 1952 and with a 25-lever frame, the majority of the windows were bricked up in the 1990s as our external view shows.* *Both M. Rhodes*

Location: *LL34 6AT*

Visibility: *From the end of the station platform.*

RHYL NO. 2

Above & above right:- *Like the other large signal box at Rhyl, No. 2 was built in 1900. It closed in 1990, but is Grade II listed and still stands at the west end of the platform at Rhyl; it is therefore included in this section. It is becoming increasingly derelict, as our view of Class 158 No. 158827 with a Manchester Picadilly to Holyhead service shows. It was larger than its partner to the east and had a 126-lever frame. By way of contrast, our earlier view of the listed signal box was taken by Dr. A.A Vickers in the early 1960s and shows the box in its heyday with a pair of diesel multiple units heading for the seaside at Llandudno; these summer Saturday trains often ran to 10 or 12 carriages.* *M. Rhodes & M. Rhodes Collection*

Location: *LL18 1DA*

Visibility: *From the end of the station platform.*

TY CROES

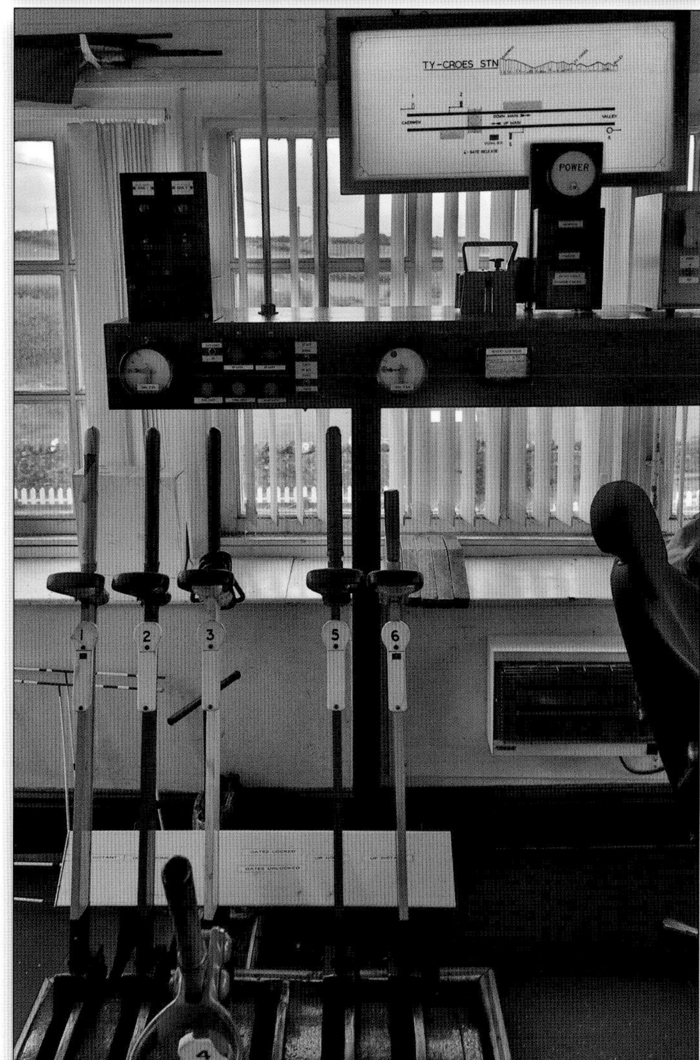

Top & above:- Opened in 1872, the signal box at Ty Croes has a 6-lever frame, reduced in size from when it was first installed. It is thought that the current frame was salvaged from the original Rhyl No. 2 signal box and dates back to 1892. Both M. Rhodes
Location: *LL63 5HX*
Visibility: *From the crossing on the unnamed road to the east of the station.*

VALLEY

Top & above:- The signal box at Valley which controls access to the British Nuclear Fuels siding, opened in 1904. It has a 25-lever frame. Both M. Rhodes
Location: *LL63 5EW*
Visibility: *From the crossing on Station Road, which the box controls.*

The Welsh Borders

ABBEY FOREGATE

Left & above left:- *Built in 1914 and replacing an older 1884 signal box, Abbey Foregate has a 93-lever frame. Our daytime view shows Class 170 No. 170511 arriving with a Birmingham New Street to Shrewsbury service.* *Both M. Rhodes*
Location: *SY2 5BY*
Visibility: *Both these images were taken from Monkmoor Road overbridge (a step ladder is needed to see over the parapet and this is just about the only place to observe the box).*

ABERGAVENNY

Top & above:- *Back in April 1985, Class 47 No. 47069 passes Abergavenny signal box with 6Z27, an extra steel train from Crewe to Severn Tunnel Junction running as a result of an earlier failure of a southbound steel train from Mossend. The signal box here opened in 1934 and replaced two older signal boxes at Abergavenny North and South respectively. It was originally called Abergavenny Station but is now simply "Abergavenny". Our internal view shows signalman Rob Blackmore at his desk alongside the 52-lever frame.* *Both M. Rhodes*
Location: *NP7 9SN*
Visibility: *Can be seen in the distance from the station footbridge.*

BROMFIELD

Right & far right:- *Local Operations Manager, Ian Rowson, chats to the resident signaller and a learner at Bromfield (both out of shot). The box here opened in 1873 and was fitted with a 23-lever mechanical frame which was extended to 29 levers in 1956.* *Both M. Rhodes*
Location: *SY8 2BT*
Visibility: *From the level crossing on an unnamed road linking the A49 and Ludlow racecourse.*

CRAVEN ARMS CROSSING

Top & above:- Looking south from the box at Craven Arms Crossing, Class 66 No. 66415 is seen heading north with a Portbury Dock to Rugeley Power Station coal train. The box at Craven Arms Crossing started life way back in 1878 as Long Lane Crossing. This box was replaced by a new box in 1931 with a 30-lever frame. The later box was subsequently damaged and rebuilt around the original frame in 1947. Further change came in 1956 when the box was renamed Craven Arms Crossing. The 1947 wooden structure was deemed unsafe and was replaced by a new building, erected around the old 1931 frame in 2000. Resident signalman Les Bowen is seen on the bells to Marsh Brook during my visit in 2013. Both M. Rhodes

Location: *SY7 9QQ*

Visibility: *From the crossing on Long Lane, which the box controls.*

CROES NEWYDD NORTH FORK

Above:- Class 47 No. 47340 is seen passing Croess Newydd North Fork signal box in 1983 with a Bersham Colliery to Fiddlers Ferry MGR service. The box here was built in 1905, replacing an older 1883 box. Originally fitted with a 45-lever frame, this was enlarged to 83 levers in 1940 as a consequence of the increased steel traffic from Brymbo Steelworks and the associated expansion in the sidings here. In 2009 the semaphore signals were decommissioned here and an NX panel replaced the mechanical frame. M. Rhodes

Location: *LL13 7NX*

Visibility: *From the crossing on Watery Road, which the box controls.*

DEE MARSH JUNCTION

Top & above:- Dee Marsh Junction signal box is remarkably a Great Central Railway construction. Dating from 1930 it was fitted with a 60-lever mechanical frame. With the closure of Shotton Steelworks in 1980 and subsequent railway rationalisation, the frame was reduced to 25 levers as our view from 1995 shows. Class 60 No. 60092 winds past the box with 6V75, the afternoon freight from Dee Marsh Sidings to Margam Yard. Both M. Rhodes

Location: *CH5 2JB*

Visibility: *In the distance from the north end of Hawarden Bridge station.*

DORRINGTON

Top & above:- Class 175 No. 175002 is seen passing Dorrington signal box with a Carmarthen to Manchester Piccadilly service in October 2013. The signal box here was built in 1872 and initially had a 22-lever frame. This was expanded to 33 levers in 1941. Both M. Rhodes
Location: *SY5 7LH*
Visibility: *From the Station Road overbridge to the south of the box.*

GOBOWEN NORTH

Above:- The signal box at Gobowen North dates back to 1884. It is fitted with a 16-lever mechanical frame. In 1987, when the 80-lever Gobowen South box closed, a release switch was fitted to the North box to allow the layout to the south of the station to be controlled by a switch panel located adjacent to the sidings for the Oswestry branch. M. Rhodes
Location: *SY11 3JS*
Visibility: *From the Chirk Road (B5069) level crossing, which the box controls.*

HEREFORD

Right & above right:- Hereford resident signalman, Richard Jones, accepts a train from Tram Inn. The box at Hereford dates back to 1884 when it was fitted with a 62-lever frame. This was enlarged to 67 levers in 1942 but then rationalised back to the current 60 levers in 1973. In 1984 an OCS panel was added to take over the work of Shelwick Junction signal box, which closed that year; it is visible at the far end of the box in our interior view. Back in 1985, DMU Set No. B429 is seen passing the box having arrived from Birmingham New Street. Both M. Rhodes
Location: *HR1 1HR*
Visibility: *From the Aylestone Road (A465) overbridge.*

LEOMINSTER

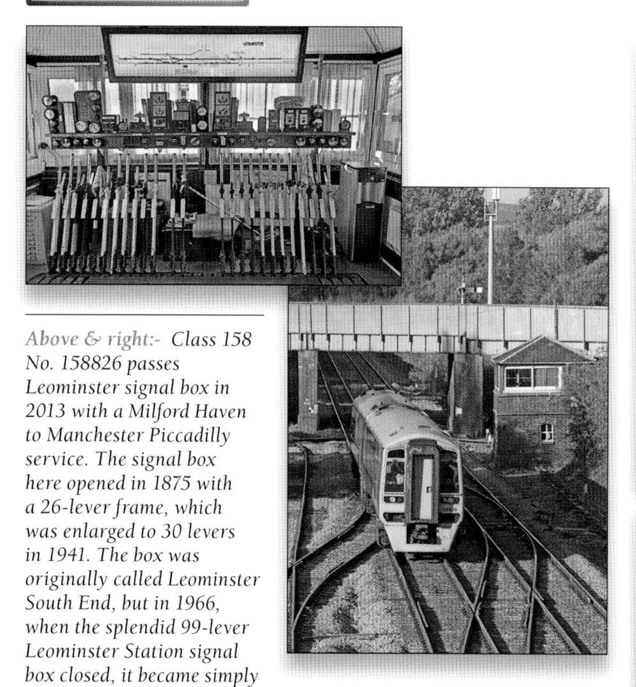

Above & right:- Class 158 No. 158826 passes Leominster signal box in 2013 with a Milford Haven to Manchester Piccadilly service. The signal box here opened in 1875 with a 26-lever frame, which was enlarged to 30 levers in 1941. The box was originally called Leominster South End, but in 1966, when the splendid 99-lever Leominster Station signal box closed, it became simply "Leominster". Both M. Rhodes

Location: *HR6 0QQ*

Visibility: *From the overbridge on the unnamed road to the north of the box linking Leominster bypass to Worcester Road.*

LITTLE MILL JUNCTION

Top & above:- The signal box at Little Mill Junction dates back to 1883. When it opened it contained a 40-lever mechanical frame and this was enlarged to 55 levers in 1938. When mechanical signalling between here and Newport was superseded in 1979, an NX panel was installed controlling the route through Panteg to Maindee Junctions and this can be seen at the far end of the box in our interior view. At the same time the frame was reduced to 17 levers and these control the track outside the box and the junction to the out of use Glascoed branch. Both M. Rhodes

Location: *NP4 0HD*

Visibility: *The box is not visible from a public place but there is official access via a gated lane off Berthin Road.*

MARSH BROOK

Above & above right:- Signalmen "Barry Cank" & "Griptonk" enjoy lively banter in Marsh Brook signal box whilst one of them is training (I forget which one!). The signal box here is said to be the oldest along the Marches line, dating back to 1872. It has an 18-lever frame and is pretty much in original condition except for new windows adjacent to the box steps as shown in our external view. Both M. Rhodes

Location: *SY6 6QE*

Visibility: *From the crossing on the B4370, which the box controls.*

MORETON ON LUGG

Top & above:- Dating back to 1943 the signal box at Moreton on Lugg replaced an older 20-lever box built in 1875. There is now a 44-lever frame as our internal view illustrates. Both M. Rhodes
Location: *HR4 8DP*
Visibility: *From the level crossing from the unnamed road which runs through the village, half a mile to the east of the village chip shop.*

ONIBURY

Top & above:- The original 1897-built Great Western signal box at Onibury was deemed unsafe and replaced by a new timber construction in 1977. The old box had contained a 24-lever mechanical frame but this was replaced by an IFS panel in the 1977 construction. Both M. Rhodes
Location: *SY7 9AZ*
Visibility: *From the level crossing on the A49, which the box controls.*

PENYFFORDD

Left & above:- Class 150 No. 150254 passes Penyffordd signal box with a Wrexham Central to Bidston passenger train. The box was built in 1972, replacing an older structure just to the north of it. Resident signalman Phil kindly strikes a pose for the photographer in front of the 25-lever frame. Both M. Rhodes
Location: *CH4 0JX*
Visibility: *At the end of the station platform.*

PONTRILAS

Above, above right, right & below:- *Signalman Dan Booth is seen at repose in Pontrilas signal box in 2013. The box opened in 1880 with a 30-lever mechanical frame and this was enlarged to 42 levers in 1910. The two external images of Pontrilas box and the surrounding signals were taken in 1963 and exactly 50 years later in 2013. The older image shows 5924 "Dinton Hall" with a Crewe to Cardiff express passing the box whilst a steam hauled freight heads north and a Pannier tank shunts the local goods yard. What a contrast in 2013 as Class 56 No. 56094 passes with an empty log train from Chirk to Newton Abbot. The location is recognisable, but tree growth has obscured much of the trackside and all the sidings are gone.* *M. Rhodes (3) & AA Vickers (M. Rhodes Collection)*

Location: *HR2 0AZ*

Visibility: *Best viewed from Highfield Farm access road above the tunnel, from where the image of 56094 was taken.*

SHREWSBURY CREWE JUNCTION

Above & above right:- Shrewsbury Crewe Junction signal box was opened in 1903, replacing an older 1883 signal box. Signalman Neil Hughes is seen in front of the 120-lever frame, most of which is still in use with relatively few white levers. Our external view, taken from north of the box, shows Class 66 No. 66620 winding into Coton Hill Sidings, past the box, with a Bardon Hill Quarry to Coton Hill Yard freight. Both M. Rhodes

Location: *SY1 1UX*

Visibility: *From the end of the station platform.*

SHREWSBURY SEVERN BRIDGE JUNCTION

Right, far right, below and below right:- Shrewsbury Severn Bridge Junction deserves perhaps a little more space than any other signal box in this book as it is currently the largest mechanical signal box in the world, with 180 levers. Sometimes called simply "Shrewsbury", the box was constructed by the London North Western Railway in 1903 after there had been signal boxes on the site dating first from 1875 and then 1884.

There have been quite a number of larger mechanical signal boxes, both in the UK and overseas, with the largest traditional "long levered" frame installed in Locomotive Yard signal box, south of York, with 295 levers. This closed in 1952. There have been electromechanical boxes with over 300 miniature levers at Waterloo, London Bridge, Bristol Temple Meads East & West and Cardiff, as well as the biggest of them all at Glasgow Central with 374 levers.

Coming back to traditional lever frames, until 1987 the largest in the world was Newton Abbot East with 206 levers. Upon its closure the crown of the largest mechanical box in the world passed to Melbourne Spencer Street with 192 levers. This was decommissioned in 2008, leaving Shrewsbury as the world's largest signal box. It is always double manned because of the length of the frame as illustrated in our internal views. Seen from Shrewsbury Castle, Class 66 No. 66617 passes the box in July 2006 with a Saturdays-only extra freight carrying scrap from Liverpool Docks to Cardiff Tidal Sidings. Our second external view is taken from Monkmoor Road, with Class 66 No. 66529 winding past with a Portbury to Rugeley Power Station coal train. The close proximity of Abbey Foregate and Shrewsbury boxes is well illustrated in this view. All M. Rhodes

Location: *SY2 6AG*

Visibility: *Both from the end of the station platform and from Shrewsbury Castle.*

SUTTON BRIDGE JUNCTION

Above:- The signal box at Sutton Bridge opened in 1913 and was installed with a 61-lever mechanical frame. Class 66 No. 66066 passes the box with a Margam to Dee Marsh steel train on 30 September 2014. M. Rhodes

Location: *SY3 7PX*

Visibility: *From the footbridge off Bretton Street.*

TRAM INN

Top & above:- In October 2013 the leaves are changing colour and falling as the RHTT passes Tram Inn with Class 66 No. 66126 leading the train. Signalman Dave Horan stands in front of the 23-lever frame and offers a train to Hereford in the 1894-constructed box. The frame was fitted in 1978, having been reconditioned after Corporation Road signal box on the East Usk Branch closed. Dave had joined the railway in 1992, appointed by "Welsh Freight" as a signalman. This led to jobs in Lime Kiln Sidings, Little Mill Junction and Park Junction, before settling as the resident at Tram Inn. Both M. Rhodes

Location: *HR2 9AN*

Visibility: *From the level crossing on the B4348, which the box controls.*

WOOFERTON JUNCTION

Above left, left & above:- Class 60 No. 60079 passes Wooferton Junction with the morning Dee Marsh to Margam steel train in October 2013. The signal box here dates back to 1889 and replaced an older 1875 structure. It was initially fitted with a 62-lever frame and this was expanded to 75 levers in 1914. With loss of the junction and goods sidings here, today's frame is just 39 levers. In the view of Class 175 No. 175005 passing with a Manchester Piccadilly to Tenby train, signalman Iain Burgoyne is unusually trackside as a signal wire has just broken and needed investigation. All M. Rhodes

Location: *SY8 4AW*

Visibility: *From the Station Road overbridge to the south.*

South Wales

BISHTON CROSSING

Above:- Bishton Crossing was built in 1941 and originally had a 10-lever frame. This increased in size in stages until in 1961 it had 38 levers. With the commissioning of Newport panel box, the crossing box at Bishton was reduced to the status of a ground frame with just three slots in the frame retained (36–38) comprising just two levers and a gap at slot 37. In addition, a 2-lever frame was placed at the other end of the cabin to lock and unlock the wicket gates, which are controlled by a mechanical wheel as our 1995 image shows. M. Rhodes

Location: *NP18 2DZ*

Visibility: *From the level crossing on the unnamed road which the box controls.*

CLARBESTON ROAD

Top & above:- The signal box at Clarbeston Road opened in 1906 replacing an older 1885 structure. Initially it was fitted with a 57-lever frame and it is suggested that this was enlarged to 80 levers in 1914. This seems far from certain as our 1982 view, taken just before the frame was replaced by an NX panel, suggests a 57-lever frame. An OCS panel was added in 1988 and with the closure of the signal box at Letterston Junction, this controlled the tracks all the way to Fishguard Harbour. Back in 1982, Metro-Cammell DMU set C813 passes the box with a Swansea to Fishguard service. Work on rationalisation and resignalling is well under way. Both M. Rhodes

Location: *SA63 4UP*

Visibility: *The box can be seen in the distance from the station and is accessed by a narrow lane off Market Place, adjacent to the station.*

CARMARTHEN JUNCTION

Left:- Built in 1956, the signal box at Carmarthen Junction originally contained a 78-lever frame. This was replaced by an OCS panel in 1985. D. Allen

Location: *SA31 2NG*

Visibility: *The box is visible from the car park of "Krazy Kids" off the A484 and also when passing on the train between Llanelli and Carmarthen.*

FERRYSIDE

PANTYFFYNNON

Above:- Pantyffynnon signal box opened in 1892 and was originally called Pantyffynnon South. This became simply "Pantyffynnon" in 1966 when the north signal box closed. It is fitted with a 21-lever frame and is seen here with the signalman exchanging single line tokens with the driver of Class 153 No. 153312 with a Swansea to Shrewsbury service. M. Rhodes
Location: *SA18 2RE*
Visibility: *South off the station platform.*

Above left & left:- The small signal box at Ferryside opened in 1884 and has a 24-lever frame. Both M. Rhodes
Location: *SA17 5SF*
Visibility: *On the station platform.*

KIDWELLY

Above:- Kidwelly signal box is a structure of two halves; the brick base belongs to the original 1885 signal box, whilst the top half of the box was built in the 1950s when the previous wooden structure became unsafe. The 1950s rebuild was fitted with a 34-lever mechanical frame and this was replaced by an NX panel in 1983. Class 175 No. 175101 passes with a Manchester to Fishguard Harbour service on 22 June 2016. M. Rhodes
Location: *SA17 4UW*
Visibility: *From the level crossing on Quay Road, which the box controls.*

PARK JUNCTION

Above & right:- Opened in 1885, Park Junction signal box replaced an older 1879 structure. Initially installed with a 31-lever frame, the box was significantly expanded in 1899 to 105 levers. This was reduced to 100 in 1920 and today the signal box still has the 100-lever frame but there are spaces where levers 86–100 should be. With the return of passenger trains to the Ebbw Vale line, the box received an NX panel in 2007 which controls the entire branch line north from Rogerstone. Our external view, taken back in 1995 (with permission), shows an unusual view of the box and junction from one of the signals. Class 60 No. 60034 passes with a Margam to Ebbw Vale steel working. Both M. Rhodes

Location: *NP20 3AP*

Visibility: *From the footpath linking St. Davids Cresent and Shakespeare Cresent.*

PEMBREY

Above & above right:- A contender for Britain's unluckiest signal box, Pembrey has been badly damaged twice in its 110 year existence. Accidents in 1912 and 1964 led to major rebuilding of the structure. Opened in 1907 and originally called Pembrey East, the box expanded from an original 3 levers to 83 levers by 1953. With the closure of the Burry Port and Gwendraeth Valley line to Kidwelly in 1984 and the gradual run-down of the sidings at Burry Port, most of these levers are now out of use. In June 2016 trains cross in front of the box with Class 60 No. 60044 hauling an empty oil train from Theale to Robeston refinery as Class 150 No. 150256 forms a Carmarthen to Cardiff passenger service. Both M. Rhodes

Location: *SA16 0RY*

Visibility: *From the crossing on Church Road, which the box controls.*

TONDU

Above & right:- Tondu signal box was opened in 1884 and originally called Tondu Middle. It is equipped with a 65-lever frame and lies just west of the station footbridge from which our external view is taken. Class 37 No. 37887 passes with a special working from Blaengarw mine to Margam, which is running to clear the coal stockpile from the closed mine. Both M. Rhodes
Location: *CF32 9DE*
Visibility: *From the footbridge to the west of the station.*

WHITLAND

Left:- Opened in 1972 and with a 39-lever mechanical frame, the signal box at Whitland replaced an 1868 construction which had contained a 43-lever frame. The "new" frame at Whitland came from the signal box at Danygraig in the Swansea Docks area. In 1978 an IFS panel was added covering the St. Clears area. D. Allen
Location: *SA34 0DQ*
Visibility: *From the Station Road crossing, which the box controls.*

Appendix I: Index to Signal Boxes

Appendix II: Railway Company Abbreviations

Barry........ Barry Railway
BR........ British Railways, later British Rail
CamR........ Cambrian Railway
CLC........ Cheshire Lines Committee
CR........ Caledonian Railway
FR........ Furness Railway
GCR........ Great Central Railway
GER........ Great Eastern Railway
GNR........ Great Northern Railway
GWR........ Great Western Railway
HR........ Highland Railway
L&Y........ Lancashire & Yorkshire Railway
LBSCR........ London Brighton & South Coast Railway
LCDR........ London Chatham & Dover Railway
LMS........ London Midland & Scottish Railway
LNER........ London & North Eastern Railway
LSWR........ London & South Western Railway
MGNR........ Midland & Great Northern Railway
MR........ Midland Railway
MS&LR........ Manchester Sheffield & Lincolnshire Railway
NBR........ North British Railway
NER........ North Eastern Railway
NLR........ North London Railway
NR........ Network Rail
NSR........ North Staffordshire Railway
Rhymney........ Rhymney Railway
RT........ Railtrack
S&H........ Shrewsbury & Hereford Railway
SECR........ South Eastern & Chatham Railway
SER........ South Eastern Railway
SR........ Southern Railway

Appendix III: General Abbreviations

AHB ... Automatic Half-Barriers
ASC ... Area Signalling Centre
BR ... British Railways, later British Rail
BSC ... British Steel Corporation
CCTV ... Closed-Circuit Television
ECML ... East Coast Main Line
ER ... Eastern Region
ERTMS ... European Rail Traffic Management System
ETB ... Electric Token Block
ETCS ... European Train Control System
GB ... Gate Box
GSM-R ... Global System for Mobile Communications - Railway
IECC ... Integrated Electronic Control Centre
IFS ... Individual Function Switch
LC ... Level Crossing
LED ... Light-Emitting Diode
LIDAR ... Light Detection and Ranging
LMR ... London Midland Region
LOM ... Local Operations Manager
MAS ... Multiple Aspect Signalling
MCB-OB ... Manual Crossing Box with Object Detectors
MCG ... Manual Crossing Gates
MGH ... Manual Gate Hut
MGR ... Merry-Go-Round
MOD ... Ministry of Defence
MOM ... Mobile Operations Manager
NER ... North Eastern Region
NR ... Network Rail
NX ... eNtrance-eXit
OCS ... One Control Switch
OM ... Operations Manager
PSB ... Power Signal Box
PTE ... Passenger Transport Executive
RETB ... Radio Electronic Token Block
RHTT ... Rail Head Treatment Train
ROC ... Regional Operating Centre
SB ... Signal Box
SC ... Signalling Centre
SCC ... Signalling Control Centre
ScR ... Scottish Region
SF ... Saxby & Farmer
SR ... Southern Region
TCB ... Track Circuit Block
TRB ... Train Register Book
VDU ... Visual Display Unit
WCML ... West Coast Main Line

PLATFORM
5

VISA
Maestro
VISA